GRANT TEXTBOOK SERIES

Volume IV
Predictive Astrology

by Catharine T. Grant and Ernest A. Grant

Copyright 1988 by the American Federation of Astrologers No part of this book may be reproduced or transmitted in any form or by any means, electronic or mechanical, including photocopying or recording, or by any information storage and retrieval system, without written permission from the author and publisher. Requests and inquiries may be mailed to: American Federation of Astrologers, Inc., P.O. Box 22040, Tempe, AZ 85282

First Printing 1988

ISBN Number: 0-86690-343-7

Library of Congress Catalog Number: 88- 70466

Cover Design: Celeste Nash-Weninger

Published by:

American Federation of Astrologers, Inc. P.O. Box 22040, 6535 South Rural Road Tempe, Arizona 85282

Printed in the United States of America

Contents

Chapter 1: Secondary Progressions, Types of Progressions — 5

Chapter 2: Progressed Ascendant, Decanate Rulers — 22

Chapter 3: Progressed Sun — 59

Chapter 4: Progressed Moon, Timing — 92

Chapter 5: Progressed Planets — 116

Chapter 6: Transits, Retrogrades — 144

Chapter 7: Birth Diurnal Charts, Cycles — 180

Chapter 8: Symbolic Directions — 192

Chapter 9: Cyclic Charts — 217

Chapter 10: Summary of Data — 241

References — 242

|Chapter 1|

Secondary Progressions

THE STUDENT OF ASTROLOGY WHO HAS progressed thus far in their studies has learned to recognize, in the natal horoscope, not only the character of the native but also the nature of the impulses that generally affect the native as years go by. The nativity is a pattern of individual potential as well as a panorama of existence as it indicates life's sensitive points. The progressed horoscope plus the transiting positions of the planets are indicators of the continuing impulses which make life a continuous whole. Fixed stars also are important but the study of them is a specialized field for future consideration.

Every child is born under hereditary conditions and into an environment that will produce the greatest opportunities for its esoteric development, if full advantage is taken of those situations. While this is not a discourse on the philosophic background of astrology, but rather on methodology and delineation, it is relevant to recognize that esoteric advancement is the purpose of life. Everyone is born with a definite purpose in life under particular conditions which will aid in the accomplishment of that goal; a purpose that is always in accord with the nature one possesses in one's own individuality. Failure to recognize this principle, or ignorance of it, is certainly a contributing cause to failure in life and, in the broader sense, the failure of entire populations to find contentment, development, and joy in life. By firmly recognizing this fact, the fullest expression of the individuality can be afforded through the personality of the native when correct delineation of the horoscope is made.

However, life and its course is not determined by the natal horoscope alone. Life is an ever–changing condition. Constantly shifting forces find their outward expression in the events of the years. The progressed horoscope is a charting of these forces plus the means of determining their nature and influence on the individual, while the natal horoscope and its delineation are a means of determining the innate qualities, modes, and quantities, as well as the avenues or nature of their expression. Thus, apparently similar planetary vibrations express themselves in different ways. *However, bear in mind that specific cosmic vibrations do not find permanent expression in the life of an individual unless they are in accordance with the indications of the natal chart.*

For each individual, then there are two forces always at play; first, the direction of life as indicated by the natal chart and, second, the constantly changing influences which have an effect upon that direction.

This is aptly illustrated by the flight of an airplane from New York to Chicago. The pilot sets the direction of the plane westward. Its objective is definitely toward the west. During the entire flight it has to overcome the frictional resistance of air, the constantly operating force of gravity, and both horizontal and vertical cross-currents of the atmosphere. If sufficient power, or force, is available through the motor of the machine and, if the intelligence of the pilot is sufficient, then the definite objective is reached and all arrive safely in Chicago. Thus, while the initial plan of that trip is definitely set, the circumstances it must encounter throughout the entire journey are constantly changing. Due to downward drafts of atmospheric currents it may be necessary to fly higher than ordinarily might be the case; due to horizontal atmospheric currents, the plane may have to be headed to the north or south of Chicago to allow for drift, and throughout the entire journey sufficient energy must be exerted to overcome the force of gravity. So it is with life itself. The weather maps, the instruments indicating altitude, wind currents, and barometric pressure, added to the intelligence of the pilot, are all contributing factors to the successful completion of the journey. Not the least of these is the intelligence of the pilot. Progression of the horoscope (with transits) is one means of determining the constantly changing influences and the time of their operation so that one might bring a safe conclusion to life's journey.

Types of Progression

For several centuries the question of methodology in the progression of horoscopes has been under discussion, even under controversy. Advanced students of astrology have not been content with the exactitude of some of the various methods adopted. Different methods seem to bring satisfactory results within certain limitations; limitations which the author thinks are due, in some measure, to the exercise of free will upon the part of man. On the other hand during recent years some methods, not only of progressing the horoscope but the actual calculation of the chart, have been advanced that can have no possible scientific basis, are not logical, and do not seem practical. The observing student will be wary of these systems until he has sufficiently mastered tried and true methods.

To be perfectly clear to the student, and by way of emphasis, take careful note of the fact that all systems of progressing or directing the natal horoscope are based upon one of two factors, either the rotation of the earth or the motion (apparent) of celestial bodies in longitude at intervals symbolic or related to rotation of the earth at given intervals of time.

Primary Directions

Apparently the most accurate method of progressing the horoscope is by Primary Directions in both direct and converse (or regressed) motion. They deal with the first cycle of astronomical values after and before birth. These are based upon the rotation of the earth upon its axis and not only require technical mathematical skill beyond the average person's training, but also are of value only when the precise moment of birth is certain.

Primary directions are based upon the first motion of the earth in rotation. During the six hours immediately following birth the earth rotates one–fourth of the complete circle. That means that about 90 degrees of longitude in the ecliptic will pass across the upper meridian. Right Ascension (RA) is this measurement in the equator. As the earth rotates parallel to the equator, precisely 90 degrees of right ascension would pass over the Midheaven. This is the equivalent of 90 years of life. Thus, planetary apparent motion in longitude would be negligible. If the Sun is moving at a rate of 1 degree per day in longitude, during this period of time it would actually move only 15 minutes, while the Moon, were its apparent motion 12 degrees per day, would move only 3 degrees in this time. From this it will be readily seen that primary directions are therefore based on the rotation of the earth entirely and not on planetary motion in longitude. This motion may be either direct or converse.

Secondary Progressions

The system in most common usage in western or occidental astrology is known as Secondary Progression, and is founded on the second cycle of astronomical values. They also may be direct or converse in motion. By this method, each day after (or before birth) is considered as the measure of one year of life. While sidereal time increases in relation to the mean solar day almost four minutes, and thus this method may at first glance appear somewhat similar to primary directions it is an entirely different matter. Secondary progressions consider primarily the longitude of the planets as they move along the ecliptic, while primary directions, based solely upon the rotation of the earth, produce all directions that will take place in about ninety years of life within six hours after birth or six hours before birth.

Secondary progressions, either direct or converse, (regressed or converse in primary direction, being backward or the opposite to the direction such motion would be during the lapse of time involved) are based entirely upon the apparent motion of the Sun, Moon, or planets during one day (one rotation of the earth) which is equivalent of one year of time. Of course, this is symbolic, but it does have the scientific foundation of the apparent motion of the Sun, the yardstick, as it were, for our measurement of time.

As the Sun, by apparent motion, moves through the circle of 360 degrees of the zodiac, in one year, so by rotation of the earth it appears to move through the 360 degrees of the circle, thus relating one rotation of the earth to one year of time. The fractional motion during any part of the day in the zodiac is to one year of time in the same proportion that it is of one day. Thus, if the progressed Moon on a given birthday is, let's say, at 14 Aquarius 00, and one year later (the next day in the ephemeris) is at 26 Aquarius 00, it moves 12 degrees by progression during one year, or at a mean rate of 1 degree each month. Therefore the progressed Moon would be at 15 Aquarius 00 one month after the birth date, 2 months after it would be at 16 Aquarius 00, and six months later at 20 Aquarius 00. The Sun's mean advance would be approximately 5 minutes each month, as its apparent forward or regressed motion in one day (one year) is about 1 degree or 60 minutes.

Radix Directions

Another method which has found some favor since World War I is the Radix System. The problems and history of astrology which led up to its advancement are ably stated by Vivian E. Robson, one of England's leading astrologers, in his book dealing with the radix system.[1] While this method was first suggested by Valentine Naibod in the latter part of the Sixteenth Century it remained for Sepharial to set forth definite evidence of its validity.[2] As has already been mentioned, Robson continued this research and has brought the method to its present degree of perfection.

Diurnal Charts

This type of horoscope is simply the calculation of a chart for the 24 hour cycle based on the rotation of the earth. Planets and luminaries keep their natal harmonic relationship (aspects) to each other but move clockwise around the angles. This marks the return of celestial bodies to their birth position on each birthday, located at the present residence. **Diurnal Charts** are used as a supplement to the natal and progressed horoscopes in predictive analysis. The planetary positions are considered primarily as they affect or aspect the four major angles. These charts may be calculated in both direct and converse motion.

Cyclic Charts

The Sun's entry into Zero Degrees of Aries marks the beginning of the solar year and a horoscope for the year in question. The basis of this determination should be apparent for it marks the natural beginning of spring (in the northern hemisphere) or renewed life, the rebirth of our hemisphere.

But people are not all born when the Sun in entering Aries; they are born throughout the entire year with the Sun moving through the ecliptic. Just so, the return of a Sun to its natal longitude and the relationship of all other celestial phenomena to that point is of great importance in determining the manner in which the ensuing year relates to the individual. It is the beginning of the native's **Solar Revolution**. If such a chart is found to be in harmony with other factors then its influence will be increasingly important.

Solar revolutions, of course, mark the beginnings of a new

solar cycle and a purely symbolic as, for that matter, are all methods of directing or progressing. But the principles upon which they are based are fundamentally sound and have stood the test of time.

All **Solar and Lunar Returns** must factor in the precession of the equinoxes in their calculations. These are primarily tools used by the branch of astrology called Siderealists. The solar revolution chart is a similar tool erected under the tropical system.

Rotational Diurnal Charts

The Rotational Diurnal is to the solar revolution as the birth diurnals are to the progressed horoscope. No research has been done comparing rotational diurnals and radix directions.

It is recommended, however, for those desiring to go more deeply into the underlying principles of astrology, particularly students who have a knowledge of higher mathematics, such as spherical trigonometry, to pursue their studies into the doctrine of the sphere. Leaders in both the field of research and teaching who are thus equipped are sorely needed in the astrological world.

Converse Progressions

Converse progressions are based on the foundation of a day for a year, as in secondary progressions, but with the movement going backward in the ephemeris to find relatable information about the same time period. At the age of 12 for example, the planetary positions in the ephemeris for 12 days prior to birth will have a symbolic significance to that person when they reach the age of 12 years, and it will be relatable to life events of this period. The final 90 days of gestation are when the embryo is considered viable, it can survive outside the womb. Converse progression then, operate on the premise that each of these 90 days corresponds to a year of life. Converse progression is said to give indications to what will occur in the native's life when they reach the age being studied. The two procedures are said to be symmetrical, and whether one moves forward or backward 10, 12 or more years, one will find information about the native relating to that year of the native's life.

Calculating Secondary Progressions

The method of calculating secondary progressions is very simple. The movement of the planets along the ecliptic from birth until the same time on the following day represents their progression during the first year of life. Thus, each day in the ephemeris stands for one year of the native's lifetime. This progressive position of the planets becomes the indicator of influences upon fate and free will during the coming year. The method of calculation is the same as for the natal horoscope.

Calculate a horoscope for a child born at 11:00 AM EST, in New York City (74°W00', 40°N42') on November 7, 1930, to use as an example. To progress this horoscope for age 22 simply count forward in the ephemeris that number of days, resulting in November 29, 1930. This will be the ephemeris date from which the planetary longitudes will be taken. Create a horoscope using that date. This will correspond to the year 1952, 22 years after the child was born.

Normally the progressed planets, the progressed Ascendant, and the progressed Midheaven are placed in an outer circle around the natal horoscope, inside the natal house cusps. The progressed horoscope for 22 years of age, with transits, is given in Figure 1.

In calculating the cusps of the houses, all other factors are identical to calculating the natal chart. (An alternate method of locating the house cusps is to add the solar arc to the natal Midheaven degree; then proceed to calculate other cusps, at the required latitude, from the progressed Midheaven. Example charts in this volume are calculated by this latter method.)
The fastest moving celestial body is the Moon. It will be noted that from November 29, 1930, to the following day, GMT, it advanced 11 degrees and 55 minutes, while the Sun moved

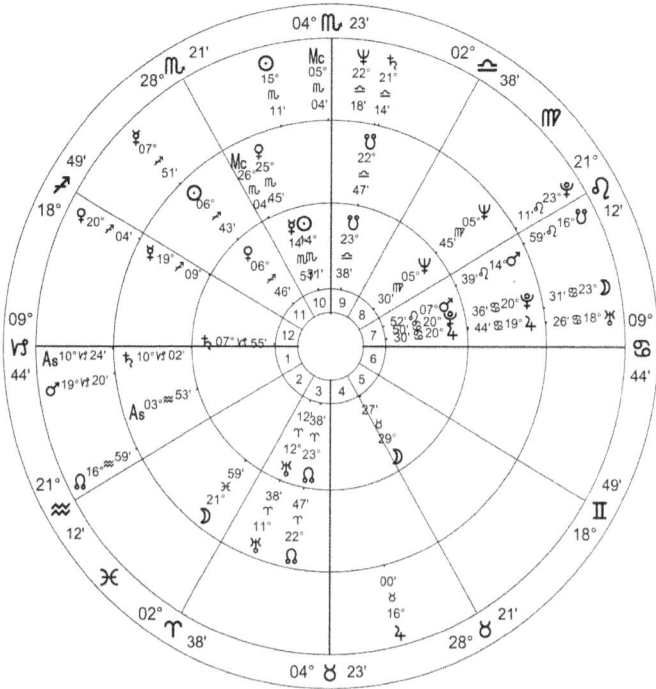

Figure 1. Natal, progressed, and transit charts for child born on November 7, 1930, at 11:00 am EST in New York City, and progressed to 22 years of age.

only 1 degree and 1 minute, Mercury 1 degree and 31 minutes, and the other planets in lesser amounts. As these are the progressed positions for the birth date anniversary, they will gradually move along the ecliptic during the year from the positions held at one anniversary to those at the next. There are 12 months in the year and with no allowance made for acceleration or deceleration in speed of their motion, they can be divided into 12 equal parts, thus progressing the planets for each month. As a matter of practical usage, however, this is usually only done in the case of the Moon.

To find the accurate progressed Moon position determine the daily rate of motion on the day (year) to be considered. Then divide the daily motion by 12 (for 12 months) to obtain the monthly motion. For November 29, 1930, the calculations are:

Moon on Nov 30, 1930 = 25♓57

Moon on Nov 29, 1930 = -14♓02

Daily motion = 11° 55'

11° 55' = (11 x 60)+55=715 minutes divided by 12=59' 35".

(Progressed movement per month for this chart only)

Progressed Moon for Nov 7, 1952 =   21♓59:00
                                  + 00 :59:35
Progressed Moon for Dec 7, 1952 =   22♓58:35
                                  + 00 :59:35
Progressed Moon for Jan 7, 1953 =   23♓58:10
                                  + 00 :59:35
Progressed Moon for Feb 7, 1953 =   24♓57:45
                                  + 00 :59:35
Progressed Moon for Mar 7, 1953 =   25♓57:20
                                  + 00 :59:35
Progressed Moon for Apr 7, 1953 =   26♓56:55

A table like this is normally calculated for the entire year which the progression affects. Aspects should be exact, with no orb, for effect.

In considering the effect and timing of directions to the radical planets, it is, of course, apparent that the influence is strongest at the time the direction becomes exact. However, as the direction under consideration may be only one of several influences operating at about the same time, the time of its operation may be slightly modified by these other influences, as would also its nature. The orb allowed in directions is much smaller than in the radical chart. It is a safe rule to allow not more than 3 degrees applying and not more than 2 degrees separating, for major aspects, although usually it will be found they operate within 1 degree orb. Directions between progressed planets, that is progressed to progressed, should be allowed a much smaller orb than progressed to radical. Also, progressed planets directed to progressed planets do not have as great an influence as those directed to natal planets. This is manifest because both progressed influences are transitory in character, while one of the influences is definitely stabilized with the radical planets.

Geographical Relocation

When a person moves to another geographical location from that in which he or she was born, it is advisable to calculate the nativity for the new location. This type of chart has come to be referred to as the **Relocation Chart**. The greater the distance the native is from the place of his birth the more important these locations charts can be. While such charts are, of course, secondary to the natal chart itself, they frequently indicate astrological influences operating in a manner not easily explained by the natal chart itself.

While the chart of the city or community in which one resides has certain influences upon the people residing in that city or community, the author has found from experience that the natal chart converted to that new location is of much greater importance as a determining factor of success or failure in that community. However, when city and community rulerships are known, it is well for the native to avoid living in those communities or cities ruled by signs in which his natal chart has malefic planets posited.

In the illustration of birth occurring at 11:00 AM, EST in New York City, when the native moved to Chicago his nativity would be calculated for the date of birth at the same Greenwich Mean time; using the table of houses latitude of Chicago for the chart, as well as the Chicago longitude correction to obtain Local Sidereal Time.

A person born in Europe and moving to America affects a marked change in the nature of these two charts – the natal and the relocated natal as shown in Figures 2 and 3. A young lady who was born in London presently resides in Columbus, Indiana, with her husband and sons. The move greatly changed the complexion of her nativity as shown by comparing the natal location in Figure 2 with the relocated position in Figure 3. Calculations were as follows:

Birth Time:

2:01 AM Double Summer Time

-2:00 time factor of DST

00:01:00 Greenwich Mean Time

17:13:58 Ephemeris Sidereal Time (12 AM)

17:14:58 Greenwich Sidereal Time

–00:00:40 Longitude correction

17:14:18 Local Sidereal Time (51N30)

To move this chart to Indiana the only calculation needs to be to subtract the longitude correction from the Greenwich Sidereal Time thus:

17:14:58 Greenwich Sidereal Time

–5:43:38 Long. correction for Columbus IN

11:31:20 Local Sidereal Time (39N12)

The lady had an extended visit to the capital of India during which she finally expressed her true solar personality more than in either home area, as shown in Figure 4.

17:14:58 Greenwich Sidereal Time

+5:08:56 Long. correction for Delhi India

22:23:54 Local Sidereal Time (28N40)

A less dramatic situation is shown in Figures 5 through 7 where a college graduate determined job placement by comparing the two most favorable offers according to the effects of relocation on the natal horoscope.

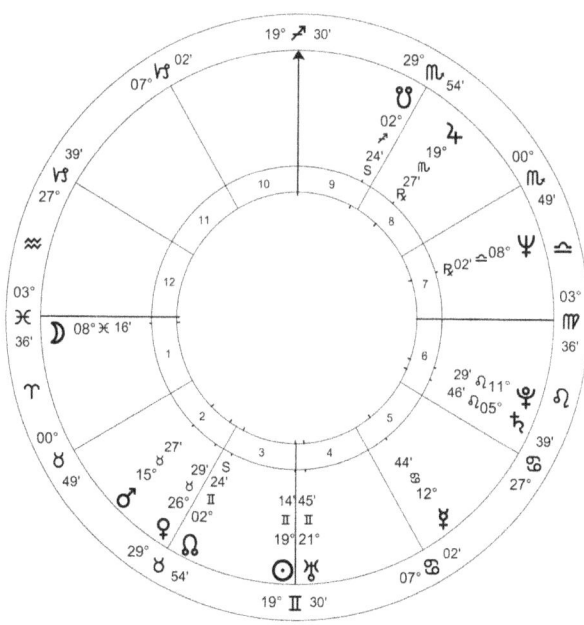

Figure 2. Natal chart of woman born in London, England, June 11, 1974, 2:01 AM British Double Summer Time. GMT= 00:01:00. Long: 00°W10', Lat: 51°N30'.

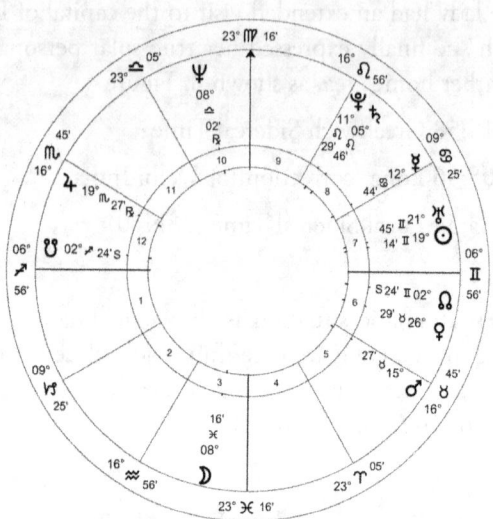

Figure 3. British born woman relocated to present home in Columbus, Indiana. 84°W55', 39°N12'.

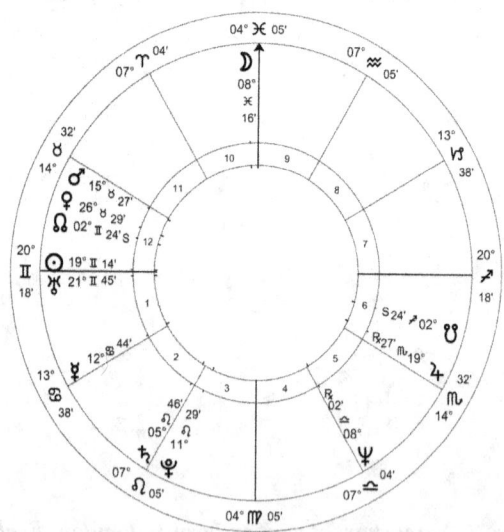

Figure 4. British born woman relocated to Delhi, India. 77°E14', 28°N40'.

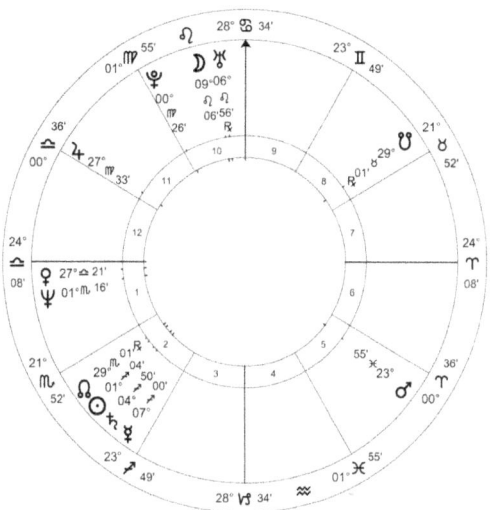

Figure 5. Graduate born November 23, 1956, in Elyria, Ohio, 4:22 AM, EST. 82°W07', 41°N22'.

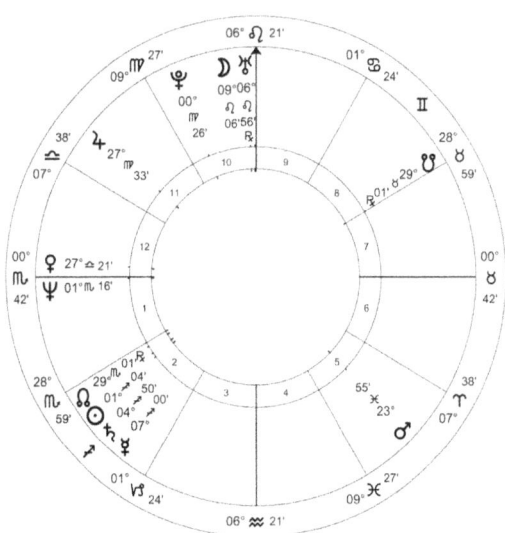

Figure 6. Graduate relocated to Red Bank New Jersey. 74°W05', 40°N21'.

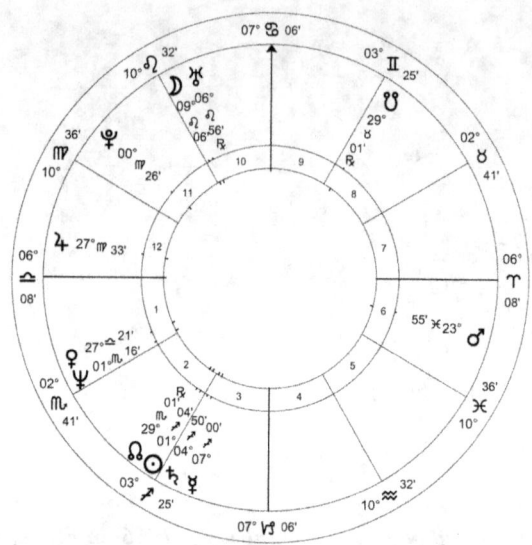

Graduate relocated to Fort Collins, Colorado. 105°W05', 40°N35'.

Additional references on Prediction:

Carter, Charles E. O., Symbolic Directions in Modern Astrology, (Macoy Publishing Co., New York, 1947.) Davidson, Ronald, Techniques of Prediction, (L. N.)

Fowler & Col., LTD, London, 1955.)

DeLuce, Robert, Complete Method of Prediction, (ASI, New York 1978.)

Doane, Doris Chase, Progressions in Action, (AF A, Tempe, AZ, 1977.)

Dobyns, Zipporah P., PhD, Progressions, Directions, and Rectification, (TIA Publications, Los Angeles, CA, 1975.)

Jones, Marc Edmund, The Scope of Astrological Prediction, (Sabian Publishing Society, Stanwood, WA, 1973.)

Leo, Alan, The Progressed Horoscope, (L.N. Fowler &

Co., LTD, London, 1969.)

Lowell, Laurel, Secondary Progressions, (Macoy Publishing, Richmond, V, 1973.)

McCormick, John, and Rushman, Carol, Deductive Interpretation of the Progressed Horoscope, (AFA, Tempe, AZ, 1977.)

Milburn, Leigh Hope, Progressed Horoscope Simplified, (Llewellyn Publications, St. Paul, MN, 1928.) Palmer, Lynne, ABC of Major Progressions, (AFA, Tempe, AZ, 1970.)

Review Questions for Chapter 1:

1. Calculate your own horoscope to an eventful year of life. Does the major event show?

2. Relocate your horoscope to your favorite city or country; repeat for an area you do not like. Can you understand the reasons now?

3. Relocate and calculate a horoscope for Astronaut and Senator, John H. Glenn, Jr., born on July 18, 1921, at 4:00 PM CDT in Cambridge, Ohio. His historic space ride was February 20, 1962; he was sworn in as a Senator, in Washington, D.C., in 1975.

|Chapter 2|

Progressed Ascendant

THE WHOLE QUESTION OF PROGRESSIONS IS one of the most troublesome facing astrology today. It has been a contentious subject for years, even centuries. The solution for some of the problems connected with it will require much research. However, sufficient knowledge has already been gained to be of great value in horoscope interpretation and the thorough student will always be alert to the development of further knowledge in this field of astrological endeavor.

To say that the progression of any particular point in the horoscope is more deserving of consideration than some other point would be a fallacy of the first order. The very nature of progressions denies this. Influences which greatly affect the life of one individual may leave little mark upon the days of another. For example, the progressed Sun arriving at a conjunction with the radical ruler of house VII in the chart of a married woman certainly would not have the marked effect upon her life that would be expected on the question of marriage in the life of a single girl.

Likewise, the age of a native at the time of a progression may have a more direct or greater influence upon him. Thus,

Saturn coming to the cusp of house IV may indicate death of a parent. This vibration operating in the horoscope of a child would necessarily have a greater influence upon the life of the native than if it were in operation in the chart of a mature person.

The entire environment of the native, as to age, experience, academic training, marital condition, etc., in all the ramifications of our complex civilization must be taken into account. The careful student will be aware of these and similar factors, thus will carefully consider all these influences in connection with his delineation of the progressed horoscope. To do so will pay rich dividends in correctly delineating the horoscope. Practice with many charts is not only desirable, but necessary so that experience may be gained.

Always bear in mind that all horoscope interpretation is based upon the natal chart. This is as fundamental as a child growing into maturity. The inherent characteristics of the child are present in the full–grown man or woman even though there have been gradual changes on the physical, mental, and spiritual levels. Environmental conditions, growth, and many other factors have all entered into the progress and development of that person. Therefore, the natal horoscope shows the inherent basic foundation upon which all interpretation must be built and the progression of the horoscope indicates the element of change, the growth of character, as well as other basic qualities of the native.

A consideration of the progressed Ascendant is elemental. Through this first house cusp and the other celestial phenomena related to it, the early days of character–forming childhood are shown in the radical horoscope. The growth and change in character will, therefore, be largely influenced by progression of this portion of the horoscope. Not only the rising sign, but the decanate occupying the eastern angle, is of great importance as well as the face and precise degree of that sign.

Bearing in mind not only sign influence and rulership, suppose three people are born, one with 5° Aries 00 rising, one with 15° Aries 00 rising and the third with 25° Aries 00 rising. Now, while the Ascendant does not move exactly at the same rate as the MC, roughly speaking it averages about 1 degree annually, except in extreme latitudes when it will vary from this mean to a great extent. All three of the natives have Mars as the predominant ruler of the Ascendant. The first has a sub–influence also of Mars (first decanate); the second has a sub–influence of the Sun (second decanate), and the third has a sub–influence of Jupiter (third decanate), as shown in Table 1. At about five years of age the third native will have 0° Taurus 00 coming up as the progressed Ascendant when, to the Mars–Jupiter influences, will be added a Venus–Venus influence from the first decanate of Taurus. The second person will not have this Venus–Venus influence entering into his life until he is about 15 years of age, at which time it will not combine with a Mars–Jupiter vibration, but with

Table 1. *The decanate rulerships according to rulers of sign triplicities.*

SIGN	DECANATES		
	First: 1°-9°59	Second: 10°-19°59'	Third: 20°-29°59'
Aries	Mars-Mars	Mars-Sun	Mars-Jupiter
Taurus	Venus-Venus	Venus-Mercury	Venus-Saturn
Gemini	Mercury-Mercury	Mercury-Venus	Mercury-Uranus
Cancer	Moon-Moon	Moon-Pluto	Moon-Neptune
Leo	Sun-Sun	Sun-Jupiter	Sun-Mars
Virgo	Mercury-Mercury	Mercury-Saturn	Mercury-Venus
Libra	Venus-Venus	Venus-Uranus	Venus-Mercury
Scorpio	Pluto-Pluto	Pluto-Neptune	Pluto-Moon
Sagittarius	Jupiter-Jupiter	Jupiter-Mar	Jupiter-Sun
Capricorn	Saturn-Saturn	Saturn-Venus	Saturn-Mercury
Aquarius	Uranus-Uranus	Uranus-Mercury	Uranus-Venus
Pisces	Neptune-Neptune	Neptune-Moon	Neptune-Pluto

that vibration built into about ten years of experience on the initial foundation of the radical Mars–Sun influence. Likewise, at about 25 years of age the first of these natives would have the Venus–Venus influence being combined with the Mars–Mars influence of his radical Ascendant, which is the first decanate of Aries, with some ten years of experience with each of the Mars–Sun and Mars–Jupiter vibrations built upon it. The student will readily see that while the same degree and sign reaches the progressed Ascendant at different ages in the lives of these natives (when they will necessarily have a different psychological outlook) the combinations of influences with the unchanging radical Ascendants are much different. Consequently, great care must be given to a consideration of these factors.

The progression of the Ascendant (or any other sensitive point) from one sign to another also changes the quadruplicity and triplicity, It may also include the passage from one trinity to another, as from Gemini to Cancer, Virgo to Libra, Sagittarius to Capricorn, Pisces to Aries. Thus, more than a single factor must be considered. In the passage from Sagittarius to Capricorn, for instance, not only is there a change from Jupiter–Mars to Saturn–Saturn, but from mutable to cardinal, from fire to earth, and from the reproductive trinity to the serving trinity. These are some of the underlying causes showing why the progression of the Ascendant (or other sensitive point) has a marked influence on the lives of most individuals. (These same considerations should be borne in mind in connection with the progression of any of the planets or other sensitive points in the chart and not alone the Ascendant.) If the change is harmonious, then it may bring beneficent influences into the life; while if it is inharmonious, it may bring conflict and distress.

While each point, on the average, progresses about one degree annually, this is not a safe rule to follow because the season of the year plus the latitude of birth cause wide variation from this mean insofar as it applies to the Ascendant and house VII, but will have less effect upon the Midheaven which is only affected by the season of the year in which birth occurred. The Midheaven progresses at almost an identical rate as the Sun.

Progressed Ascendant in Aries

First Decanate of Aries Ascendant

This influence brings a marked change into the native's life. More than this, it marks the establishment of a new cycle in the life of the native. The old is cast off and the new is taken on, and life is quickened. Intellectual activity and ambition comes to the fore. With its expression depending on the age of the native. The urge to leadership becomes strong. The wits are sharpened and the native finds himself in a better position to take full advantage of opportunities presented. Indeed, he will now largely create his own opportunities through personal initiative unleashed. Instead of depending on others, as under a Piscean influence, he seeks gain in worldly affairs by individual efforts. Personal force is intensified, which under affliction may bring disaster through rash actions or undertakings made without thoughtful preparation, thus bringing loss upon himself. It might also bring some kind of inflammatory disease, depending, of course, upon the nature of the afflictions in force then.

Suppose one native born with the third decanate of Aquarius rising has now reached about 35 years of age, while another person, born with the first decanate of Pisces rising, has now reached about 25 years of age. The innate characteristics of the first native will be Uranian–Venusian insofar as the radical Ascendant is concerned, while the second native will be of the double Neptunian (according to the old authors Neptune–Jupiter) type. The influence of a double Mars vibration on the Uranus–Venus character will be vastly different in the first case from its expression in the Neptune–Jupiter or double Neptunian second case. For, in addition to the factors illustrated above, certain other fundamental data must be applied. There are three (among others) definite cycles or divisions of life as marked off by the progression of the Moon. The first of these is that period during which the Moon makes its first progression through the zodiac, roughly the first 28 years of life. The second division is that period during which the Moon makes its second progression through the zodiac and the third division is from that time, about 55 years of age, to the end of life. These three divisions of life are marked. The first is essentially one of physical growth; the second, one of mental growth; and the third, one of spiritual growth. The progression of the chart of the man born with the third decanate of Aquarius rising will be in that era of his life which is definitely a period of mental growth, thus the influence of Aries coming to his Ascendant might be a time to give rise to inventive ability or eccentricity; while in the case of the younger man, he is still in the period of the first progression of the Moon, so that his ambitions might more aptly be turned to material gain of a rather mysterious kind or under circumstances that would be little understood by others. Of course, it might also imply spiritual development turned to "mystericism" for material gain. The main point is this: the age of the two persons would have a definite clue as to the underlying mode of expression of the ambitious development.

Second Decanate of Aries Ascendant

The influence of this decanate, Mars–Sun, is to shift the desire of ambition to the realization of ambition. The Sun (fixed-fire) is always a steadying and concentrating influence. Whereas the first decanate of Aries brought into focus the ambitious urge, just as the first decanate of Aries in the natal horoscope is one of pioneering spirit often without definite aim, so that same decanate brought into being a sub–influence of this same type. Now, in the second decanate, definite purpose is indicated by the native. The urge to accomplishment is elevated and expressed in concrete form so that success can be wrought. Likewise, while the urge of Mars is felt, the influence of the Sun decanate of Aries is to ennoble and elevate that urge. At an age in life when such things command attention, it will give stronger purpose to love affairs or speculation, while if the native is older or married, it gives greater interest in the matter of children.

The energy of Mars, properly directed by the Sun, gives the finest type of people. Of course, much depends on other factors in the natal horoscope as well as progressed positions, but the second decanate of Aries coming to the Ascendant (personal affairs), is probably one of the most marked positions for personal success, if the native has reached maturity. As always, age is an important factor. Regardless of age, however, the second decanate of Aries progressing to the Ascendant, and in a natal chart that indicates fine character, brings out a loftier spirit thus freeing the character from the material element.

It may not be amiss here to point out that the second decanate of any sign progressing to the Ascendant tends to lend direction and, to some degree, stability to that which was started in the first decanate of that sign. Just as the fixed signs are always placed between the cardinal and mutable, so the second decanate is between what may be roughly called the cardinal and mutable decanates, although the use of this term for the decanates must be used rather advisedly, remembering another factor.

The first decanate of the masculine signs is always positive or outgoing force. The succeeding decanates are always feminine or receptive in their character. Thus, the second decanate of Aries is negative, feminine, receptive, and subordinate to the overall positive nature of the entire sign. It is these very characteristics which cause it to give direction to the energy of the first decanate. Reflection is the keynote and when plans are made or when energy is abundant, it is reflection that will always give direction to its usage. These principles must be applied in consideration of the progressed chart, whether it be to the Ascendant or to other points in the chart.

Third Decanate of Aries Ascendant

The third decanate of Aries is what we may call the mutable position for the combination of Mars energy with Jupiter's lack of tenacity tends to diffuse the energies. The Mars energy is not lacking, but merely lacks direction. After the success of the second decanate comes the energetic exuberance of the third. The element of change is rather from the stability of the Sun to the nonetheless ambitious Jupiter, but with desire to change from one thing to another. As Dr. F.R. Wheeler has aptly put it, "The indiscipline of Sagittarius added to Aries provokes the spirit of revolt and rebellion; whereas the influence of Jupiter added to Mars is apt to bring strong desire for religious or judicial reform. Often, lack of tenacity destroys the opportunity for success. This is particularly true if the radical Ascendant is in Pisces. Nevertheless, this is a fine period in life for travel, religious or philosophical study, and for the development of interest in the metaphysical world. Money may either come or go easily, depending to a large extent on other factors in the horoscope. The native may become extravagant, but then wealth may come easily at this period.

Perhaps one of the greatest lessons to be learned during this approximate ten–year period is to control impulsiveness. If the natal chart indicates high and lofty character, such impulse and expansion will aid in the development of a loftier spirit and the desire to search deeper into the esoteric truths of life. Such search, however, will be more along orthodox lines the further along the decanate progression goes. Desire for spiritual truth is keener here, but it may be lacking in direction unless the chart is otherwise strong. Of course, on the lower planes, such impulsiveness is not beneficial for it implies lack of caution leading to disputes.

This decanate in its closing degrees begins to prepare the native for the gradual change that will take place with the coming of Taurus to the Ascendant.

In progressed horoscopes another factor to remember is that when the Ascendant is in the first decanate of a sign this makes it possible for the second decanate and, perhaps all the third decanate of that sign to also be found in house I.

Thus when other than the first decanate is on the Ascendant, it means that the next succeeding sign is gradually passing up through the first house. The student will readily see, therefore, that all of this element of change is astrologically explained as gradual. Character itself is something that is gradual in its development. It is not made overnight, although it may be destroyed that quickly. Just as physical growth of a child into manhood or womanhood is a gradual process, so character itself is a gradual process which the horoscope explains.

Progressed Ascendant in Taurus
First Decanate of Taurus Ascendant

Here the element of change is very pronounced: from Aries to Taurus, from Mars–Jupiter to Venus–Venus, from fire to earth, from cardinal to fixed. The energy of Mars is dying out and the determination of Taurus is increasing. The first impulses usually felt are those of a material sort. Just as Taurus is the natural second house sign, so its influence here tends to financial affairs. The materialism and practicality of the sign, however, under favorable influences indicate an ability to make good use of the gains attained. Ambition has subsided to a large extent but perseverance in the maintenance of the objectives already reached and the desire for financial security is stronger. Here is where the passive side of this negative decanate shows forth. The reckless ambition of Aries is a thing of the past but the security of a dollar in the bank speaks out in its place. Of course, under affliction, the stubbornness and obstinacy of Taurus may be productive of losses for practically all losses indicated in the chart will be due to these characteristics.

Another rather strange, and seemingly unrelated, factor which may come to the fore is the development of a psychic sense, particularly if the native has Pisces rising in the natal chart. Certain degrees of the first decanate of Taurus (6 degrees to 8 degrees specifically, and 4 degrees to 12 degrees generally) are definitely indicative of psychic ability in the natal chart and, if other factors in the natal chart indicate psychic ability , it will usually be developed during the progression of the second face of this decanate over the Ascendant.

Second Decanate of Taurus Ascendant

While Taurus is a feminine, negative, and passive sign, this decanate is the most aggressive of all. It is the masculine, positive, and out–pouring decanate of Taurus, mutable in its characteristics. As the change is from Venus–Venus to Venus–Mercury, it may mark a period of critical ability which aids professionally or it may end in useless discussion. Again the intellect comes to the fore and mental faculties are awakened to great activity of an analytical nature. Under affliction, however, this may produce nervous strain requiring hospitalization. In any event, the mildest of afflictions will bring some nervous strain.

This is the practical decanate of Taurus and the Venus–Mercury influence tends to strong mental practicality. Reasoning ability is increased, logic is reasonable, and the native, if professionally engaged in mental pursuits, may find this a period of great monetary gain through the development of these characteristics. All mental pursuits should be pushed if other favorable influences are operating coincident with the second decanate of Taurus on the Ascendant.

Third Decanate of Taurus Ascendant

The gradual passage of the Mercury decanate into the past and the upsurge of the Capricorn decanate of Taurus lends stability, with passive ambition, to the character. While this is also a slowing up process, a sort of putting on the brakes, it gives greater insurance to the success of whatever commands the interest of the native. It is indeed a strong influence as relates to the occupation or profession for Capricorn and Saturn are house X influences naturally, with cardinal ambition. (This decanate is an excellent place to note the blending of astrological influences for in it is the negative sign, stimulated by a cardinal type of decanate, which is inherently passive and which is preparatory in its action for the coming mutable masculine decanate of Gemini.) The influence of Saturn on Venusian characteristics, as indicated by this decanate, is entirely wholesome and worthwhile unless there is affliction between these two planets in the radical chart. Saturn is always a difficult planet in its influence but, when one is able to blend its vibrations harmoniously with the remainder of the chart, it is not only stabilizing but is also productive of great honor, success, and responsibility. As it is the money sign this may be and usually is, reflected in increased income – notwithstanding the fact that Saturn is a planet of restriction. Perhaps it may more properly be said to be a stabilization of financial outlook. Of course, it means also that income will be produced only by hard work through the stability of fixed sign Taurus. It also brings responsibility, or a sense of responsibility.

Emotionally, because of the double influence of earth (Taurus and Capricorn), there will be hindrances, delays and difficulties, but it will encourage the cultivation of higher virtues of a more lasting character. Affections may be stabilized or may be destroyed. One extreme or the other is expected; there is no middle road. If they are stabilized then the influence of the succeeding mutable sign will have little effect on the emotional life; but, if they are destroyed, then the sign Gemini coming to the Ascendant may bring a lack of purpose in life that is destructive of all that man considers worthwhile. Thus, the finest counsel is to work for stabilization of the affections and emotional life. Certainly that which is emotionally ephemeral will be destroyed by this double earth influence, while that which is practical and stable will be intensified and beautified.

Progressed Ascendant in Gemini

First Decanate of Gemini Ascendant

When the Ascendant progresses from Taurus to Gemini, the element of change is exceedingly pronounced. Not only is it a change from the stability of Taurus to the mutability of Gemini, but it is from earth to air, from the passive ambition to active intuition. The action of this change depends much upon the rising degree of the radical horoscope. For example, should the nativity have the closing decanate of Aries rising, a change comes early in life, and the Ascendant's progression through Taurus will prove a stabilizing influence on the tendency to diffuse the energy of Aries (Mars). But after this experience has been accomplished, the mutable intuitive qualities of the first decanate of Gemini too often tend to bring about complete scattering of the energies through lack of definite objective. The native loses some of his tenacity and unceasing change must come; seeking this change the native often lacks definite purpose. Thus, the ambition of Aries and the energy of Mars (its ruler) brings strong reaction from the stabilization loaned by Taurus when the Ascendant moves into Gemini at that age in life when Jupiter (35 to 42 years) has sub–rulership. Unless the native has learned well during his Terrain apprenticeship, intuition runs wild when Gemini's first decanate appears.

Great changes in the native's outlook will undoubtedly be effected, due largely to new experiences, both mental and material. The tendency, however, will be to superficiality. Mental activity will abound in almost all directions. The mental awakening which will come sends the native searching in all directions to learn with little depth to though.

If the native has Pisces on the Ascendant natally, this activity may be in the direction of philosophy, religious impulse or experience, and emotional instability; with Aries on the radical Ascendant the mixture of cardinal and mutable will activate desire for variety because these natives have intense mental activity; and with a Taurus natal Ascendant (if it be the second or even the third decanate), the clairvoyant and/or clairaudient power is brought to the fore. But for Taurus generally, it creates difficulty in finances brought about by lack of direction and instability in the native's reaction.

However, it must be borne in mind clearly, that all of these suggested influences of progressions are dealing with analytical astrology rather than synthetical. In the process of synthesizing the progressed horoscope, each chart must be considered as a whole in the same manner as when synthesizing the radical or natal horoscope.

Second Decanate of Gemini Ascendant

The second decanate of Gemini is much more stable than the first. Whereas during the years of the progression of the Ascendant through the first ten degrees of Gemini there was mental restiveness and lack of direction, when the second decanate is reached by the Ascendant (while the activity is still apparent in the native's mental outlook), discernment, judgment, and balance begin to adjust and direct the thought. Here is the blending of Mercury with the Libran decanate under sub–rulership of Venus. Whereas in the second decanate of Taurus, the Mercury–Venus influence was motivated primarily by the characteristics of Taurus, here the blending of these two planets is similar but with the seventh sign characteristics predominantly manifest rather than the second sign. In Taurus, also, the dominant planet is Venus while in Gemini this dominant influence rests in Mercury.

The native will probably react to this influence in one of two ways, if not in both. First, marriage and the seventh house affairs are strongly influenced. Sometimes this decanate in itself will bring about marriage or in any event, it stimulates the fact of marriage in the life of the native. Naturally the environments of age and circumstance must be taken into account. Second, the native may espouse some cause, doctrine, or philosophy and actively express life through it. The native will also find association with other people more pleasant and productive of mental gain or material good.

This decanate brings about mental readjustment, enhancing the opportunity for real progress. This finds reflection in relieving financial strain, for the energies are focused on definite objectives and no real success can come without such foci. This decanate also brings a measure of contentment. However, a predominate characteristic of this second decanate of Gemini is lack of outward desire of material gain. Inwardly, there is a desire for sufficient amount of the world's goods to carry out definite mental studies without suffering from want of life's necessities.

Third Decanate of Gemini Ascendant

The Aquarian decanate of Gemini increases the objectivity of the native's mental and material progress for which both of the preceding decanates have been preparing him. The age of the native must always be considered in connection with these progressions. By and large, however, the third decanate of Gemini brings a degree of surety and security to the native. It is a climax to the mentalism of Gemini as a whole. However, inquisitiveness does not cease when the Ascendant progresses to the third decanate of Gemini; the Uranian impulse simply is added to it. The native searches deeper for knowledge, which often has to do with the occult. The mysterious intrigues the mind and the desire to know that which is hidden is keener. Reason takes the place of intuition. Science takes the place of faith, although the degrees of supreme faith are generally recognized as the twenty-third degree of Gemini and Sagittarius. The native becomes more progressive and success is attained (depending again somewhat upon the environment of age and circumstance, although this success may come even in the teen years as well as late in life).

In considering the third decanate of Gemini, do not overlook the influence of Saturn. Remember according to Manilius, Ptolemy, and the ancients, Saturn is the ruler of Aquarius. Advanced students must never lose sight of this fact (and the further fact of the rulership of Jupiter over Pisces). Saturn gives depth with success when harmonious as it also stimulates research along stable lines. Thus there is this mixture of Mercury–Saturn–Uranus blending with the natal horoscope which, when harmonious, is a sure influence for deep mental progress.

This decanate brings new friends and associations and stabilizes association with others. As to whether this is beneficial or detrimental will depend on afflictions in the horoscope as a whole.

The third decanates of Gemini, Virgo, Sagittarius, and particularly, Pisces, are sometimes referred to as preparation decanates for they are preparatory to greater changes, particularly in the case of Pisces. These changes are marked by the passage from one trinity to another. They are the climax of their own trinity so the third decanate of Gemini marks the climax of mental activity as it relates to itself.

Progressed Ascendant in Cancer
First Decanate of Cancer Ascendant

Again, consider the strong element of change from air to water, from mutable to cardinal, and from the intellectual to the emotional. The change from Mercury–Saturn–Uranus influence to the Moon–Moon influence stirs the emotional side of life deeply. Much, of course, depends upon profit the native gained through the experiences of the last decanate of Gemini, for decanates through which the Ascendant progresses are but the foundations upon which succeeding decanates are built. If the preceding decanates' influences have been beneficial, then here is their finest expression. As Dr. Francis Rolt–Wheeler has said, however, "If the preceding decanate has only built up intellectual vanity, then the sensitivity of this decanate will prove a trap." The emotional and imaginative side of life permits development of domestic matters at their best, the making of personal attachments that bring joy, and the cultivation of the finer instincts of man.

The home ties of the native begin to take on new form and mean more. Instead of self dependence is found home dependence with its new sense of responsibility. The maternal or family instincts will be aroused. Desire for home and family (again depending to some extent upon the age of the native) will be paramount. The world has been viewed through the eyes of

Gemini, and now the native is content to find his acre of diamonds in his own backyard. This instinct is probably stronger in the first decanate of Cancer than in either of the other two.

Second Decanate of Cancer Ascendant

This is perhaps the most unfortunate of the Cancer decanates for here the Scorpio–Pluto influence is added to that of the Moon. Usually deaths in the family circle bring suffering and distress. The combination of the influence of Moon and Pluto is always disruptive, and when added to the nature of Scorpio (the eighth sign) it too often sets the termination of life for those held dear by the native

This disruptive influence also may act upon the character of the native (depending again somewhat on age) making him secretive, jealous, and ill–tempered. Passion takes the place of maternal love, love itself is displaced by jealousy, and ill–will takes the place of friendship. Thus, disappointment and a souring on life may be the result.

This is also a rather dangerous period. As the Moon rules the fluidic content of the body, particularly the blood, and Mars (co–ruler of Scorpio) has to do with infectious fevers, there is some danger of infectious diseases or blood disorders brought about through contact with others. Care and caution must always be exercised during this period. Indeed, this is a difficult decade in the life of all natives with its degree of danger being largely measured by the natal horoscope.

Third Decanate of Cancer Ascendant

Life is not a series of unrelated events; everything arises from a prior cause. The contentment, joy, success, and well being of the native having his Ascendant progress through the third decanate of Cancer is measured largely by the manner in which he reacted to the second decanate of Cancer. This Moon–Jupiter–Neptune decanate, following a second decanate of the higher nature, will express itself through higher emotional development. This is indeed a subtle influence on the life which may express itself in occult development or in emotional religious experience as differentiated from the intuitional intellectual experience of Gemini.

To the negative vibration of Cancer is added the negative influence of the watery sign Pisces, sometimes influencing the native to be receptive to fatalism and all that it implies. Indeed, in this decanate is the first of the watery fatalistic degrees, 28° Cancer 00. Likewise, if the lower nature of Pisces should be dominant in influencing this decanate, the parasitic nature of Pisces may be brought forward as negative, leaning, and dependent without energy or desire to progress.

On the other hand, with the influence of Jupiter blended in this decanate, the native is being subconsciously influenced toward the spirit of universal love. If the native has learned well from the experiences of the second decanate of Cancer, then compassion, benevolence, charity, and hospitality find expression here.

Health factors should be carefully considered when this decanate represents the progressed Ascendant because hospitalization for one cause of other is usually shown. These are often the result of infectious diseases commenced during the progression through the second decanate.

Progressed Ascendant in Leo

First Decanate of Leo Ascendant

The cool, moist passiveness of the Moon–Neptune–Jupiter decanate gives way to the hot, virulent, determined outpouring of energy of the double solar decanate of Leo. The easy-going negative nature of Cancer with all of its sensitive qualities gives way to the positive, self-assured leadership qualities of the Sun. How marked this change will be must necessarily depend on the natal horoscope, particularly the rising degree and the position of the Sun. But a new element of power enters the very soul of the native and self–reliance becomes more manifest. Thus the soul is brought into a state of consciousness where individual feeling and emotion take the place of personal attachment.

The vitality is strengthened, health may improve, the disposition may become more cheerful, and the whole outlook on life seems bathed in the golden beauty of the dominant solar vibrations. This decanate strengthens the body, mind, and soul. Whether changes will be manifest along proper lines, of course, depends much upon the native's progress through the past influences which have been cast upon the mold of his life. But the vibrations of this decanate revitalize, stimulate, and energize every phase of life's interests and activities.

When directed along proper paths success comes in affaires de coeur, in the material aspects of life, and in the relationships with others. A more magnanimous nature is developed. Afflicted, this decanate may influence the native to vanity and disreputable interests, but on its better side, generosity, philanthropy, good character, love of pleasure, and full enjoyment of life's best gifts will predominate.

In consideration of both the natal horoscope and, more particularly, the progressed chart three qualities enter into the being of every individual: heredity, environment, and character. These three factors indicate the inherent qualities with which he is born, the changing factors of life (of which he is a part), and the real destiny (destination) of the native. Alan Leo has referred to them in this fashion:

"Heredity supplies the vessel, pure or impure according to past causes in previous lives by an affinity of physical particles, like attracting like.

Environment gives conditions in which expression may be made of the latent qualities inherent in the soul, and it harmonizes with the actual needs and requirements of the soul in order that the latter may obtain its freedom from the fate of other previous lives by paying off the debts it has incurred and by developing those traits of character for the lack of which the continued evolution of the soul, at the point then reached, would be delayed.

Character is that inherent quality of the soul which it brings with it as an asset, and is the root of merit through which it is either susceptive and conformable to its environment, or rises above and dominates.

In this sense Character becomes Destiny."

Whether or not the student accepts the philosophy of Alan Leo, the ever-changing conditions of life will be apparent from this comment. Causation is indicated by changing planetary and zodiacal positions in the chart, thus the blending together and the continuity of the whole pattern being largely shown by the progression of the angles (particularly of the Ascendant), which has so much direct relationship to the innate qualities of the native himself.

Second Decanate of Leo Ascendant

Here is the intermingling of the qualities of both Leo and Sagittarius (Sun and Jupiter). To the determination and stability of the Sun's own sign is added the ambition of Sagittarius; thus, in its higher plane, marking success, conservatism, respect for law and order, and a philosophical, if not religious, attitude of mind. On the contrary, in its lower nature, the poorest qualities of the native will be emphasized with a strong desire for gambling, speculation, and disrespect for conventions. The influence of the experiences of the preceding decanates on the life of the native must be observed. In any event, there is an expansion of activity, with good usually predominating, thus making success. On the material plane, however, it may bring complete loss through risky ventures and speculation, but even this will succeed in driving home to the native the need for acceptance of a philosophical attitude productive of future good to him. To one man the gain of a fortune may mark success, while to another the greatest possible success may come through material loss. Contrariwise, the gain of a fortune may spell the ruin of all that is worthwhile within another. Successful interpretation of how these influences will operate depends largely on how well the radical horoscope has been interpreted.

The second decanate of Leo also brings other mental expansion through travel, long journeys particularly. And, as Jupiter is the Great Benefic, it may also bring expansion in business and financial matters through the conservative ambitious leadership this decanate bestows.

Third Decanate of Leo Ascendant

When the influence of Aries is added to the influence of Leo, some danger is brought to the native for the influence tends to over–expand and go to extremes. If success has been marked in the second decanate, then this decanate may easily invite disaster for the moderation of the second decanate (which was a large contributing cause of such success) will give way to impulsiveness with a tendency to rash and hasty actions.

To the native's determination is added a quality of self assertiveness including domination of situations and people which may destroy much of the good heretofore accomplished. In the well–balanced horoscope, however, Mars energy added to the Sun produces a period of great energy, enterprise, and progressiveness. Impulse of emotion, under the control of the mind, will stimulate the finest qualities inherent in the native. The pioneering spirit of Aries is combined with solar energy and, properly directed, it aids in the successful accomplishment of life's objectives. While this is predominantly a mental decanate in the heart sign, the tendency is to blend intellect with emotions which produces truth, and the courage of conviction to enable one to carry out principles through all obstacles and difficulties.

Progressed Ascendant in Virgo

First Decanate of Virgo Ascendant

The change from the Sun–Mars decanate of Leo to the double Mercury decanate of Virgo is indeed marked. Discrimination, a critical frame of mind, and fine analysis with more thought than has been applied previously mark this period of life. Rash and fiery independence is superceded by thoughtful discrimination In the place of leadership has come the force of service. Virgo brings modesty and a retiring attitude, thus turning the native to be a willing servant.

With this sudden change from Leo to Virgo often comes impairment of health, nervous tendencies, and disorders which are difficult to combat (if suggested in the natal horoscope). Difficulties with inferiors and affairs not working out in just the manner desired, both bring about worry and distress. This decanate may even bring occult or psychic qualities and interest to the fore but, in any event, after the excitement of the Sun–Mars decanate of Leo, this Mercury–Mercury decanate of Virgo brings the native into a period marked particularly by its lack of excitement, a sort of letdown from the thrill of existence previously experienced.

Second Decanate of Virgo Ascendant

When the Saturn decanate of Virgo begins to rise, a period of increased ambition, perseverance, and tact brings new experience to the native. A more scientific attitude is developed, and depth of learning becomes marked. Interest in searching out scientific truths stimulates the native to higher planes, while it may have a tendency to make him melancholy at times (if the natal chart is not of a high vibration). Opportunities for advancement will accrue and the native will gain through his own perseverance or endeavor. This decanate brings some public recognition through services rendered to mankind generally or through the personal merit of the native. Saturn increases the activity and, with the discernment of Virgo added, success is marked by the native's industry.

If there is much affliction to this decanate, the desire to rise in life may stimulate the native to dishonesty or may make him a victim of the trickery of others. Here again, the inherent qualities of the natal chart must be taken into account. The average student will pick out those portions of these lessons which apply to a particular horoscope. Thus, it will be agreed that there cannot be too much repetition of counsel that may keep the student from erring in even a single horoscope.

Third Decanate of Virgo Ascendant

The critical and, at times selfish, side of Virgo here gives way to the intuitive and receptive phase of its influence for in the third decanate the blending of Mercury and Venus influences softens the harshness of criticism. This Taurean decanate also brings improvement in financial affairs, thus creating a more cheerful and hopeful outlook. This is a very fine period along almost all avenues of life's expression and natives with Ascendants progressing through this decanate should be counseled to take the fullest advantage possible of it, on the higher plane, to prepare themselves for the full enjoyment expected with the first decanate of Libra.

There is a tendency to be more obstinate or sometimes stubborn, which may be turned to good account when properly exercised. The combination of love and intellect (Venus and Mercury) is always stimulation to a sympathetic understanding of the problems of others and, if the horoscope be a high quality radically, it will bring true obedience with an eager desire to learn and advance. But, to most persons, this decanate brings improved conditions with progress and contentment, unless afflicted so there are serious losses through neglect of duty, love of self, and materialistic tendencies generally.

Progressed Ascendant in Libra

First Decanate of Libra Ascendant

The progress of the Ascendant into the first decanate of Libra is not as radical a change as it might seem for it is only a change from Mercury–Venus to Venus–Venus. True, it is an alteration from earth to air, and material to intuitional, but it is almost always for benefit and that native is not aware of change until it is accomplished. Life will become calmer with greater balance foreshadowed by a period of greater ease. Finances may be more secure and life in general will follow a smoother course. There is a balancing between good and evil, so the native takes surer account of his own position in life. His attitude toward life and others will be more balanced, so he can seek out new friendships and contacts with a keener desire for fraternal fellowship.

This next ten years or so of life means much, for upon its foundations of justice or injustice will be built the experiences that influence the remaining years of life. The decisions made affect the future strongly. Likewise, the native will be influenced more by others; in particular a single individual is likely to make a strong mark on his life. This may be through marriage or entering into a business partnership. To the progressive native this change brings opportunity for clearer understanding of the human values of life and any animal side to his nature will be left in the past while he progresses into the social and humanizing attitudes toward life.

The age of the individual has an important bearing on this period for thus will be indicated the rising degree of the natal horoscope of which these new and changing vibrations must be made a part.

Second Decanate of Libra Ascendant

This also marks a very favorable period in life usually for the Saturn influence is added to that of Venus with Aquarian significance, giving not only direction to the cardinal qualities of Libra, but lending perseverance, stability, a sense of values, and loyalty to the native. If already married, it brings about a deeper understanding of the marriage relationship and will stimulate the higher qualities of love toward one another. If not married, it may bring about a union of the affections with one of the opposite sex who has a deep sense of loyalty and devotion. Pure platonic love may be found here. Opportunities are created for excellent and long duration friendships on real foundations of appreciation.

The native's own mental attributes will be stabilized and he is given a greater responsibility to the whole social order, thus releasing a sense of independence and freedom coincident with the inner awakening of a more social and artistic sense, which is more or less latent in all humans. The mind will be more refined and attention directed toward subjective types of study. It brings group association with gain through societies, public gathering, and organizations. The humanitarian side of the nature is stirred profoundly and the native may become interested in a study of character and humanity. Purity of thought and refinement of nature are the key notes of this decanate.

Under heavy affliction, however, this decanate may bring to the foreground open enemies, for it is an innate quality of this angle of the heavens. Either permanent friendships or lasting enmities are made. In the latter case, the native will be forgiving, unless Leo is rising in the radical horoscope when other factors must be considered. Gains or losses through partnerships may be shown. The peace–loving nature of Libra plus the staid qualities of Saturn and the originality of Uranus, however, usually are productive of good to the native. Considered in the light of the Uranian qualities and Aquarius, these factors of friendship may be brought about suddenly and from unexpected sources, but to consider the influences in the full knowledge given by the ancients plus recent discoveries it means a Venus–Uranus–Saturn vibration. The influence of Uranus in its true perspective, the higher scale of Mercury, means no difficulty should be encountered here for the function of Uranus is summed up in the word brotherhood, and when the Brotherhood of Man is individualized, all of those faculties will be developed as exemplified in the loyalty characteristics of Saturn–Venus.

Third Decanate of Libra Ascendant

Here is another combination of Venus and Mercury, in a

cardinal airy sign. Fondness for intellectual pursuits is stimulated, particularly as it relates to the arts. In the final analysis this decanate gives refinement to the intellect and a discriminating sense of true pleasure in living. Activity is mentally greater and success can be assured through the development of literary ability. The smaller affairs of life take on more importance and the native gives greater attention to them. The outlook is cheerful and hopeful, as it always is when Venus and Mercury combine under favorable circumstances with their vibrations being focused upon a sensitive point in the chart.

However, this decanate is the combination of the Gemini nature of Mercury's influence, rather than that of Virgo. Thus this Gemini decanate of Libra is more diffusive, giving a wider mental interest and acquisitiveness for all matters relating to music and art.

Progressed Ascendant in Scorpio
First Decanate of Scorpio Ascendant

The change from the Venus–Mercury decanate of Libra to the double Pluto decanate of Scorpio is one of the most marked for good or ill in the whole zodiac. If the native has absorbed the higher vibrations of Libran influences which have been at play upon his Ascendant as it progressed through that sign, then he may expect great advances during this period of life when the dynamic energy of Scorpio's vibrations dominate the progressed Ascendant.

Each of the planets (but not the Sun and Moon) according to the ancients, had rulership over two signs which were referred to as their diurnal thrones and nocturnal thrones. The planet Mercury's diurnal throne is Gemini, while its nocturnal throne is Virgo. Venus has her diurnal throne in Libra and nocturnal throne in Taurus, while the Mars diurnal throne is Aries and his nocturnal throne in Scorpio. The observing student will note the variation in the influence of these planets, as well as that of other planets, in their diurnal and nocturnal signs; for in each of these they act through different quadruplicities and trinities and, in some instances, different triplicities. Thus, Venus in her nocturnal sign acts through fixed–earth, which is manifestly much different than when she acts through Libra, which is cardinal–air. Likewise, Mars acting through the fiery cardinal sign Aries, will exert a much different influence than when he acts through the watery–fixed sign Scorpio. Great Martian energy is always difficult to manage and when it becomes a fixed energy in a watery sign it is very liable to stir the emotional side of the native to a degree that might bring disaster. Hence, the lessons of Libra, and how well they have been adapted, mark greatly the native's reaction to the first decanate of Scorpio when such a pronounced change takes place–for the intellectual activity of cardinal Libra to change over to the emotional, energizing nature of Scorpio is a marked difference in mode of expression. Even though the recently discovered planet Pluto now rules Scorpio, Mars remains the co–ruler.

This position will awaken any latent possibilities in the nature as well as give a stability which, rightly used, may promise great success in life. The personality is aggressively determined which can bring successful culmination to ambitious desires, making the native appreciate his inherent powers. This is one of the most dangerous decanates of the entire zodiac. Its natural tendency will be to make him secretive, jealous, and sarcastic, which if permitted to run uncontrolled will bring disaster, but when controlled and directed properly will stimulate to accomplishment.

This is a decanate of growth. If Libra is on the natal Ascendant without affliction, this decade of life promises tremendous growth, spiritually as well as materially and intellectually. If Virgo is on the natal Ascendant, it directs the vibrations more to the mental side of life than to either physical or spiritual. In any event, the nature of the growth, whether for good or ill, depends largely upon influences which have been at play during the preceding years of life as well as the native's reaction to them.

Second Decanate of Scorpio Ascendant

The second decanate of Scorpio, with its Pluto–Mars–Neptune–Jupiter vibration, is generally a very critical period in life. Many unique experiences are brought to the native, but the lack of harmony between these planets, with the fatalistic side of Neptune pushed forward, brings much sorrow to the native. There is danger of confinement, usually due to poor health, but the warning should always be given to be very guarded and careful in all actions, whether related to health or partnerships. Temptations will come during this period bringing possible treachery or harm through the opposite sex. The expansive characteristics of the Jupiterian influence, plus the emotion of Mars and Pluto, stimulate the passions. The contradictory nature of these vibrations indicate water with a loss of energy which might even break the morale of the native. However, if the earlier lessons of Libra and Scorpio have developed the native into the higher planes, then he will rise above temptations and be strengthened by successful combat. Minor troubles will then have little or no effect.

This decanate, through its waste characteristics of a combination of Mars–Pluto–Jupiter vibrations, often brings needless expense. This may be reflected either through the native, the marriage, or other partners in life. Caution and care must be exercised in all matters and, no matter how subtle, all temptations should be left behind. The native's greatest battle in life is going to be fought out during this ten–year period, which can permanently make or mar.

Third Decanate of Scorpio Ascendant

In the Cancer decanate of Scorpio, are vibrations which are far from harmonious. The Pluto–Mars–Moon decanate brings sorrow to the home life. Alan Leo, in referring to this decanate, says, "It will bring deaths into the family circle and cause domestic changes of a troublesome type. It will incline the native to be sarcastic, and will cause him to be exceedingly receptive to psychic symptoms of all kinds; it is not a good period that it heralds, and will bring very many strange experiences into the life while it lasts. To those who are making great progress it will bring a very strong leaning towards the occult, and a love of all things mystical. To those who are in any way receptive to its vibrations it will cause romantic and peculiar attachments, though nothing very favorable will come out of them. It seems to indicate changes that are enforced rather than sought.

Certainly this is a period of life when great caution must be exercised for the explosive qualities of this combination can be quite harmful. The native should control anger and impulses at their start to develop so far as possible a passive nature as the problems fall upon him. Over–stimulation should be avoided as it is detrimental to the nervous system; also the avoidance of all forms of alcohol, drugs and stimulants should be urged.

Scorpio is influenced greatly by the force of the radical Ascendant and the absorption of the higher vibrations of preceding decanates and signs. Scorpio is the testing ground for the native upon which will be built foundations for the beneficent influences of Sagittarius when they arrive or the shifting sands which will destroy the values of Sagittarius.

Progressed Ascendant in Sagittarius
First Decanate of Sagittarius Ascendant

When the progressed Ascendant reaches Sagittarius the native feels as though his burdens are being lifted. A more cheerful outlook is foreshadowed; a philosophical attitude towards life and its problems develops, for this is the sign of the higher or abstract mind. His outlook will be more independent so latent ambitions will come to the fore and be marked with some degree of success. The release from Scorpio vibrations may even make the native feel so carefree that it will prove harmful through the scattering of energy over too many interests. Note the change from fixed water to mutable–fire.

These changes are not sudden changes. The orb of influence of the cusps extends over several degrees and as these degrees move forward only about one degree each year, during the closing years of one sign the influence of the next sign, or even decanate, begins to be felt in the life, Likewise, it must also be remembered that the progressed first house continues to extend over 30 degrees of oblique ascension so that on the average 30 degrees of the zodiac may be extending some influence on the first house at all times. Certain it is that the influence of the next sign will be strongly felt during the year immediately preceding the cusp arriving in that sign and, in a lesser degree, will be felt for at least two years before. In the case of changes from one decanate to another this period may be cut in half for all general work.

The influence of the first decanate of Sagittarius may also bring material gain as well as mental buoyancy. Faith and hope increase and, with these, may come a desire to take up philosophical studies. Much, of course, depends upon the radical horoscope but, if a natal chart indicates ability for law, religion, philosophy, and the development of the abstract mental processes, now is the time to develop them. This is a good period usually for travel and a long journey, to some foreign land, may be successfully undertaken. Interest in physical development will be stimulated as outdoor exercise and games engage the interest. Increased love of freedom is also shown.

However, if there is serious affliction, this decanate of Sagittarius brings a rebellious spirit with a corresponding disregard of the conventions, of law, and of religious belief. A careless and indifferent attitude towards life, others, and ambition may be expressed. The keynote to success during this period of life seems to be expressed only through the native's ability to concentrate beneficent influences and bring success.

Second Decanate of Sagittarius Ascendant

The ten years marked by the Aries decanate of Sagittarius

again brings together the influence of Jupiter and Mars. Expansive–explosion seems to be the keynote to this decanate, as these two planets would imply. The native will show forth an independent and impulsive mental attitude in new experiences, upon which he acts impulsively and without proper forethought. Rashness seems to dominate actions. Lack of control and self–assertiveness directed towards new interest are shown.

The danger lies largely in an impulse to go from one extreme to another. While this decanate entails some danger, it is primarily danger from within the native himself, rather than from without. On the other hand, if the natal chart indicates an over–cautious person, the stimulation of this decanate may prove to be a driving force that can bring success. These natives usually have Scorpio or Libra rising natally and neither sign alone indicates a tendency to be overly cautious (although Libra does give balance), the result being that, when the second decanate of Sagittarius is reached by the progression, lack of self control brings disaster. This decanate, through its Mars influence, also brings liability to accidents. The mind and intellect are keen and bright.

Third Decanate of Sagittarius Ascendant

The third decanate of Sagittarius lends a stabilizing influence to the impetuousness of the second decanate. While the native may make some impulsive attachments, the influence of Jupiter plus Sun (for Leo is the sub–ruler), unless heavily afflicted in the natal chart, rarely bring deep–rooted difficulties. Rather the fixity of Leo is borrowed by the intuition of Sagittarius resulting in a highly beneficial influence. The native should learn to exercise caution in dealing with others, particularly where the emotions are concerned. This decanate may bring a certain type of idealistic marriage.

This is, indeed a poor decanate for those tempted to gamble and speculate unless the natal chart is so indicated, in which event the native will gain much. In other words, it either predicts great gain or great loss; there is no middle course. Thus it will be seen that great values can be obtained while the Ascendant is progressing through this decanate if great caution and care are exercised.

Progressed Ascendant in Capricorn
First Decanate of Capricorn Ascendant

The active, and sometimes diffused, stimulation of the third decanate of Sagittarius gives way to the coldly methodical attitude of Capricorn. Industry, perseverance, and endurance supplant enthusiasm and scattering of energies. A more diplomatic attitude on the part of the native will be apparent; his own ambitious desire to excel and force ahead in a business-like course, carefully planned. Though the radical chart may not indicate the inherent ability necessary to attain desired success, nevertheless the impulse given to the native's whole attitude will bring rewards measured only by the inherent characteristics indicated in the natal horoscope. If the native is progressive, here will be the opportunity he has been seeking.

As this is the sign of diplomacy, it may bring political pursuits, public office, or positions of great trust and honor. If the progressed horoscope is favorable as a whole at this period then the native may expect great success through personal industry, careful forethought, prudence, and thrift. If it is unfavorable by progression and he has not made wise plans under the influence of the third decanate of Sagittarius, then the next decade of life will be laborious and dull, high ideals will fall by the wayside, and monotony will make existence boring. This may develop, or may even be caused to some extent by a selfishness on the part of the native. All astrologers are agreed that, in its highest vibration, this decanate of Capricorn leads to a love of service to others.

Second Decanate of Capricorn Ascendant

Whereas the first decanate of Capricorn brought method and direction to the ambitious nature of the native, the second decanate brings persistence and acquisitiveness. Here is the blending of Taurus vibrations with those of Capricorn, resulting in stability and progress: Financial advantage under favorable vibrations is indicated strongly. The practical side and common sense attributes of the native's nature come to the fore. Professional or employment conditions improve and relationships with employers are more beneficial. A personal sense of responsibility becomes the basic philosophy, not merely a desire to work for material gain. The higher the vibrations of the natal chart, the greater the success which will come during this period. However, with heavy affliction, the native works hard for little pay and life becomes even more monotonous through the emotional side of the Venus influence. The natural impulse of a Saturn–Venus influence is intense loyalty so the higher the vibrations the greater the purity of purpose, of contact with others, and of freedom from the physical.

Third Decanate of Capricorn Ascendant

Alan Leo said that the third decanate of Capricorn "will make the native practical and adaptable in his ambitions, causing the latter, however, to be tempered by a discriminative and critical frame of mind." Experience shows that this particular decanate, combining influence of the Virgo qualities of Mercury with those of Saturn, gives a stronger tendency to selfishness than perhaps any of the other thirty five decanates of the zodiac. The most difficult lesson to be learned is that of discretion and discrimination, for there is a strong tendency to concentrate upon personal viewpoints and either refuse to accept or ignore the point of view expressed by others. Self is more important than others. Sometimes the success marked by the preceding decanate goes to one's head and the sense of human rights is lost. On the favorable side of this influence, though, it gives a deep understanding of the values of life through critical analysis; but on lower planes, selfishness, worry, and anxiety predominate with consequent effect upon health.

Progressed Ascendant in Aquarius

First Decanate of Aquarius Ascendant

With progression of the Ascendant to the first decanate of Aquarius, a very definite era is marked off in life. While there still remains a strong Saturn–Saturn influence (for the ancients considered this the diurnal house of Saturn), the influence of Uranus–Uranus vibrations are strong, and the function of Uranus is to tear out old foundations if they have been built upon shifting sand in order to rebuild them on solid ground, thus giving greater security. Old conditions pass and new conditions arrive. New friendships are made and the tendency to consider self gives way to a new concept of others, fraternal, feelings or a philosophy that recognizes and engenders a feeling of universal brotherhood. The native may join organizations into which he may throw great energy in a keen desire to better conditions generally. Idealism along entirely new lines takes the place of practicality, but withal there is a certain stability which seems to direct the native. Intensity of purpose marks the personality. All of this applies principally to the more highly developed types, but even to the very average there will be mental stimulation, new associations, and changed conditions. In this latter type, there is a desire to express personal views, to assert private rights, and a tendency to accumulate wealth in the form of land, buildings, and real estate. If seriously afflicted, it may bring false friends in the new associations, pretentious friends to whom he must be subservient. This decanate thus brings difficulty, sorrow, and trouble. The native takes on qualities that appear queer, eccentric, or unorthodox. These changes, whether for good or ill, may come about suddenly, perhaps more suddenly than any other change in the progressed Ascendant from one sign to another.

Second Decanate of Aquarius Ascendant

With the second decanate Aquarius shows the way to a deeper interest in intellectual pursuits. Here is the blending of Uranus–Saturn–Mercury (Gemini decanate) manifesting originality in research, in finding out, in determining for himself the whys and hows of things. The keyword of Aquarius is "I know", and the desire to know is strong in this second decanate. Literary taste will be developed and the native will find he is passing though a pleasant, but a refining, fire. The missionary spirit may even here be developed, perhaps for some non–secular organization or some new philosophy (or really for some emphasis upon a particular point of some old philosophy, for that is exactly what most new philosophies and "isms" are). Because of the cooperative and friendly nature this decanate develops within the native, various forms of assistance from others may come to him through relatives and friends. Discrimination and judgment mark dealings of the native. This is a strongly mental decanate.

Third Decanate of Aquarius Ascendant

Whereas the first two decanates of Aquarius gave a feeling for universal brotherhood and fraternal attachments on a general scale, this third decanate marks close personal attachments which the native will inevitably make. It is a strong influence for marriage on a high plane. The physical vagaries of marriage are negligible, but the mental and spiritual relationships and personal fellowship with another is strongly indicated. As it is the Libra decanate, there is greater mental balance, serenity, and peace. The forcefulness and sureness of Aquarius is still apparent, but with a tenderness not expressed in the preceding decanate. Marriage may be accomplished with a foreigner or while traveling. Under affliction, the native may be misunderstood, which would have a strong psychological effect upon him. But his faculty for appreciating other points of view will be strongly developed during this decade and he may rise above these difficulties, due primarily to his own ability to discern, differentiate, and balance. This decanate may also, if other indications support, bring forth a development of clairvoyant power. Interest in the occult is keen and the mental ability to understand deep truths of occultism is strong. While the Ascendant is progressing through this decanate the native will almost always be able to take full advantage of favorable influence in his horoscope for this is definitely a decanate of the domination of will which can be expressed to the fullest extent.

Progressed Ascendant in Pisces

First Decanate of Pisces Ascendant

The preceding decanate of Aquarius was an influence to prepare the native for karmic conditions with which Pisces surrounds him. If he has learned the philosophic Aquarian lessons well, then the difficulties and problems which are now being presented will not have the depressing and saddening effect they might otherwise bring. The melancholic side of nature is brought to the fore; deep brooding over conditions, or worry, may bring depression and despondency. If fear is latent, here it will become active. Troubles over which he has no control will surround him. Ill health may bring confinement. Expression of the emotions and feelings becomes difficult and an inferiority complex may develop. The native himself will prove to be hospitable and the difficulties of friends, loved ones, and those of whom he is fond will weigh heavily upon him and command much of his interest. It takes a strong natal chart with very favorable vibrations to overcome the difficulties of this first decanate of Pisces, and even then the import is restrictive.

Second Decanate of Pisces Ascendant

Sensitivity is the keynote for this decanate under the sub–rulership of the Moon (Cancer). Sympathy for himself and others will be strong. Domestic difficulties and troubles abound during this period, much depending upon the nature of progressions otherwise in effect, which in any event cause much emotional disturbance. Under this influence, also, a romantic attachment may be formed; strange events take place which are difficult to understand and will cause distress unless exceedingly great care is exercised. This is a decanate of absorption and, unless the native exercises a positive attitude of mind in regard to others, he may become subject to detrimental subjugation.

Friends prove parasitic and the tendency to permit domination by others is strong. If inherent clairvoyant or clairaudient power is indicated in the radical horoscope, the opportunity for mediumistic development will be here presented, but great caution must be exercised for when mediumship is practiced, the drain upon physical resources is strong. Under unfavorable vibrations, practice of phenomena should be avoided at all times and under all conditions.

Third Decanate of Pisces Ascendant

The third decanate of Pisces is the most fatalistic in the entire zodiac. Deaths, sorrows, estrangements, and depressing difficulties abound, so it takes a strong heart and great courage to control destiny during this period of life. The native will be inclined to worry and will be emotionally affected by conditions that seem unfavorable. It is a period when the emotional nature is strong and the passions may be re–awakened. This is a Neptune–Jupiter–Pluto period in life involving the passionate sign Scorpio and, during which, there will be a continual clash between the physical passions and the spiritual longings of the soul. The native who conquers by control is then prepared to enter this new cycle of his existence marked by the progression of the Ascendant into Aries. It is the highly developed soul which conquers the third decanate of Pisces for karmic conditions are at their strongest, reaching a climax at the twenty–eighth degree as the Aries influence begins to make its presence known. The native should exercise every power within himself to conquer this decanate by using self control along all lines. He should not become addicted to drugs, alcohol, or other stimulants for through such habits come disaster.

Character From Progressed Ascendant

While the foregoing chapter dealing with the progressed Ascendant does not purport to be complete the elements necessary for a proper delineation of character, insofar as the progressed Ascendant molds character, are set forth. This is analogous to an analysis of the horoscope which is necessary before individual interpretation is undertaken. In the following chapters, the progression of planets will be discussed.

It remains important not to lose sight of the fact that the life of man is not a disconnected series of events, but rather part of a continuous whole which events influence, either constructively or destructively. Each type of influence is built upon the foundations of what has preceded it and all of the material must be considered, rather than just a segment from it.

Review Questions for Chapter 2

1. Which transition of the progressed Ascendant from one sign to another makes the greatest change? Which makes the least?

2. Trace the progression of your own Ascendant through a normal life span.

3. How could a study of progressions and cycles aid psychologists in understanding actions of their patients?

4. Do you comprehend how marriage partners may be affected by progressed changes in their personal lives? Explain.

5. Will honors and rewards come by progression if they are not indicated in the nativity? Why?

|Chapter 3|

Progressed Sun

Ptolemy indicated that the ancients considered the Sun, Moon, Ascendant, Midheaven, and Part of Fortune as the **Prorogators** of **Significators** of the horoscope or the timing factors; while the remaining heavenly bodies were the **Promittors** or influences being brought into play.

The different celestial bodies indicate influences of varying natures. For example, as Alan Leo has stated this matter, "Saturn has proved by experience to have cold, binding, and restricting influence; Mars on the contrary is hot, expansive, and explosive in his influence. Again, Jupiter is a warm, temperate, and harmonizing planet; Venus a brightening, cheerful, and loving influence, while Mercury comes between these four and acts as a receiver for each in turn, absorbing, and reproducing the influence in a more or less modified condition, it being found to affect the mind more directly than any of the other planets." The influence of Mercury, therefore, is primarily a psychological influence.

These differences in the natures of the various bodies as well as the nature of the differences must always be carefully borne in mind. With practice will come a subconscious consideration of them but at the outset the student will have to guard carefully, for lack of consideration of these important matters will easily lead him into error and improper interpretation.

Quoting further from Alan Leo, whose instruction on these matters are perhaps more comprehensive than those of any other single modern writer, he says:

"The Sun is the ruler of the will and motive or moral power, that which is summed up as the individuality, the solar rays being colored and modified according to the sign through which they were passing at birth. This individuality is either permanent in its expression of the mind, or unstable and changeable, according to the state of the native's progress in evolution. It is modified by the planets aspecting the Sun, in the same manner that the feelings and emotions are modified by the planetary positions and aspects affecting the Moon.

The pure individuality of all human beings is represented by the Sun apart from the sign through which any one soul receives its rays during any separated earth life."

The Sun thus is the motivating power in the horoscope of each individual, the dynamo of existence. Thus, as it expresses itself through the mind, the Sun is a strong indicator of the mind. In this manner solar movement, both through the signs of the zodiac and in relationship to other celestial phenomena, becomes the most important factor in the horoscope. This does not imply, however, that the effect of the Sun's directions will necessarily be the most influential in outward or observational expression. On the contrary, the fact that no solar directions may be in operation during a given period does not mean that this period of life shall be devoid of action or that events will not occur. The age, environment, and other factors which go to make up life, and as are indicated in the chart as a whole, must be taken into account. The death of a person may bring tragedy to one life or may pass with indifference in the life of another. But the lack of solar directions does mean that the individuality of the native will not be as strongly affected.

The duration of solar directions has long been a matter of

some concern to researchers in the field of astrology. There is one school of thought which contends a direction of the Sun continues to manifest itself until the Sun comes to the direction of another planet. Another group has advocated that its influence continues from the time of an exact direction until it moves by direction to the same aspect with that planet progressed. The author's experience found it much safer, and more in accordance with logic, to use the time of exact direction as the strongest but, due to orb of influence, the Sun's vibrations may begin to be felt a full year before the direction is exact and may continue a full year beyond that time. If some other sensitizing aspect, such as the progression of any other planet to a direction of the Sun's position or to the planet to which the Sun is directed, occurs or if an eclipse, lunation, or full Moon happens on the same point of longitude or even sometimes in the case of transit of a major planet to the sensitized points, then in either of these instances the influence indicated by the position of the Sun and the other body, will definitely occur at that time. For precise and exact timing, however, add other methods to those of progression such as the solar or lunar return horoscopes and the rotational diurnal or birth diurnal charts, the rotational diurnal chart being related to the natal or progressed charts.

Another matter of some importance in considering either the progressed Sun or other progressed planets, is to note the overlapping of direction. Suppose, for example, that radical Mars is 17 Taurus 00, radical Jupiter is 20 Taurus 00, and the Sun by progression comes to a direction of Mars. During the next three year the Sun is progressing to the same direction of Jupiter. Vibrations established by the Sun–Mars direction may lay the foundations for vibrations to be established under the Sun–Jupiter contact. Likewise, when the Sun comes to a direction of the mid–point between these two planets at 18 Taurus 30, there will be a strong influence established of Sun–Mars–Jupiter combined, which certainly may be brought into action if indicated by other factors in the progressed or transiting charts.

Dr. Francis–Rolt–Wheeler has laid down six definite rules for considering the progressed Sun, which are:

1) It is necessary to consider the strength and character of the sign into which the Sun has progressed. The Sun's force will be greater if it has progressed into Aries, the sign of its exaltation, or into Leo, the sign of its dignity. It will be weaker if it has passed from either of these signs into a sign where it is peregrine, and still more, if it has passed into a sign of either detriment or fall. By this may be judged much of the degree of stimulative character which the Sun will give to the planet with which the direction is made.

2) It is necessary to consider whether this is a direction from the progressed Sun to a radical planet, or from the progressed Sun to a progressed planet, a radical angle, or a progressed angle. Not only are directions progressed to radical always the more important in themselves but, in the case of solar directions, this importance is augmented because of the deeper rooted forces.

3) Remember the character of the solar force in the radical horoscope. A good solar direction in a progressed horoscope can not be interpreted with the same strength in a nativity where the Sun was weak radically. For a fundamental rule in progressed interpretation is that it is only modification of natal influences, not the setting into action of an entirely new combination.

4) The nature of the planet with which the direction is made is of importance. A direction to Mars is different from one to Saturn. A direction is interpreted different from an aspect. For example, Sun in Libra in house V square Moon in Cancer in house VIII might, if other factors were coordinating, indicate the death of the mother in that year; but the same position in aspect should be interpreted in the terms of the native's own health and character. The action, not the meaning, is relevant.

5) The position of the directing planet is important by strength or debility, in a positive or a negative sign, in which quadruplicity, or in what triplicity. All directions, except conjunctions, squares, and oppositions (when the same quadruplicity must needs be involved), must not only consider the nature of the Sun and the planet, but the conflicting elements of these two quadruplicities; all directions, save trines, must consider in the same way the interplay of differing triplicities. Since it is beyond the human brain to compute the myriad possibilities, one must learn early in their education to exercise a sense of selection and to seize upon the dominant note. Sun opposition Saturn radical, from house X to house IV, is by no means the same as from house II to house VIII. The Sun in Aquarius opposition Saturn radical in Leo is very different from Aries to Libra. Sun cardinal sextile Saturn radical, mutable is not to be interpreted in the same way as Sun fixed sextile to Saturn radical, cardinal. Sun–fire square Saturn–water does not give the same indications as Sun–air square Saturn–earth, and so forth. In brief, when a solar direction is seen to be acting on a progressed horoscope for the year under consideration, it should be carefully synthesized.

6) The student must guard himself against overstatement. There is a strong temptation to give a long description of sincere analysis, the effect of which is to give the native a disproportionate opinion of the importance of the direction. And never must the student allow himself to slip into the error of reading a progressed map as though it were natal. The interpretive technique is entirely different.

7) The author adds to the foregoing that the natal position of the Sun must also always be taken into account.

What is said here of the solar directions, to a greater of lesser extent, is true of all directions. It will be noted in the second of these considerations that reference is made to a direction of a progressed planet to another progressed planet. In view of the fact that secondary directions are often considered as symbolic, some competent astrologers have advanced the idea that there can be no influence exerted from two symbolic positions and that therefore the progressed planets cannot have any influence from a direction to another progressed body with which the author cannot agree in its entirety. The progression of planets by secondary directions is not exactly symbolic for it is based upon apparent secondary astronomical motion of the heavens. An interpretation, or the timing of its influence even, may perhaps be considered symbolic but then, philosophically at least, all of the experiences of this physical life are symbolic in that they are a reflection of the macrocosm and only real in a transitory sense. Therefore, the influences to be expected from the direction of one progressed planet to another progressed planet do not manifest in the same manner as a progressed planet to a radical body. Also the influence may be still further mitigated by other directions to the radical positions simultaneously in effect, in which case they may merely indicate a trend in relationship to these other influences.

The natal chart is basic and a progressed chart cannot show influences which are not inherently shown in the nativity. Thus, if radical Sun and radical Jupiter are harmoniously configurated, progression to a favorable vibration will be stronger than it would be in a horoscope lacking an aspect between Sun and Jupiter. Likewise, if Sun and Jupiter are evilly configurated to each other in the radical horoscope, little permanent value can be expected to culminate under a favorable progressed direction between the two planets.

Progressed Sun Through The Signs

The progressed Sun (or any planet) is not interpreted in quite the same manner as the natal position. The radical Sun is concerned with the basic qualities of the ego at birth, the foundation upon which this life's expression is to be built; the progressed Sun shows the nature of the influences that are to be brought into being in the development of the ego, the construction of life's expression, and the edifice to be erected on that original foundation. The expression of life is determined fundamentally by the position of the radical Sun while progressions through the signs and decanates, with the other planetary vibrations being constantly brought into play from varying positions, indicate the type of energies necessary for the development of that person.

Suppose for example, that a light bulb is turned on. By passing colored screens in front of that bulb, rays of light will appear to take on colors comparable to the screen's color and density. The rays of light appear to be acting differently and their effect will vary as a result. But, the original bulb is constantly emitting identically the same rays of light. There is no variation in the bulb itself but only in its appearance and effect as contravened by the colored filters.

Thus, one born with a well fortified Sun in Capricorn in house IX and Mercury also in Capricorn, receiving a trine aspect from Saturn in Virgo, would indicate a person with a deeply intellectual mind, a research student of philosophy. The progression of the Sun through Aquarius would find him searching for original truths as they relate to philosophy and its application to mankind in general. When the Sun progressed into Pisces, these truths might be applied to spiritual premises as applying to everyday life. When the radical Sun finally progressed into Aries, the motion into cardinal fire would bestow a fearless attitude in the presentation of these truths, with a stimulating intellectual keenness that would facilitate their definition. But the original foundation was not the pioneering spirit of Aries, but rather the research ability indicated through Capricornian coloring and the Saturnian influence of the radical chart as related to the mind. In other words, the radical horoscope showed the innate qualities, while the progression of the Sun (and other planets) showed the development of those qualities and the trend in expression they were expected to take. Had the natal Sun been elsewhere and the planets directed to the same progression it would not have given such inherent abilities although there might have been a temporary research interest with sufficient ability to carry it through.

Thus, it will be seen that the Sun is representative of the mind, the desire, and the expression of life itself, while the signs of the zodiac are the indicators of the coloring which will be given to this expression; thus giving us the clue to the mode of expression – the tone. (Just as the houses are the avenues of expression.) Bearing all of this in mind, here are the keynotes of the progressed Sun through each of the twelve signs.

Progressed Sun in Aries

This is a period of invigoration and renewed energy, the beginning of a new cycle for the soul and its development as it moves up the spiral of progress. The old cycle has passed with Pisces and the new will be marked by new hopes, new ambitions, and new desires. The position of the natal Sun will largely indicate inherent qualities but this is a period of marked change with new objectives to be attained. Depending upon the radical chart, as well as the nature of progressions in effect at the time the Sun moves into Aries, will be the question of whether these will manifest as the higher qualities of intellectual ability, patriotism, bravery, and self reliance, or whether the lower qualities of deceit, exaggeration, and selfishness will hold sway. In any event, it predisposes to periodic rash acts which, if the radical Sun is in Pisces, will prove detrimental to the native or fatalistic in operation; if the radical Sun is in Aquarius, they may be without proper forethought. It is a period of either great advance on the higher planes or retrogression, temporarily, on the lower planes.

Progressed Sun in Taurus

This, through the qualities of Taurus, is a time of stabilization. The impulsiveness of Aries is replaced by the carefulness and firmness of Taurus. Aims and objectives envisioned by Aries may find their realization through the stabilization of the native's efforts while the Sun progresses through Taurus. A certain pride marks this period of life but there is also a sympathetic understanding of the problems of others. In its lower qualities this period may be affected adversely through obstinacy and stubbornness of the native as well as a dogmatic attitude toward the views of others. If the natal Sun was in Pisces, there may be psychic development, particularly through the first ten years of the progressed Sun in Taurus. A fondness for food and raiment, as denoted by Venus, becomes apparent which, if under affliction, will bring later distress physically. Life itself, on the whole, will take a more steady course and if the radical Sun was in Aries, there is a marked letdown in activity.

Progressed Sun in Gemini

During this period of life there is great mental progress for good or ill. If the native's radical Sun was in Aries, and unafflicted, this will be a period when versatility, teaching ability, and general mental perception are enhanced. These people make the finest kind of teachers of advanced learning, with the pioneering qualities of Aries blended to the intellectual qualities of Gemini. In its lower plane, however, there is fickleness, lack of purpose, and diffusion of the energies so that the superficiality abounds. This is a period which may also be strongly marked by travel with a view to broadening the intellect. Inquisitiveness distinguishes this era in life as the native desires knowledge of how the rest of the world lives.

Progressed Sun in Cancer

This is really a period of conflict. While Alan Leo calls it a period of "tenacity of mind, keen memory, firm will, and kind thoughts," it is a period of conflict. The Sun is a fixed, fiery body whose nature does not fit well into the cardinal–water nature of Cancer. Progress is slow and, depending upon the natal chart as well as progressions, this will be a period when the native's own sensitiveness may prove an obstruction to progress. Cancer is an emotional sign, while the Sun is a mental body. When these two qualities conflict, there is a question of which will dominate. If emotions control the solar influence, then there is a mental lack of satisfaction, while if mental qualities dominate the emotions, the restrictions imposed are detrimental to the emotional stability or feeling of satisfaction. Particularly is this true while the Sun passes through the Scorpio–Pluto decanate of Cancer. This period also, if under affliction, may indicate the death of a parent. The conflict between mind and emotions produces changeableness, instability, and may even, through the emotional influences, give a desire for the sensational. Withal, this is a period when the native's attentions are turned to home and home conditions.

Progressed Sun in Leo

Naturally, progression of the Sun into its own sign should bring forth the loftiest qualities to be found in the native. Here is an opportunity for great harmony, mentally and emotionally, with the pure emotions and an affectionate nature. This position of the progressed Sun will, through the native's own perseverance and stability, mark the degree of success which he may attain in life. In its lower vibrations arrogance, domination, and love of display can destroy the opportunities for success otherwise shown. It might also show forth a sensual side of the nature, particularly if the radical Sun is in the second decanate of Cancer and afflicted. Of course, the first decanate of Leo is the strongest position for the progressed Sun, but to the second decanate will be added an ambitious impulse which, if well directed, brings success.

Progressed Sun in Virgo

Virgo is a mental sign and the progress of the Sun to this place in the zodiac shows a period in life when discrimination plays an important role. Mental attributes will be keener and more analytic. It does, however, as a rule indicate a period when the native will be more interested in the details of life than in its broader aspects. Understanding may come through keen perception. In its lower vibrations, the native is self–deceptive and selfish, with a hypercritical outward expression to those whom he contacts. This is a period when the health may not be so good due to the diffusion (mutable sign) of the Sun's energy in this earthy sign.

Progressed Sun in Libra

The progress of the Sun through the first six signs of the zodiac marked the positive half of this cycle of the soul's progress. Its entrance into Libra is the beginning of the passive, receptive, or negative half of this cycle. The influence of the Sun is not so great (outwardly) in Libra because here it is in its fall, but it does balance the intellect and gives a clear concept of the realities of existence. Everything will now be balanced. Both sides of questions coming up for determination will be weighed carefully. Association with others will become a deeper desire of the native with satisfaction only through such contacts. In fact, the progress of the Sun into Libra often is the time of marriage although consider factors bearing on this question from other parts of the chart. A greater desire for cooperation is manifest and opportunities for self expression in contact with others are prevalent. The very paradox of this occurs however, if the nature of the vibrations are inharmonious and the native finds himself ostracized and isolated from those he likes because of his own attitude of unfairness and separation. It usually takes rather severe afflictions to bring out the baser qualities of this influence from Libra so the position of the Sun here is to that extent usually more man if est in harmony, pleasantness, and sincerity.

Progressed Sun in Scorpio

Sun progressed into Scorpio energizes the mind, sharpens the wits, gives intelligent judgment, and adds profoundness to the thinking processes. The mental attributes may even take on a mystical turn which proves valuable. Earnestness in all undertakings marks the native and a serious outlook upon the problems of life becomes more apparent. The higher qualities of Scorpio seem difficult to acquire, but when they are attained the native becomes courageous, sacrificial, and worthy. In its lower qualities the person with the Sun progressing through Scorpio may be sarcastic, cynical, and cruel. Much depends upon radical and progressed positions of all the planets in a correct determination of this influence. This is a sign of regeneration and the native may, particularly while the Sun is in the second or third decanates, experience a religious transformation which finds its fullest expression as the Sun progresses into Sagittarius. Scorpio is a sign that makes or breaks many people; it is a sign of extremes.

Progressed Sun in Sagittarius

The religious experience of Scorpio becomes the religious intelligence of Sagittarius. Philosophical, prophetic, and generous in outlook and attitude toward others, these persons find great satisfaction in aiding the downtrodden. Sympathies are broadened and self development and self expression become strongly man if est. Here again may be indicated journeys, particularly a missionary life, whether in foreign lands or in the home community. It is difficult for real success because of the desire to accomplish too much. The ambitious nature is stimulated. On its lower vibrations, progressed Sun in Sagittarius will make the native unreliable, shallow, and rebellious intellectually.

Progressed Sun in Capricorn

Ambitions are further stimulated by progressions of the Sun into Capricorn, but this is desire for personal advancement. The opportunity for public recognition comes during this period of life. Prominence and publicity, (Capricorn is the advertising sign) are indicated. The reasoning ability is more sagacious and profound. There is a desire for service as well as willingness to labor for success. Professional and social success may be achieved. In its lower nature, Capricorn gives the progressed Sun's influence along lines of selfish ambitions, self interest, and a desire for self glory. Progress may seem slower and more effort required to accomplish one's ends, but with the maintenance of a level head, Capricorn often brings the greatest benefits to the native. The first decanate indicates its influence largely through the profundity of the intellect, out of which the second decanate reaps material gain, and the third decanate general public recognition.

Progressed Sun in Aquarius

This period marks a great change in the native. He passes from the selfish nature of Capricorn to the universal brotherhood of Aquarius. Outlook on life undergoes a marked change as wider understanding of human nature and its attendant weaknesses gives greater purpose to life. The assistance of others, without hope of remuneration or reward, stimulates the native to unusual accomplishment. The Uranian influence of Aquarius, however, is one of extremes, and in the baser vibrations this becomes indifference, pride, and dogmatism. This period may also mark the beginning of an era in the life of the native when he seeks to accomplish the unusual. Unorthodoxy in all matters may affect him and, if other vibrations are favorable, success will be attendant because of his unique methods. This is also a period of self appraisal. Often, the search of self as marked by the Sun progressing through the third decanate of Aquarius lays the foundations for a religious experience growing out of his progress through Pisces.

Progressed Sun in Pisces

The coloring of the zodiacal sign Pisces on the progressed Sun makes the native philanthropic, hospitable, and profoundly sympathetic. It also indicates a period when fate will seem to play an important part in his life. In its highest vibrations, which rarely are attained by contemporary people, Pisces gives to the progressed Sun an understanding of the highest spiritual qualities which man can possibly apprehend or comprehend. Some degree of progress is certainly made by all when the favorable vibrations are present, but these qualities cannot always be measured by normal standards for they are on a higher plane. Esoterically this position of the Sun is a summing up of the experiences of the cycle which the native is now completing. If he has leaned his lessons well, then the finer qualities of the Piscean influence will be man if est and his life will be an example of all the finest qualities found in man. If, on the other hand, he has been manifesting through the baser vibrations of the various influences in his experiences throughout this cycle, then Pisces will give him qualities of indolence, parasitism, and dependence, with the attendant fatalistic impulses, which will make life a misery to himself and all whom he contacts.

Progressed Sun Aspects

The fundamental nature of the planets involved in the directions is now to be taken into consideration. The radical, or natal, horoscope must always be borne in mind, as it is fundamental to a determination of how the progression is likely to operate. No consideration of the progressed horoscope should be undertaken until the natal chart has been carefully delineated.

Data presented in these chapters must be interpreted in light of the fact that the sign through which a planet is progressing will affect the vibrations established at the time, both as to quality or color and as to strength and weakness. Furthermore, the mundane houses in which are located the progressed planet and the planet to which progression is made, as well as the houses over which they have rulership and their natural homes, must all be taken into account as indicating the plane of action involved in the progression.

It will thus be clear that all possible factors involved could not be set forth within the limits of a single volume. The problem is further complicated by the need to consider both decanate and face of each sign through which the progressed planet is moving. Hence, only that fundamental information is presented which the student needs for sound astrological interpretation.

The Sun and (according to the ancients) the Moon, Ascendant, Midheaven, and Part of Fortune – which Ptolemy calls the prorogators – are perhaps the primary foci of all horoscopes; hence their progressions are of vital importance not only with respect to the influences affecting human life but also as the agency through which evolutionary changes take place in the soul. But the Part of Fortune can probably be omitted in secondary progressions, since its value as a timing element seems to be greater in primary directions. Remember also what has already been taught concerning the Sun's relationship to the mind.

The material presented here deals with progressed bodies and their aspects in relation to the radical position of the body aspected. To a lesser degree, and in a transitory manner, the same general influences may be observed as between progressed position and progressed position. Evolutionary changes of the inner self are not thought to occur in the latter case, the indications observed being rather regarded as temporary and transient mundane conditions.

The orb allowed for progressed planets is also of importance; the author's experience has been that a wider orb should probably be allowed for conjunctions and parallels of declination than for other directions. However, in all directions it must be determined whether or not planets harmonize with the signs or houses in which they are placed. While the time element is exceedingly difficult to define, the wise student will not allow more than one degree applying to an exact aspect, or more than one degree after the exact aspect has been completed. In the case of the Sun this would approximate one year before and after the time the aspect becomes exact, in the case of the Moon – slightly less than one month before or after. With slower planets, which may be within one degree of exact for many years, the author's practice is to limit the duration of the direction to not more than three years in any event, timing it more precisely by the progression of the Sun, the Moon, or the Ascendant (or any combination of them). Some astrologers allow as much as three degrees of orb for directions of both the Sun and Moon, and this author has done the same upon occasion.

At least one astrologer has adduced evidence in favor of limiting parallels of declination to not more than three minutes, and other aspects to not more than 15 minutes of longitude – with corresponding time elements measured by the speed of motion of the celestial body – when the precise moment of birth, or other time for which the chart is set, is known and a very accurate chart can be calculated. In any case, the student will always find it safer to impose restrictions on the factors being considered in the horoscope, thus avoiding interpretations which are without astrological foundation.

When no Sun directions are in force, life will run a smoother course without fundamental changes affecting the native directly and permanently. Also the force of other influences emerging during this period will be somewhat mitigated, whether for good or ill.

Conjunct Sun Progression to Natal Sun

Favorable directions of the Sun to its radical position increase the native's vitality and energy, as well as to improve his health. His abilities are likewise enhanced, with consequent recognition by superiors (in employment) or by the public (if in a professional position). New responsibilities and undertakings during this period are more likely to lead to success, and this is a very successful period of life generally if other indications corroborate.

When progressions are unfavorable (such as the semi-square or square), the health may be upset, the vitality weakened or disorganized, and the attainment of success will demand greater than ordinary effort. The Sun reaches the semi–square of its radical position at about 45 years of age, and it is well known that more failures occur at this age than at any other. But this condition may be completely overcome by other influences in the chart. For example, if Mars rules house X cusp, and the progressed Sun forms a semi–square to its radical position, while Mars at the same time trines the radical Sun by progression (to which it is, let us say, favorably disposed in the radical horoscope), the difficulties due to the Sun's unfavorable position will be largely mitigated, and the native will be very successful at this time.

It is thus easily understood why a set of indications of the influence of progressions cannot be set forth to cover every horoscope. Astrology depicts life, and life is complicated.

Conjunct or Parallel Sun Progression to Moon

The conjunction, or parallel of declination, of the progressed Sun with the radical Moon is the most important period of life for the native. It brings on great changes and for this reason is often considered a critical period. If favorable vibrations are operating at this time, particularly if the radical Sun and Moon are favorably disposed, it is a period of improvement, advancement, and success. This is often a time of marriage, social advancement, and both mental and moral progress. New friends may appear, and the native's credit and honor are enhanced. The native has more self confidence, so this brings opportunities for advancement. This may be a period of exceptionally good or exceptionally poor health, particularly in female charts which are subject to strong psychological influence by the Moon. In the case of females also a threat to the health may give rise to fevers, especially in the bloodstream. Other than in health matters this direction affects the female less strongly than the male (except that it may bring an opportunity for marriage, if the native is eligible).

Favorable Sun Progression To Moon

This is a particularly favorable and fortunate period in life, its strength depending on the relationship between the luminaries in the natal chart. The outlook is bright, the health is good, and the mind is cheerful. Almost all the native's efforts lead to success and gain, and at this time the energies should be directed along lines where success is most desired. The major progressions (sex tile and trine) of ten bring marriage, unions, agreements, or attachments of long duration. Opportunities will arise in all areas, and success will depend upon their fulfillment. The native should certainly push all affairs during this period when lunar progressions and lunations coincide favorably.

Unfavorable Sun Progression to Moon

This is a period of disorganization, disintegration, unhappiness, and dismay which may affect both honor and reputation (the natal chart should be studied). The health will be generally poor, so the native will feel restless and debilitated. He should not undertake new enterprises or ventures since financial losses threaten, but should be passive, reserved, and retiring. Crises in the native's life are marked by such unfavorable progressions, particularly if the progression forms an opposition, with separation from loved ones, death, disappointment, and difficulties of the kind indicated by sign and house position as well as by the radical positions of the bodies involved. The emotions are deeply stirred and careful thought must be given to all matters if difficulties are to be avoided.

Conjunct, Parallel, or Favorable Sun Progression to Mercury

The outward effects of these progressions are not as noticeable as with the other planets, for Mercury is a reflecting planet. Thus the Sun conjuncting Mercury will indeed stimulate the mental processes and confer a strong inclination to study, but it will also form progressions to any planet aspected by radical Mercury in the natal chart and thus must be interpreted in the light of the planet which Mercury reflects. However, these progressions are important for the consciousness, as they develop the mentality to a higher station. Opportunities arise for travel, writing, and literary work (if in harmony with the natal chart). The native will find it easier to adapt to new surroundings, and the desire to undertake new ventures will be strong. However, this is primarily a period of mental quickening.

It should also be mentioned that the semi–sextile position with Mercury is usually as strong as the sextile progression to other bodies.

Unfavorable Sun Progression to Mercury

The Sun can never progress to opposition with Mercury, since this planet can never be more than 28 degrees from the Sun radically. In fact, in any ordinary life it can never be moved in direct motion to a wider progression than the trine (and this only when the native is past 90 years of age). Unfavorable progressions of the Sun to Mercury usually produce a period of worry, anxiety, and mental difficulty, this depending largely on the planet reflected by Mercury in the natal horoscope. The native will be unsettled and indecisive. He should be careful in dealing with anyone of the type represented by Mercury's house and sign position and radical aspects. This is also an excellent time for the native to react passively to conditions for, unless otherwise indicated by the natal horoscope, this is a period of temporary difficulty which can be measured and mastered to be used as the base for future accomplishment.

Conjunct or Parallel Sun Progression to Venus

In the horoscope of a single adult of marriageable age, and frequently even in the chart of a married person, this period almost invariably marks the union of the native's affections with another of the opposite sex. It is an emotional period of a strongly benefic nature (unless Venus is very afflicted), most often leading to marriage. This time often marks the birth of a child. It is a period of prosperity and success, when the native enjoys life to its fullest. Since Venus is a money planet, financial success is usually indicated, and the native should aggressively push his affairs and opportunities to a successful conclusion. The benefits of this conjunction or parallel of declination would be overcome only by strong malefic influences from other quarters. The native's social life will be intensified, and permanent friendships contracted. Every opportunity should be seized, since the native's activities during this period can lead to much benefit. The affections are stimulated, and the native is drawn into closer sympathy and contact with others, particularly of the opposite sex. Note the sign and house position of radical Venus as well as the house which it rules.

Favorable Sun Progression to Venus

Also a period of great satisfaction to the native, this one greatly resembles the conjunction of progressed Sun, only lacking the emotional intensity. Financial and social gain are indicated, so opportunities should be aggressively accepted. Prior attachments or relationships with others will here culminate in unions such as marriage or a business partnership. Hence the primary aim of this direction is happiness. This period is excellent for investment and speculation (if the natal chart concurs), and great gains are possible. In fact, this period is fortunate in every respect.

Unfavorable Sun Progression to Venus

This is a period of emotional stress and possible financial loss, with domestic difficulties arising over money matters. In any event, the emotions are so disturbed that the native is distressed and exhausted, with severance of home ties and loss of friends. The native should exercise care so the emotional instability arising will not give rise to aggression, delusion or harmful thought and actions that might affect him or her permanently. Under this influence death may come to a friend of the native.

Conjunct or Parallel Sun Progression to Mars

This is usually considered a very dangerous period, stimulating the native's rash impulsiveness, and much depends on the radical positions of both Sun and Mars. The feelings and passions are intensified (especially in a feminine horoscope, where these progressions often indicate an opportunity for marriage, largely for physical or over emotional reasons). The native must take care not to act on impulse or emotion; difficulties are avoided only by thinking through and premeditating all of life's activities. The native suffers from the overstimulation of the Sun and Mars in these positions (both being fiery bodies). However, in the horoscope of a timid person or one with an inferiority complex, this position may remove such tendencies and thus prove beneficial. The native will be restless but very independent; he should be very cautious, since, under this powerful emotional stimulus, irritability and quarrels can bring on sudden and unexpected disaster. While these directions are in force the native may show off by being extremely extravagant and liberal. But, on the other hand, the energy, activity, and enterprise accompanying such vibrations can bring success, if guided by self-restraint, forethought, and intelligence (and if the natal chart corroborates).

Favorable Sun Progression to Mars

This is a forceful influence for success, stimulating the native's enterprise, energy, and strength of purpose. In a feminine horoscope this progression often indicates marriage or the birth of a child. While the emotions are strongly accentuated, there is also mental stability. This is an excellent time for new business ventures, as well as for travel. The ambitions, energy, and desires are awakened. The native is more courageous, but again the explosiveness of Mars may force him to act too quickly. Good health and strong physique are indicated. The principal difficulty indicated by any direction to Mars is a strong tendency to follow desire rather than will with the force being intensified if this direction occurs in an angular position.

Unfavorable Sun Progression to Mars

These mark periods in the native's life when disaster is always close at hand, physical as well as mental or emotional. The health will be affected by fevers, so great care must be exerted to avoid accidents. Loss of friends and loved ones is indicated, through death or through the native's own foolishness. The native is belligerent and argumentative, which brings on occupational as well as social and domestic difficulties and estrangement from loved ones.

There is danger of scandal, disgrace, and loss of prestige (depending, of course, on the natal chart). The reputation may suffer, rightly or wrongly. The native must be cautious and discreet to overcome the difficulties of this critical period. His health may be impaired by feverish illness brought on by his own indiscretions. If Mars rules house VIII, this direction may indicate end of life, but here the greatest caution is needed (particularly as concerns one's own horoscope) for the astrologer's emotional involvement may lead him to false conclusions. The native will be tempted to take great risks which should never be attempted. He should not follow the inclination, which is strong under this stimulus, to rush headlong into any of life's activities. Alan Leo says that the period during which the quadratures progression is in effect will be remembered for years to come, while that of the opposition to most, if not to all, will prove to be the most memorable period of life.

Conjunct or Parallel Sun Progression to Jupiter

These are two of the most powerful influences for good which may come into any life. The conjunction or parallel of Jupiter (representing the native's higher mental attributes) and the progressed Sun (representing the mental expression of these attributes) bring to the fore the finer qualities of character, resulting in social success and general good fortune. Once realizing that the parallel of declination is the inception of whatever is indicated by the sign and house position of the bodies involved, the student will appreciate that this marks an important epoch in the native's real development or evolution. The strength of these influences endures for years. Of course, the parallel may occur at the time of conjunction, quadratures, or opposition of the planets involved (or near that time); if it occurs when either of the latter two angles are in effect, the losses or difficulties implied by these progressions will be met philosophically and with fortitude, so that they are somewhat mitigated. In the case of the conjunction, however, or the parallel which may occur at the same time, the health is improved, finances are stronger, and success is marked. These vibrations may have a strong emotional tinge, in which case the native will form unions and make attachments of great benefit. But there is a dangerous tendency to over–expansion, over–enthusiam, and excessive ambition. Note the radical chart carefully, as well as the progressed Moon and lunations. Jupiter is physically the largest planet in the solar system, and (if the radical chart is favorable) its influence for good seems to outweigh all other influences of other bodies. Therefore, the union of solar vibrations with those of Jupiter points to great success in a venues indicated radically; the good to be derived from this conjunction can be destroyed only by a total over–expansion of the interests combined with foolish extravagance.

Favorable Sun Progression to Jupiter

This again is a period of great good fortune. While not as permanent as the conjunction, it is definitely marked by prosperity, good health, social gain, and accomplishment of the desires. Strong attachments may be made, any new undertakings will be successful, and conditions surrounding the native will be beneficial in every way. These vibrations often bring a deep and lasting religious experience which gives the native a new and different outlook on life. His spirits are buoyed and he has a deeper insight into religious truths with their value for facing the problems of life. Favorable progressions of the Sun to Jupiter may even indicate marriage of an idealistic character or to a wealthy person. These progressions are definitely to be used for developing character, spiritual advancement, material gain, or social prestige. In many horoscopes all of these may be accomplished. Again, depending upon the radical positions of the planets and their strength, these directions may bring fame and prominence. These are definitely periods in which the native should take the fullest advantage of the benefits offered, particularly along religious lines.

Unfavorable Sun Progression to Jupiter

Unfavorable directions of the Sun to Jupiter, while not destructive of character, are dangerous for the native's material affairs. Domestic and social matters are also affected adversely, and financial losses are to be expected. In fact, all of the native's interests and activities will be subject to very trying vibrations. Death or separation are indicated (usually of some relative or in-law) but the native will not feel the loss deeply unless his nativity indicates him to be highly emotional. Friends may request loans during this period; however, they should be rejected, since such loans will not be repaid without recourse to law. The native will be surrounded by hypocrisy and, because of Jupiter's connection with the sign Pisces, he should guard against treachery and deception. Social and religious disputes will cause more annoyance than loss, but legal difficulties may bring serious disappointments.

The radical position of Jupiter must not be overlooked even though it is difficult to imagine any harm emanating from the vibrations of the Greater Benefic. What appears detrimental, even under the opposition of the progressed Sun to radical Jupiter, often turns out for the native's benefit. Disappointment may result from his exaggerated expectations more than from any actual loss or hindrance. Bear in mind the expansive qualities of Jupiter and the intellectual qualities of the Sun. When these two natures are under inharmonious vibrations, much temporary dissatisfaction may result from the native's overconfidence, exaggerated expectations, ultra–magnanimity, or excessive self assurance by affecting either the health or the mind. He should endeavor to maintain a true sense of proportion as well as a sincere and equitable attitude, toward all people and in all things.

The native who conquers these progressions is destined to make great advances. The influence of these inharmonious vibrations may be so subtle as to be unnoticed until the native is too deeply enmeshed to extricate himself.

Conjunct or Parallel Sun Progression to Saturn

These directions are usually very unfavorable; Saturn's coldness intercepts the vital forces of the Sun so the native's constitution is weakened and debilitated. During this period he will be very susceptible to disease and great care must be exerted to avoid long lasting or chronic illnesses. The circulation will be poor and the native will be susceptible to deep–seated colds, etc. He may develop a suspicious nature and thus apprehend difficulties and danger. A restriction has been placed on him, its effect being largely measured in terms of the qualities indicated in the natal chart. The native will confront heavy responsibilities and, if other influences are favorably, hard work and intense application will make this a highly successful period. If the native reacts favorably to the conjunction of the Sun and Saturn, this will be an epoch in the evolution of his character, but, all in all, the distress usually indicated here is such a heavy burden that most break under the strain and become subject to the lower vibrations of this influence. This is certainly a time for maintaining a cheerful outlook and a stout heart, as these will greatly aid in overcoming the psychological barriers encountered. The native should never succumb to the natural tendencies of these vibrations but should overcome them by energetic action rather than following the line of least resistance.

Favorable Sun Progression to Saturn

The primary benefit of these vibrations is that they stabilize the native's life by steadying his mind, thus building his character. While not conferring any great material benefit, they present opportunities for the assumption of broader responsibilities and for success if the native is willing to work arduously. He will become friendly with older or more settled persons who prove in every way reliable and beneficial. These vibrations indicate permanent attachments; the nature of these influences being to lay the foundation of future success rather than to bring any immediate gains. The other indications in the progressed horoscope must be carefully considered but, knowing that Saturn's virtues are industry, patience, perseverance, chastity, and refinement, the native will readily understand how to interpret their import when the entire horoscope is considered. If prior influences have so warranted, this period is the culmination of the native's success in life; he is given positions of trust and responsibility, his abilities are recognized, and his reputation elevated with the consequent gains entailed. It is a period of self appraisal and concentration which, if properly directed, can be most beneficial for the individual's whole life (the foundations laid at this time being permanent).

Depending again on the radical horoscope, this may be an exceptionally favorable period for investment and purchase of land or property. It is definitely not a period for speculation but rather a powerful influence for investment from which future profit may be reaped.

Unfavorable Sun Progression to Saturn

This is one of the most trying periods in the native's whole life when everything he does seems to go wrong and all activities encounter obstacles, hindrances, or unaccountable delays. He will be beset by domestic difficulties and his own health may be impaired by chronic or wasting illness. The death of friends or relatives may produce an enduring depression or melancholy. As always, much depends on the radical horoscope. The opposition directs vibrations at the native himself and his footsteps are dogged by sorrows, trials, and disappointments of all kinds. There will be a strong tendency to lose hope and look at the dark side of every event. The native is at war with himself so his own moral character is severely tested. He should avoid resorting to alcohol or drugs to buoy himself up during this period, since any habits contracted will be difficult to lose and the best way to conquer is to avoid. In this time of life he may lose his esteem for others, so hope should be carefully cultivated. It is also a period when others lose their esteem for him, requiring cultivation of an optimistic outlook. But the dark cloud over his life will pass and leave behind a deeper appreciation of real values. The native should not succumb to despondency and moroseness.

If the native's radical horoscope has the Sun and Saturn in trine aspect to one another, when the Sun comes to an opposition with Saturn by progression, it will then be sextile to its own radical position. Trine of Saturn and the Sun in the natal horoscope is preeminently beneficial; thus there is promise of real benefit at the outset of life. The malefic opposition of the progressed Sun and radical Saturn will occur at about sixty years of age making two sets of vibrations in effect: one benefic and the other malefic. The benefic is not only the original promise but also the permanent influence. The influence of the malefic is not permanent and its power to harm the native is strongly mitigated by the radical positions of these two bodies.

The student will readily see why the natal positions of planets involved in progressions must be noted. Again, these influences will be further affected by the zodiacal positions of the Sun and Saturn in both the natal and progressed charts. And note further that the avenues of expression through the various houses will differ. Thus in all horoscope delineation, especially in predictive astrology, the influences to be noted are extremely intricate and great care is needed. Similarly, angular, succedent, or cadent house positions will aggravate or ameliorate the influence as well as strengthening or weakening the vibrations.

Conjunct or Parallel Sun Progression to Uranus

These directions mark an epoch, as do the conjunction or parallel of declination of the progressed Sun with all other major exterior planets. With Uranus they particularly mark mental changes and expansion of the horizons of the native's thought, in concrete practical affairs as well as in abstract philosophical ones. Sharp and sudden changes in outlook are to be expected; the native will develop new and original ideas which he would formerly have considered highly unorthodox. He may take an interest in astrology, the occult, metaphysics, or philosophy. In any case, this is a period of change, with sudden attachments or equally sudden estrangements of friends and loved ones. Intimate associations are to be anticipated during the course of these influences. However, the changes brought on by these vibrations are mental and objective rather than material and subjective. The native will suddenly encounter strange and peculiar experiences which may make him irritable and excitable, especially when transits of emotional or mental planets aspect the radical or progressed positions of either the Sun or Uranus. These vibrations definitely influence the making and breaking of friendships more than any other positions in the horoscope.

Favorable Sun Progression to Uranus

This is an exceptionally fine period in which to develop a constructive and original view of life or to undertake new interests, travel, or studies (such as astrology or occult sciences). These vibrations will make the native appreciate the true Uranian teachings of the universal brotherhood of man; the expansion of his interests along these lines will yield success in all his efforts. This is also a strong influence for joining philosophical or ritualistic organizations and societies. It is excellent for travel, speculation (particularly in matters concerning travel, electricity, and aviation), and for general expansion. These influences often bring about a romantic adventure of novel character. The gains to be made under such favorable directions occur suddenly and unexpectedly. The native will have many original ideas; his ingenious and inventive interest in affairs of life will bring new friendships.

Unfavorable Sun Progression to Uranus

Alan Leo states that the square of the progressed Sun to natal Uranus is the worst aspect known (except, possibly, for the square of progressed Mars to Uranus). And certainly the suddenness with which either acts, and the damage which may ensue, warrant great care and caution while they are in force. Without any prior notice, all affairs seem to go wrong, with financial losses, severe disappointments, divorce, and sudden estrangements. The native will be unsettled; these vibrations sometimes bring about a complete nervous breakdown. Disorganization is the keynote; this is preeminently a period in which the native should maintain a resigned and equable attitude, for he is surely being tested in the crucible of experience. He should endeavor to be passive and calm, as everything will tend to annoy him. Travel should not be undertaken. The native will tend to impulsive and radical acts; his rashness may be so extreme as to lead to ignominy and disgrace. Caution must be exercised in all dealings with others, so all forms of disputes or legal conflicts should be avoided. In this period the native should mistrust his own judgment and depend largely on that of others; he has a strong tendency to be erratic and this inclination to act hastily or on very slight provocation may lead to disaster. There is also great danger of disgrace through relations with one of the opposite sex.

Conjunct or Parallel Sun Progression to Neptune

The nature of this direction is exceedingly difficult to explain with Neptune's influence being so elusive and difficult to explain that mere words hardly suffice. The epoch in the native's evolution set out by these directions is strong indeed, being marked by spiritual development of the highest order. So few persons respond to the high vibrations of Neptune that many astrologers consider it a highly malefic influence. This author does not agree since, if the emotions are not too strong, anyone can learn to put forward the higher nature with which he is endowed and develop the better qualities within himself. If this is done, the direction of the Sun to the conjunction or parallel of declination of Neptune, while mysterious and incomprehensible to the average person, will bring out a spiritual experience or psychic awakening which will give the native a full appreciation of the purpose of existence not understood by others. Very little material effect is to be expected from this direction although, if the progression occurs at a time when other malefic influences are manifest, the blending in of the progressed horoscope may indicate great losses of a mysterious nature. The Neptunian vibrations will prevent the cause of the losses from being well understood, but these vibrations are not themselves the cause.

Favorable Sun Progression to Neptune

Rather than conferring direct material benefit, these vibrations give a feeling of contentment, ease, and assurance that everything is going well. Prosperity and riches may come (if other indications corroborate), but Neptune increases their volume to unexpected proportions rather than being the cause of the gain. Religious exaltation is also indicated. The native may take a deep interest in the arts, becoming proficient in music, painting, or some other creative outlet. Here, perhaps, is found the motivation for the deepest inspirational experience of which man is capable.

Unfavorable Sun Progression to Neptune

The moral aspect of this influence must be stressed, for degradation, disaster, and disgrace are indicated if the native cannot control his emotions by exercising self restraint and willpower. Difficulties are brought on by rash actions, often involving drugs or the opposite sex. The emotional nature will be deeply depressed, and, in the case of neurotics or physically sensitive persons, the moral fiber is so weakened as to bring physical ruin on the native who does not control himself. This influence seems stronger in male horoscopes than in female, although in the latter the native may be brought to the depths of despondency by the psychopathic conditions foreshadowed. Under these directions the hardest battle to be waged is with one's own soul. Alan Leo, who was preeminently a philosopher, has said that, "All the antagonistic forces of the lower nature, or the undeveloped part of man, rise up and seek to swamp him, and powerful indeed must he be if he can breast them. Only the pure can do so, and even they must prepare to see their cherished schemes totter in apparent confusion to the ground. Failure, however, consists not in failing to maintain, but in ceasing to strive; and for the overcomer the reward is great."

Conjunct or Parallel Sun Progression to Pluto

This aspect is a powerhouse of potentials. The progressed Sun in this position can run into its own emotional baggage bringing up old wounds and dramas, bringing crisis, extreme moods, fears about control, attempts at control and possibly the loss of control. There will dramatic change in the native's life, perhaps even the life path; and change brings crisis even though the change may be very much needed. Old desires may come up for the native that will prove key to discovering hidden potentials. These potentials, if left unacknowledged, will explode onto the native's life stage, creating more crisis. If there has been relationship break-down, the native may resort to vengeance or displays of emotional anger that may surprise even the native. There could be a craving for power and the tendency to over-do, and the native's natal chart will provide a background for this that will help to navigate the possibilities. There will be extremes in the native's self esteem, and the feeling that there should be dramatic changes in the life. This can manifest as the desire to change residence, appearance, relationship, career or religion, depending upon where in the chart aspect falls. There is potential for secrecy here, and also for hidden emotions and emotional outbursts.

Well aspected, this position of Sun and Pluto can bring deep, powerful transformations that will bring life–long benefits to the native. Clear thinking, and This is a result of having transformed crisis into personal power through perseverance. The native has integrated the pain and loss felt during life, and now uses the strength and wisdom gained to accomplish that which she or he truly desires.

Changes occurring during this combination of powerful forces have long range consequences. Other aspects, house position, and sign location of both celestial bodies determine the final outcomes.

Favorable Sun Progression to Pluto

A favorable blending of the personal focus of the Sun with the group planet Pluto will assist the native in searching for a deeper understanding of his relationship to life in general. This may take the form of lengthy psychoanalysis or it may be change in religious or spiritual disciplines. Increased willpower and self assurance at this time enable the native to assume positions of leadership otherwise denied to him. This is a good period to become involved with groups working toward ecological understanding, volunteering with battered children or wives, exploring ancient archaeological digs, or investigating psychic phenomena. On the higher levels it is a period of major growth and self understanding.

Unfavorable Sun Progression to Pluto

When the progressed Sun opposes or squares natal Pluto the native will be quite domineering and dictatorial. Often this attitude arises out of a fear of being overruled by others. It is a defense mechanism behind which the person conceals his personal weaknesses. The heightened consciousness of his inadequacies stimulates him to either blatantly combat any effort to assist him or, going to the other extreme, he becomes utterly dependent upon an aggressive individual.

This progressed aspect brings sudden and harsh removal of material possessions as well as beloved relatives and friends. Of ten these releases are necessary in order for the native to develop new values necessary for changing directions in his life style. This is not time to tamper with occult phenomena.

Review Questions for Chapter 3

1. What is the basic difference between the Sun progressing into or out of zodiac signs to the progressed Ascendant changing signs?

2. Are aspects from progressed planets different from aspects between two natal planets? How?

3. Review the criteria for considering the progressed Sun.

4. Is it necessary to consider the natal Sun strength to evaluate progressed Sun?

5. How is your present progressed Sun affecting your own activities?

|Chapter 4|

Progressed Moon

The position of the progressed Moon is next in importance after the progressed Sun, but in horoscopic delineation the mutual relationships of the other heavenly bodies should always be considered before those of the Moon, not because the directions occurring among the planets are more important (since each horoscope must be considered in itself and the mutual directions are simply the connecting links at a given time between the soli-lunar forces in effect), but because the Moon is one of the primary timing factors for influences which may come into being later. Hence it is probably better procedure to take the influences operating through mutual directions before considering the Moon as a timing factor.

The vibrations established by the Sun's progression are far more subtle than those of the Moon as becomes obvious when it is recalled that the Sun is the inner self and the Moon the outer self. The Sun represents the soul, and its development is necessarily subtle. The Moon is the soul's expression, through personality or otherwise, in everyday life. Hence, the Moon is important mainly for its influence over the outward expression of life. The Sun's progress through the zodiacal signs represents the progress of the native's soul, while the Moon's progress through the houses of the horoscope represents the native's progress through life.

Naturally, the horoscope must be interpreted in the light of the native's age, environment, ambitions, and outward or material expression of life.

Life can be divided into three major periods, each represented by the Moon's progression through the zodiac and its return every 28 years to its natal position. The first period is one of physical growth, and interpretation of the horoscope during this period should normally relate to the material expression of life. Thus, during the last quarter of this period (from 21 to 28 years) every ambition promised in the natal chart is stirred strongly. In this age youth desires to save the world, young men see visions which they want to go out and conquer.

The second revolution of the Moon (from 29 to 55 years old) is one of mental growth, and the chart will be affected by this. The third period, from about 56 years of age to the end of life, is an era of spiritual growth.

The influence of the progressed Moon as a timing factor in the horoscope cannot be overemphasized. As already pointed out, the Sun's progression to an exact aspect with a planet is highly important and will always initiate the vibrations indicated by the Sun's progression into force some time before or after the exact direction. Assume, for example, that the progressed Sun comes to exact conjunction with Venus one month after the birth anniversary for which the progressed horoscope has been calculated. Assume further that the Moon, progressing at more than 13 degrees a year (more than 1 degree per month), reaches a significant position in relation to this aspect of the Sun two months before the birth anniversary, that is three months prior to the exact direction by the Sun. The Moon will cause the Sun's influence to be felt three months before its direction is exact. Similarly, if the Moon reaches the exact direction later, it may delay the Sun's vibrations until the Moon has progressed to this sensitive point.[5]

The student should not misinterpret the emphasis on the

Moon's position as emphasis on her influence. This influence in the horoscope is of major importance, as is the Moon's progression through the horoscope. But if it makes contact by direction with sensitive points in the horoscope with which it has no natal relationship, and no other vibrations impinge upon this point at the time, the direction may pass without any perceptible impact. At best it will prove a temporary and transient condition or event, since the Moon's influence passes quickly. Thus, at times her influence is hardly noticeable, and at other times it seems a potent force for arousing vibrations which materially affect the native.

The student is again cautioned to study carefully the natal horoscope; the influence of the progressed Moon will be greater if the native is affected emotionally by the events of life rather than mentally or psychologically. On the whole, however, lunar aspects must be considered in the light of the solar and mutual directions in effect as the Moon progresses through the horoscope. Only then may they be regarded as having a permanent effect on the native and such years of life are eventful. In other years their effect is less certain, especially if the native is not emotional.

To illustrate the foregoing: when the progressed Sun and progressed Moon came to a quadrature of Saturn, it signified the death of someone in whom the native was interested, however the Moon's progression to the square of Saturn with no other directions in effect may only indicate a cold (particularly in the head) or, in a feminine chart, a temporary lowering of the vitality. The first has a permanent impact on the native, while the second is only a passing matter.

Excess emphasis should never be placed on lunar directions from month to month. They must be blended with other changing celestial phenomena and then regarded largely as chronometers of these other influences unless the sign and house rulership of the Moon is involved. If lunar directions are favorable at a time when other directions are unfavorable, the Moon will always mitigate the unfavorable ones so some good will come to the native (its nature being indicated by the Moon's directions and the other orbs involved). Similarly, if lunar directions are unfavorable at a time when other directions are favorable, any permanent benefits will be lessened and vitiated by the Moon. When the Moon's progressed position coincides with other progressed positions at a given time, she adds power and influence whether for good or ill.

Progressed Moon Through the Houses

Since the Moon has more to do with outward expression, her influence in the houses of the horoscope is of major importance; the signs of the zodiac are, in a sense, subordinated to the houses as the function of each sign is to give tone, color, or strength to the influence (or to the timing of a vibration) focused there.

Progressed Moon in House I

Progression of the Moon over the Ascendant into house I usually produces change. While this is true for the Moon's progression over any angle, in the case of the Ascendant (and, to a slightly lesser degree, the Midheaven) this is a change from inner to outward expression. The angles always mark cycles in human development and, since the Ascendant is the first house below the earth, it is the first house of exteriorization, of outward expression. As all six houses below the earth (I to VI) relate to the personality, and all six houses above the earth (VII to XII) to the individuality, this is a time of personal expression and change whose nature will be determined by other factors of the horoscope. Emphasis is laid upon the formal side of life, all such matters being brought to the fore.

In interpreting the Moon's progression into house I, the student should note the sign on the Ascendant and its force in the natal horoscope. Next the character of the change should be considered: it may be abrupt, depending again on the sign involved and the Moon's strength in that sign. Particularly in feminine horoscopes, progression of the Moon over the Ascendant may indicate a change in health conditions. If ill, the native may take a turn for the better; if well, his health may become impaired. In any event, note the solar (and mutual) influences in operation, for coincidence between the Moon progressing through house I and solar progressed vibrations marks a major period in the native's life – one of change from the previous period.

The author has on occasion, found the combination of solilunar forces operating at this time to bring about marriage, completely changing the native's mode of life.

Progressed Moon in House II

The Moon's progression through any house brings to the fore the matters relating to that house: hence, in house II finances are important for the more than two years during which the Moon moves through this mundane position. If the native has previously been in financial difficulties, and the Moon's position here coincides with favorable directions otherwise, there will be a release from financial restrictions. Opportunities for investment and financial advance may arise. But, on the other hand, if there is serious affliction the native should be cautious in his finances; unless extra precaution is taken, there will be definite losses and this is an unfavorable time for speculation of expansion.

This again illustrates the great value of astrology. The warning is given by the nature of the malefic vibrations by the angles formed (whether semi-square, square, sesquiquadrate, inconjunct, or opposition), by the nature of the bodies involved, and by the houses over which they have dominion or in which they are posited.

Progressed Moon in House III

In this period the native is drawn closer to brothers, sisters, and relatives generally; however, whether this will be advantageous or otherwise is indicated by the other directions in operation during the Moon's movement through house III.

The native's mentality will be quickened, and this may be expressed as restlessness (because of the Moon's changeable nature) - depending in large degree upon the sign on the house III cusp and other natal qualifications. Under affliction this may be a period of worry and depression; under benevolent directions it may be a period of worry and depression; under benevolent directions it may be one of mental progress and adoption of a series of progressive views. Alan Leo states, "the objective consciousness will be far more active than the subjective and by these means stimulated and rendered more inclined to think deeply." Opportunities for educational advancement should be eagerly accepted during this period; learning will be easier for him during these two and a half years than in almost any other period (with the possible exception of the Moon's progress through house IX).

Progressed Moon in House IV

The Moon's progression over the Nadir and through house IV usually marks a critical period in the sense that either great good or much difficulty may be encountered. Changes in the home are indicated and, under affliction, the passing of a parent (usually the father) is indicated. Divorce or separation may come if the natal horoscope indicates marital difficulties. On the brighter side, however, there may be highly beneficial changes, with old conditions coming to an end and new ones commencing. Note any other directions operating during this period.

Deep occult significance attaches to the position of the Progressed Moon. Alan Leo, who has perhaps studied the occult side of astrology more deeply than any other modern astrologer, observes, "From an occult standpoint the Moon's passage through this house is favorable, as it will precipitate many things that have been held in suspension; there will, moreover, be an occult vein running through the native's consciousness, whether he recognizes it as such or not, this being one of the psychic houses in all of which the Moon has some strength, being able to receive vibrations that are active in the nativity."

As this is the natural home of the Moon, its strength for good or ill is manifestly enhanced; it can be the basis of great and permanent improvements if the native can control his tendency to domestic restlessness. Since this house rules property of all kinds (land, real estate, mines, etc.), advantage should be taken of any promise in the natal chart of gain along these lines.

Progressed Moon in House V

The Moon's progression through house V promises a period when speculation can lead to great gain or great loss, the native having a strong tendency to act in such matters on hunch. The nature of any other influences in effect at this time should be carefully determined. The application of reason to all matters should be encouraged as this is an emotional period when the heart and inner emotions are stressed over those of the outer self; fiery emotions over watery emotions, emotions of the heart over those of the senses.

Life's pleasures will be emphasized, and the native will want to have a good time. Interest in the opposite sex may be stirred or the native may fall in love. If other factors corroborate, in a female chart, birth or loss of children may be indicated. All matters normally ruled by house V come to the fore. Again, the native should strive to be ruled by reason rather than by his emotions.

Progressed Moon in House VI

The progressed Moon's movement through house VI is important for diet, health and hygiene. The natural tendency is for the native to become sick; if serious afflictions are operating at this time, the sickness becomes permanent and may be chronic throughout the latter years of life. In this period the native should definitely be on guard. If the native has indulged too freely in the pleasures of life indicated by the house V position of the progressed Moon, house VI position is the time to pay the piper. Care should be taken with the diet and all factors influencing health should be attended to carefully. All afflictions of the Moon in this period will affect the health. The physical system must be carefully regulated, thus preparing for an improvement in health as favorable vibrations are later established.

The Moon in this position will also bring changes in the native's work and employment. Promotions and loss of position are both possible; employees or servants may leave, or new ones may come.

Progressed Moon in House VII

The Moon's progression over house VII cusp marks another cycle in the native's life. Just as the houses under the earth represent the exteriorization or formal expression of life, so houses VII to XII represent life's philosophical or internal (psychological) expression. The native's relations with others change markedly, with opportunities for marriage, partnership, or some other definite contact with others for good or ill – depending upon the promise of the natal horoscope and the progressed directions operating at this time. Especially in male horoscopes (and because of the Moon's association with marriage) this position indicates marriage rather than some other affiliation, unless it is organizational work relating to the public. As always, age and other environmental conditions must be taken into consideration, but the careful person will avoid marriage or a partnership if the progressed Moon in this position is afflicted.

Progressed Moon in House VIII

Death is close to the native when the progressed Moon is in house VIII. The aspects formed are of importance in signifying the relationship of the person or persons passing on. If affliction involves house XI, death of a friend is to be expected; if IV or X, that of a parent or of the spouse's parent; if V, that of a child; III, of brothers or sisters; IX, of the spouse's relatives, and so forth. If the progressed Moon is under favorable directions during this period, the native will benefit from death through an inheritance or legacy.

House VIII is also a major occult house so the Moon's passage through it awakens an interest in the occult. If directions are favorable, this should be developed by the native, as the birth of some psychic power may be indicated; but if directions are unfavorable, the native should be careful not to be led astray.

Progressed Moon in House IX

The progressed Moon coming to the cusp of house IX and passing through it almost always brings interest in travel for business, pleasure, or whatever other reason shown by the planets involved in the vibrations. The success or failure of the journey is indicated by other directions operating at the same time, but this is generally a favorable period of life in that the higher intellect is emphasized. Occultism, religion, and philosophy are stimulated, bringing a broader understanding of the fundamentals of life. This period usually offers the native the opportunity to evolve to some extent from his lower nature into a higher plane. Such opportunities should be seized, as they will bring, joy and fullness of life in the years that follow. Any evil directions in effect generally indicate difficulties which the native will have to overcome in order to elevate himself. This is the house of the abstract mind; all aspects of the mind are stimulated, not only the intellect but also the intuition.

Progressed Moon in House X

The Moon's progression over the Midheaven and through house X is next in importance after its progression over the Ascendant. It is directly related to two particular phases of life. The first, as might be expected, is the native's position, occupation, or profession. Under favorable influences the changes effected mean great gain and added responsibility for the native with opportunities for advancement. This is an excellent time to seek favors from others or public recognition. In the second place, this is a period of moral adjustment involving the native's honor and reputation. If the Moon is afflicted, there is grave danger of events affecting these adversely depending on the nature of the afflictions and the planets involved. The native must act with caution and forethought; circumstances which appear unimportant will play an important role for good or ill.

Progressed Moon in House XI

This is a decidedly beneficial period with the Moon's progression through house XI stimulating the native's hopes and wishes, associations, and friendships. Even under affliction, while a time to be wary of contacts and relationships with friends, it is not necessarily a time of difficulty or trouble. New associations will be made and will be permanent in nature if vibrations from other bodies are favorable. As the native's own desire for friendship will be stimulated during this period of slightly more than two years, he should cultivate new friends and be assured of their sincerity and good wishes. They may prove of great value when the Moon moves on through house XII.

Progressed Moon in House XII

This period is the most apparently fatalistic of the native's whole life. Even when directions are favorable, he may be deeply affected by the restrictions, limitations, sorrows, and difficulties which arise at this time. Much depends on the zodiacal sign involved; how permanent the influence of this distracting period will be during the remaining years of life depends on the aspects and other factors in the chart. This is the third, and the most emotional, of the karmic houses. The Moon, by its very nature, is stronger in this house and all the native's earnings during the Moon's entire revolution will be paid in full now.

But this house's occult nature gives the native an opportunity to strengthen himself inwardly to confront circumstances. His sympathies are aroused, and the deepest emotions of which he is capable may be stirred. If he is unbalanced the native may be affected psychopathically. He may tend to develop an inferiority complex. But he must always be on guard against others. If he has not created enemies in the past, he need have no fears of the Moon's progression here; but if he has been domineering, egotistical, or riding roughshod over others, this is the time of reckoning, and he pays in full.

Progressed Moon Aspects

While the Moon is a primary timing factor, it has its own characteristics and effect on the progressed horoscope just as on the natal chart. Lunar directions, especially when they act as timing factors, are measured largely by the degree to which they corroborate solar or mutual directions. If not in accord with these other factors, lunar directions may pass with little or no effect, and this must be remembered in the following analysis. Too strong an influence should not be attributed to the progressed Moon unless other factors contribute at the same time.

The student is also cautioned to regard lunar directions as directed to the longitude of the radical planet as well as, to a lesser degree, from the progressed Moon to the progressed planet. For example, the progressed Sun has a slightly different influence on the position of the radical Moon than the progressed Moon on the position of the radical Sun. In connection with the influence of the progressed Sun on the progressed Moon and vice versa, however, other factors must be considered to determine which body is exerting preponderant influence: the house positions (both radically and by progression) of the Sun and Moon, their sign positions, the elevation of one planet over the other, or other progressions in effect. Herein lies the art of synthesis; no definitive law can be applied to an art and each horoscope must be determined on its own merits.

The influence of lunar progressions is not long-lasting, not more than a month with the interior and faster moving planets but longer with the exterior, slower moving ones. Thus, with

Saturn, Uranus, Neptune, or Pluto they are two to four times as long as with Mercury or Venus. The whole question of the exact orb to be allowed is of great concern to research workers in astrology and opinions vary greatly. It is always better to adopt a conservative approach than to make interpretations which are wrong at their inception. Naturally, when a planet is in a friendly zodiacal position (longitude) its influence will be longer lasting than when it is in an unfriendly position. Likewise, its influence for good is stronger in favorable signs. The converse is also true.

Conjunct or Parallel Moon Progression to Sun

This native's life will definitely change for good or ill, depending upon all other factors of the natal and progressed horoscopes. The Moon's emotional stimulation of the ego (Sun) activates the native to initiate new undertakings. This direction is probably more influenced than any other to any planet by the conditions in the natal and progressed horoscopes. It may make the native ambitious and aspiring, bringing him new friends and social advancement particularly if the Moon is stronger than the Sun in the natal chart. It often brings marriage, particularly in a male chart. If the native is a female, the health may be adversely affected by the conflicting natures of the Sun and Moon and the Moon's influence generally on the female organism. As always, however, other factors must be taken into consideration.

All in all, this direction is more favorable in male horoscopes than in female. Radical changes invariably occur in the native himself or in his environment, affecting his future. The native may become restless, with plans failing to materialize, if other progressions are not operating or if there are no strong transiting positions of planets. If the Moon is simultaneously making aspects to other sensitized positions in the horoscope, the solar force is added to that of the Moon, stimulating and encouraging it. Individual effort is aroused and this influence will ultimately yield favorable conditions even though at the time it may appear otherwise.

Favorable Moon Progression to Sun

The vitality is strengthened, and the native's health improves. His mental outlook improves also, he becomes more ambitious, and his efforts are crowned with success. Home conditions improve, as do the conditions of work or profession. All undertakings initiated under this influence have good chances of success; it is a time to make new friends, form partnerships, and to seek favor or cooperation from superiors. Satisfaction of many of the native's hopes and ambitions is indicated. This is a favorable period of life (if other factors in the progressed horoscope corroborate), limited only by the natal chart. The most favorable progressions in a chart for either material, spiritual, or physical gain are trine of the progressed Moon to the radical or progressed positions of the Sun.[6]

Unfavorable Moon Progression to Sun

Plans go awry; disorganization is the keynote; the native's domestic life is threatened, sometimes with respect to the health of a family member. The native will be disagreeable, and changes may bring about business losses. If the natal chart shows separation from parents, the spouse, or others, this is the time when that occurs. Honor and reputation may be affected, depending upon other aspects in force. The native's own health is threatened (through the Moon's relation to the digestive system) and this may affect his whole constitution. Malefic progressions of the Sun and Moon occur about every seven years, but many people remain perfectly healthy for the first 40 or 50 years of life. Thus, it is clear that these directions of the Moon must be interpreted in the light of other factors in the horoscope. Approximately every 28 years the Moon comes into opposition with the Sun, and this is usually a very critical period, the climax of a series of influences bringing anxiety, worry, and disappointment. Separation or divorce may be indicated by the other progressions. The native's feelings and emotions suffer, and all disputes should be avoided.

In considering directions between the Sun and Moon the student must remember that these are two of the three influences affecting the hyleg (the Sun or Moon may be the hyleg of the horoscope) and, as such, its influence is great on the native's health and well-being. Not that afflictions of these two bodies by direction cause end of life, but the native's general health will be good or bad as measured by the constitutional qualities, heredity, and other factors indicated in the natal chart. Furthermore, the Sun and Moon must be considered with more care than other bodies because of the psychological impact of impaired health on the native's ambitions thus affecting his chances of material gain and advancement.

Conjunct or Parallel Moon Progression to Mercury

Great mental activity with changes in philosophy and viewpoint is shown now. Since Mercury is a neutral planet, these changes will reflect the nature assumed by radical Mercury as well as other progressed factors operating at this time. This direction will bring changes of all kinds, new friends, and advancement. Intuitive qualities are developed and latent mental qualities may come to the fore as well as presenting opportunities for study, travel, and intellectual development. The mind is more alert and receptive to new ideas; the native comes to understand his own mental abilities with their strength and power. He should devote this period to study, as his interest is stimulated in intellectual matters. But lack of concentration often coincides with these progressions so the average person cannot attempt to acquire knowledge in a number of subjects without dissipating his intellectual energy, thus wasting talents which could otherwise be put to good use. The greatest lesson, therefore, to be learned at this time is to concentrate on certain subjects and store the knowledge for future use.

Favorable Moon Progression to Mercury

This is a very fortunate period, with success limited only by the native's innate intellectual ability. Under these aspects the mind grows rapidly, enabling the native to use his mental talents to good advantage. Travel (a mode of education) may be indicated; literary undertakings and other business pursuits will thrive and prosper. The mind is alert and active. While the wise use of these favorable influences and characteristics is largely determined by other progressions in effect, the native can do useful work leading to immediate or future gain. He should take maximum advantage of these favorable progressions between the Moon and Mercury, as they lead to rapid promotion, advance, and gain. This is generally a favorable period for the finer things of life, and for everything related to the intellect; the characteristics acquired by the native at this time will stand him in good stead later in life.

Unfavorable Moon Progression to Mercury

This is a very fortunate period, with success limited only by the native's innate intellectual ability. Under these aspects the mind grows rapidly, enabling the native to use his mental talents to good advantage. Travel (a mode of education) may be indicated; literary undertakings and other business pursuits will thrive and prosper. The mind is alert and active. While the wise use of these favorable influences and characteristics is largely determined by other progressions in effect, the native can do useful work leading to immediate or future gain. He should take maximum advantage of these favorable progressions between the Moon and Mercury, as they lead to rapid promotion, advance, and gain. This is generally a favorable period for the finer things of life, and for everything related to the intellect; the characteristics acquired by the native at this time will stand him in good stead later in life.

Unfavorable Moon Progression to Mercury

In this period the reverse will occur of all that has been stated about favorable progressions between the Moon and Mercury. It is unfavorable for all affairs of the type indicated by the natal chart positions of these bodies and of any other planets operating at the same time by progression or transit. Care must be exercised before signing any papers. Both the native's home life and his conditions of employment will be subject to disturbance; changes may be forced which will be detrimental to him. The native's mind is activated too intensely for his own good; he is liable to overstep the bounds of propriety and throw discretion and moderation to the winds. Quarrels and disputes should be avoided and great care taken to guard the reputation. The native is likely to suffer from misinterpreting the conditions around him. This is a bad period for travel. The native is inclined to worry and be over-anxious about his own affairs. Great caution is necessary with the other directions in effect indicating the avenues from which trouble may be anticipated.

Conjunct or Parallel Moon Progression to Venus

This is a very fortunate and delightful time of life and, in a male horoscope, may indicate marriage to a very attractive woman. In a female horoscope, it may mean the birth of a child which is usually a daughter. Not only will the native benefit directly from this good fortune, but it will also give him a bright outlook upon all affairs of life. It is essentially a period of gaiety, with all the feelings and emotions being pleasurably excited. Emphasis is on the social side of life, with the emotions being stimulated by new friendships. This is an exceptionally fine time for contact with others; while this influence is strong only for a limited period of time, the friendships made will be lasting. Since Venus is a money planet, this may be a good time for investment and for purchase of things ruled by Venus. Refining and purifying the personality, these vibrations confer finer qualities of character.

Favorable Moon Progression to Venus

All that has been said of the conjunction and parallel holds true here as well. The mind will be clearer and more lucid and the native's affections will be stimulated. His emotions will find an outlet in friendships, contacts, and activities. Depending upon other directions in force (and on the limitations of the natal chart), this period may bring social success, monetary gain, a firmer character, and all the finer things of life generally.

Unfavorable Moon Progression to Venus

These progressions indicate emotional disappointments; if corroborated by other major influences, they can cause upheavals which will definitely be detrimental to the native, much depending upon the signs and houses involved. An oversensitive condition is created which is difficult to cure, so the native's feelings are disturbed and uncertain. When these progressions are in operation, everyone to whom the native is bound by ties of affection is likely to be involved. Domestic affairs are disarranged and ties of affection may be broken. If the progression is one of opposition, there may be deaths in the family circle or grief may come through the ill health of those whom the native holds dear. The native should be receptive at this time rather than aggressive, negative rather than positive. He should take things philosophically and guard his friendships carefully.

Conjunct or Parallel Moon Progression to Mars

The native should now exercise the utmost caution in all his dealings and actions, as the natural tendency is to impulsive and rash behavior. The Moon being a passive, emotional, non-resistant orb and Mars being dynamic, fiery, and full of energy, the Moon is overstimulated when it reaches the sensitive point of Mars with its passionate materialistic energy so the result is often sexual excess destructive of the native's better nature. If he has a naturally passionate disposition from the natal chart, the overstimulation of this aspect will often wreak great harm; if uncontrolled, the direction of the Moon to these positions provokes extremes. This direction is also associated with accidents - largely due to the native's rash impulsiveness. Care must be exercised in forming attachments and friendships during this period; it is dangerous for all personal matters, as all latent desires are accentuated. Especially in a feminine chart, these progressions will bring marriage or the conception of children - love children as they are sometimes called.

Favorable Moon Progression to Mars

The mental processes are stimulated, and the native becomes very active along the lines indicated in the chart during this period. She wants to broaden her experience, becomes open to new ideas, and if she can be prudent and avoid the excesses due to the overstimulation by Mars, this period will favor business ventures; but the native should remember that any directions between the Moon and Mars are unfavorable in themselves because of the completely different vibrations from the two bodies. The native will be courageous during this period but the influx of mental energy, as well as the stimulation of the physical energies, indicates extreme courses of action. Whether or not the native can control her lower or animal nature will depend greatly upon the value of favorable vibrations of the Moon and Mars to each other. Any direction between the two stimulates the impulsive and passionate side of the nature as well as the mental nature. This is a good period to plan and arrange personal affairs. Any good coming to the native will be measured largely by her ability to control her impulses. If she can do so, success is indicated in almost all affairs due to the stimulation of the energies and the wholesome mental attitude accompanying it. Force used wisely is a power for good; force dissipated, however, wasted the energies and leaves the native weak.

Unfavorable Moon Progression to Mars

These unpleasant aspects will be mitigated only by powerful favorable conditions in the natal chart or through progression. Unless the native has complete mastery of himself, sorrow and trouble are almost inevitable from this position whether it be square, opposition, or even minor aspects.

Much depends on the native's attitude toward his surroundings; he tends to be hasty, rash, and inconsiderate, but again the radical chart must be consulted. He should avoid travel and not enter into agreements or sign papers. Control over the passionate nature is essential; the tongue should be held in check, and quarreling should be avoided. The health should be watched closely as there is a tendency to feverish and inflammatory conditions. He should pay attention to his diet. Excitement is to be avoided, since this arouses the worst side of the passionate nature. He should be discreet in his relations with the opposite sex, as reputation may be lost through some intemperate or hasty act. He should guard against all actions which might bring on scandal.

Conjunct or Parallel Moon Progression to Jupiter

This is a very benefic direction which will bring improvement in all of the native's affairs. Social and financial gain may be expected along lines otherwise indicated. This is a peaceful and prosperous period, hence favorable for travel and for the commencement of new undertakings. The native will enjoy life and more fully appreciate its pleasures and experiences. He should take maximum advantage of his opportunities for the greater the exertion he makes, the greater will be the gains.

Favorable Moon Progression to Jupiter

These are the finest periods of life, for not only is the native successful in all undertakings, but his achievements are recognized by others. The mind and disposition are improved, and financial and social gain are indicated. This is a fine period for investment which, if other indications corroborate, will bring gain and prosperity. Opportunities will be presented of all kinds not the least of which are spiritual opportunities which confer honor, uprightness, and kindliness toward others.

Unfavorable Moon Progression to Jupiter

Jupiter is such a great benefic that he can do little harm so the primary difficulties of these directions are those brought on by extravagance, poor judgment, and undue generosity. The native may indulge in excesses particularly in matters of diet and health. Illnesses marked by blood impurities are shown so the native must learn to be careful and temperate in everything related to health. While financial losses are indicated, gains may also come at this time - not legitimate gains but ones due to others' losses. These progressions may bring legal difficulties and upset spiritual affairs; all excesses must be avoided, and if the native does this, no harm can befall him.

Conjunct or Parallel Moon Progression to Saturn

This is definitely a period of restrictions with the native's actions and interests being retarded and delayed by worries, disappointments, and anxiety. In a feminine chart, this is an especially poor period for the health as the system is debilitated by circulatory difficulties. Friendships may be broken and the native's mind will be burdened by petty annoyances of all kinds. This is time of depression for deaths may occur among those close to the native. He should also guard his health. This is not a good period for domestic, financial, or business matters; sometimes, however, it has more steadying than a harmful effect. At this time the native should rather plan for the future than act in the present.

Favorable Moon Progression to Saturn

A highly stabilizing vibration and favorable in every respect is brought by this combination of energies. The native will stop and take account of himself. Gains will come through persistence and tenacity. The native may have new responsibilities which will help stabilize him; opportunities will arise which enable him to orient himself more harmoniously to life and his environment. He will be more serious and give more attention to personal matters, all of this helping to build character. Thus he will be more prudent, careful, and trustworthy which will bring him honor and credit. This is a fine time to secure permanent employment: although it may at times prove laborious, it will be lasting. This is a period generally for permanent gains.

Unfavorable Moon Progression to Saturn

In feminine horoscopes this is a particularly bad period for the health. Disappointments come from all directions and new undertakings are to be avoided. The native's life enters a critical period when financial difficulties arise and domestic problems come to the fore (often through the death of a family member). The whole course of life seems to be upset. However much the native strives to get ahead, all progress is blocked so he should retire from the active life and devote himself to planning for a time of more favorable vibrations. Disappointments will make the native gloomy and depressed; he will be despondent, brooding, and incapable of seeing the brighter side of things. The health is poor and the vitality low. He should not place trust in others and all associations should be with younger persons rather than with older. Sorrow and grief may come. This influence is certain to incline the native to fearfulness and timidity so he should guard against it by being firm, resolute, and positive. Mental depression can be avoided by associating with those who are cheerful, joyful, and bright. This is one of the most somber periods of life.

Conjunct or Parallel Moon Progression to Uranus

While most astrologers consider this progression as wholly malefic, the author cannot agree. Being a planet of high vibration, Uranus is difficult to attain at mankind's present stage of development, but in many charts of high vibration its influence is wholly benefic. These progressions bring strange experiences, generating out-of-the-ordinary circumstances and conditions. In horoscopes of high vibration this period may mark the development of ideals which are unorthodox but progressive and encompass all of mankind. But most charts are not sufficiently evolved to accept these higher manifestations of the planet; consequently, it must be considered primarily in the light of the experience which may be anticipated. Unusual friendships and attachments are formed. Sudden upsets in plans and domestic arrangements may be expected, bringing estrangement and the dissolution of long-standing ties. This is not a good time for the general affairs of life because conditions change too suddenly and become rapidly exacerbated. The native's intuition will develop; he will become interested in occult subjects and may be overtaken by a latent fate or karma. Unsound foundations will be destroyed and new ones built.

Favorable Moon Progression to Uranus

While Uranus thus brings some favorable material gains from unexpected sources, the permanent gains from these favorable contacts are more occult in character, affecting the inner consciousness. Important and beneficial changes will be effected and the native's own magnetic qualities will be stimulated. He will take up new interests, progressive subjects, and new ways of thinking. Since this planet rules astrology, it often leads to a study of this subject. It is a favorable time for changes and they will be for the better. The native should seek to advance his interests under these vibrations. New friendships may be formed with unusual and remarkable people and sudden gains may be anticipated from speculation or investments. This is also a time when many people join secret or occult societies and organizations.

Unfavorable Moon Progression to Uranus

Judged from the ordinary viewpoint this aspect is indeed highly malefic, with sudden and unexpected changes occurring in the most unusual way and from unusual sources. The native suddenly finds himself faced with conditions which are difficult to gauge and thus difficult to overcome. Under these progressions he should not initiate anything, for the changes brought about will probably bring regret and insoluble problems (unless the prior conditions were so termite-ridden as to be unbearable). Opposition of the progressed Moon to natal Uranus is in every way trying, for (if the natal chart or other directions corroborate) home ties and everything previously held dear will be destroyed and the native will find himself in an entirely new situation. But here again the natal chart must be studied carefully since these progressions operate at regular periods in life and such conditions do not befall everyone; this analytical approach is often offset by other indications in the natal chart.

Conjunct or Parallel Moon Progression to Neptune

All progressions of the Moon to Neptune are difficult to explain. Their major influence seems to be on the native's subconscious due, perhaps, to the fact that Neptune's vibrations are greater than those of Uranus and thus bring the native into contact with strange individuals, sometimes with parasites. The native may also have strange dreams and be afflicted by weird or psychic impressions. Astrologers are not yet able to define their effect on the native. It is believed that thought transference, telepathy, and psychometry may be experienced at this time, if the native is inclined that way. Other aspects should be noted. The native is inclined to be fearful.

Favorable Moon Progression to Neptune

The native seems to change his consciousness and assume a more receptive mental attitude. Favorable psychic manifestations or dreams may occur. If he will maintain an unbiased mind, he may have some highly interesting experiences.

Unfavorable Moon Progression to Neptune

Because the deceitful nature of some Neptunian vibrations (as they are presently understood) the native should be on guard against being taken advantage of by his friends. He will fret much and experience emotional upsets. He should also guard carefully against contracting habits which will later prove detrimental, such as drugs or alcohol.

Conjunct or Parallel Moon Progression to Pluto

Because of the emotional sensitivity of both of these bodies the native may feel quite unstable during this period. Great lamenting of past relations and acquaintances comes to the fore. There may be a strong, and unreasonable, desire to move away from the site of current problems or dissatisfactions. This is not a good time for public appearances because of the native's increased vulnerability. Conversely, the heightened sensitivity may bring revealing spiritual or psychic experiences if denoted in the natal horoscope.

Favorable Moon Progression to Pluto

Awareness makes it possible for the native to show compassion to others, especially women. This is a good period to instigate a new dietary regimen. Understanding finally comes about long-awaited questions.

Unfavorable Moon Progression to Pluto

Other than being quite disruptive these aspects must be interpreted in view of the other factors in the natal and progressed horoscope. The native often retreats into his own private shell and suffers alone. The changes may come from within or from outside forces but are always long lasting.

Review Questions for Chapter 4

1. Calculate the progressed Moon positions for the current year for your own horoscope. Estimate activity, then keep a journal or daily log to ascertain the accuracy of your predictions.

|Chapter 5|

Progressed Planets

ELIMINATION OF MUTUAL ASPECTS IS A serious error; the relative positions of all celestial phenomena are a continuing expression of the same forces in the sense that the events of the next six months of life are a continuation of the previous six months. Since life is a continuum, with each part a segment of the whole, all cosmic vibrations (as indicated by primary and secondary astronomical motion) are continuing forces affecting the individual life. Thus, they must all be taken into account to the degree that strength is marked by natal and progressed positions. However, movement from one progressed position to another is recognized as simply the relationship between two symbolic points, bearing a more transitory and impermanent influence.

The intrinsic influence of some heavenly bodies is probably greater than that of others, aside from house, sign, and directional position. Thus, most astrologers agree that the directions of Jupiter, Mars, Venus, and Mercury are next in importance to those of the Sun, Moon, Ascendant, and Midheaven, and the influences should be judged in accordance.

Bearing in mind the difference between a progressed direction to a radical planet and to a progressed planet, now consider the mutual aspects among these various bodies - bearing in mind

Aspect	Distance in Zodiac	Symbol	Nature	Keyword	Orb
Conjunction	0°	☌	Variable	Preeminence	8°-10°
Semi–sextile	30°	⚹	Favorable	Growth	1° 2°
Semi-square	45°	∠	Unfavorable	Friction	2° 3°
Sextile	60°	✶	Favorable	Opportunity	5° 6°
Square	90°	□	Unfavorable	Obstacle	6° 8°
Trine	120°	△	Favorable	Ease/Luck	6° 8°
Sesquiquadrate	135°	⚼	Unfavorable	Agitation	2° 3°
Quincunx (Inconjunct)	150°	⚻	Difficult	Adjustment	1° 2°
Opposition	180°	☍	Conflict	Separation	8° 10°
Parallel	0°	∥	Variable	Intensity	1° 2°

Table 2. Major Ptolemaic aspects of the horoscope.

that this is analysis and not synthesis (see Table 2).

One of the chief defects of astrologers, in interpreting mutual directions or other kinds of progressions, is to reach conclusions without weighing all of the factors involved. That is why the following considerations should be carefully weighed before attempting to determine the operation of a direction. It is assumed, of course, that the natal chart has already been delineated and studied carefully. The order in which the following are enumerated is not important, since they must in any case be synthesized, and the order of significance will vary according to the natal chart:

(1) the nature of the action of the progressed planet

(2) the nature of the radical planet or (in directions between progressed planets) the nature of the planet to which progression is made

(3) the sign in which the radical planet is placed;

(4) the house in which the radical planet is placed is exceedingly important as it indicates not only the

strength of the influence but how the influence may become manifest;

(5) natal relationships to the radical planet from other bodies;

(6) the sign and house rulership of the radical planet;

(7) the relationship between the progressed planet and the radical planet in the natal chart;

(8) the sign position of the progressed planet's natal place;

(9) the house position of the progressed planet's natal place;

(10) the relationship between the natal position of the progressed planet and the natal places of the other planets.

Remember also that when a direction falls in a cardinal sign or angular house, its action is more forceful, direct, and speedy; when in a fixed sign or succedent house, slower and more lasting; and when in a mutable sign or cadent house, coming on quickly and passing away almost as quickly. While other considerations must also be borne in mind, these are fundamental.

As the student knows, the greater a planet's distance from the Sun, the slower its apparent motion through the zodiac. Directions are made by the faster moving body to the slower moving one; thus, the planet closer to the Sun is usually making directions to the one which is farther from the Sun. However, when one planet is retrograde while the other is direct in apparent motion, they are said to be in mutual application to each other. These facts should always be borne in mind in horoscope delineation, as it is very important for reaching a correct determination. But in the case of the retrograde planet, the slower moving body is usually the one which must be carefully studied; the slower planet usually indicates the nature of the vibrations established while the faster indicates the manner of its expression. For example, if Mars comes to a direction of radical Jupiter, with radical Jupiter and progressed Mars both in direct motion, this indicates Martian influence on Jupiter; but if Jupiter is retrograde in the radical chart and Mars, by direct motion, comes to a direction of Jupiter, this is a Jupiterian influence culminating in explosive action with Mars. This principle is often overlooked and leads many astrologers astray in their interpretations. If the student is careful at the start of his delineation, he will be saved much trouble later.

Exterior planets (Jupiter, Saturn, Uranus, Neptune, and Pluto) move so very slowly by secondary directions that they hardly leave the radical position during the average lifetime - that is, they will usually remain within the orb of their radical positions so it seems hardly necessary to consider their individual progressions. Planetary distances are shown in Figure 8.

Progressed Mercury Aspects

The warning is again repeated that astrologers must always remember the secondary or mirroring character of Mercury.

Conjunct or Parallel Mercury Progression to Sun

When the Sun (or any other body) progresses to the radical place of any planet, including Mercury, the solar vibrations blend with those of the second body and temporarily color or stamp the vibrations of the second body. If the second body, however, were progressing to the position of the radical Sun, it would temporarily color or stamp its vibrations on those of the Sun plus the latter's radical position and environment. The vibrations emanating from the position of the radical body are fixed and continuous, while those of the progressed (or even transiting) body are superimposed upon them, thus coloring or stamping them. In other words, the radical body and its vibrations are influenced by the progressed or transiting one.

Conjunct Mercury Progression to Natal Mercury

Mercury aspecting its natal position stimulates the intellect and disposes the native to the study of other subjects. If other directions are favorable, this is a favorable period for all

Mercury-related matters; if other directions are unfavorable, this is an unfavorable period for such matters, with much worry, disappointment, and difficulty. There is also a strong tendency to nervousness and anxiety which may cause a breakdown in the health.

Conjunct or Parallel Mercury Progression to Venus

The native's mind and higher emotional nature are brought into harmony, and his whole outlook on life is cheerful, beneficent, and happy. This is a very beneficial period which elicits much good, both social and mental, from friends, partners, and family members. This is usually a good period for finances also. Note the planet which Mercury reflects; while this is a comparatively weak influence, unless the two were mutually aspected at birth, its value is increased or decreased according to the lunar directions in operation at the time. Mercury is probably more dependent on sign, house, and other factors than any other body; consequently, much greater care must be given to these conditions than with any other celestial body.

Favorable Mercury Progression to Venus

This is another very beneficial period for mental, social, and financial gain particularly through friends and associates of the family. During this period artistic qualities indicated in the natal horoscope will become highly developed, for opportunities for advancement are strong. Of course, aside from conjunction or parallel, the strongest favorable aspect is the sex tile (for few persons live to such an age that Mercury and Venus form a trine to each other). This is a good time for traveling and making changes, and the aspect of Mercury to Venus almost always brings about changes of the nature indicated by the planet which Mercury reflects natally. This is a time to cultivate mental qualities. It is also the climax of the native's ambitions and aspirations.

Because of the neutral nature of Mercury itself, lunar directions must be carefully considered.

Unfavorable Mercury Progression to Venus

Whether semi-square or square, this direction hinders and delays the benefic influence of Venus and upsets the mental equilibrium of Mercury. This does not suggest insanity or mental disease, but rather that the native's innate mental qualities are not in harmony. The semi-square may even pass without making its influence being felt unless lunar directions in effect at the time determine otherwise. A square between these two planets however, causes a forcible separation of the thinking principle from habitual feelings and conventional thoughts, domestic customs and hidebound observances of all kinds (progressed Mercury square radical Venus), and under the other direction (proposed Venus square radical Mercury) the feelings in their new expansiveness are at war with fixed habits of thought, and artistic enlightenment is therefore likely to result at the cost of some sacrifice to any pedantic tendencies there may be in the native's disposition. This disintegrating influence brings the native all kinds of financial and domestic disappointments and difficulties as well as undermining his relations with his friends. Social disturbances will usually occur.

Conjunct or Parallel Mercury Progression to Mars

The beneficence or malevolence of these vibrations is largely to be measured in terms of the natal chart. The combination of Martian fiery, determined energy and the mental qualities of Mercury creates the danger of mental explosions in the form of rash acts, hasty decisions, or foolhardy courage. It makes the native acute, enterprising, and ambitious plus stirs him to greater activity along the lines indicated by the house and sign positions of the bodies, but there is a permanent danger of overestimating personal powers with consequent indiscretions which may prove exceedingly harmful. Perhaps the greatest lesson to be learned in this period is at all times to be discreet in relationships. The native tends to over-confidence and aggressive assertion of his own capacities. His mind is inclined to be bright and cheerful, but in this period he may be the target of fraud or sharp practices. The whole nervous system is excited and overstimulated. Caution must be exercised in everything. If the native has learned self-control, the mental stimulation found here will benefit all matters indicated by the natal and progressed positions of these planets.

Favorable Mercury Progression to Mars

These vibrations stimulate and quicken the mental faculties, bringing good judgment and gain through intellectual pursuits. The native is sharp, bright, and active, and this is a fine period for new mental interests. His relations improve with his family as well as with those who serve or minister to him. If he knows how to apply the mental stimulation conferred during this period of life, he will benefit both mentally and materially for his own ambitions, enterprise, and speculative abilities are stimulated and urged forward. This is a good influence for the health and especially for the nervous system. If lunar directions corroborate by making favorable directions while these influences are in effect, general success will be limited only by the native's own ability to keep control of his great energy (as indicated by the natal chart).

Unfavorable Mercury Progression to Mars

This is one of the most difficult directions possible in a horoscope (depending, of course, on the natal horoscope to a large extent), making the native dishonest, tricky, and rash. He exaggerates, is impulsive, and utterly disregards the rights of others. This can bring him into disrepute and dishonor. His strongly pugnacious attitude (mental rather than physical, its interpretation depending on the natal chart) arouses opposition and discredit from every quarter. He should be especially careful in his dealings with relatives and inferiors (influence of Gemini and Virgo). Indiscretions lead to financial difficulties. He should think twice before signing any documents and, as far as possible, have little to do with the law and lawyers. Ill-repute, libel, and scandal will hover around him at all times. Harnessing the mental energy is difficult and there is always danger of mental explosion. Disputes and travel should be avoided. The nervous system seems in a state of shock and mental energy may be applied irrationally to life's problems. This is a period in which to guard against accidents and inflammatory diseases. Start no new undertakings, but rather cultivate a passive nature, as only in this way will such inharmonious vibrations be conquered.

Conjunct or Parallel Mercury Progression to Jupiter

As one of the most favorable possible influences on the mentality, the value of this aspect is limited only by the limits in the natal horoscope. It indicates good judgment, intellectual plus, at times, spiritual advance, social advances and financial gains. The native will make friends who will be useful to him; not only will conditions improve as regards his immediate family, but his contacts and relationships with in-laws will also be excellent. The whole mental outlook is improved, finding expression in cheerfulness, joy, and a hopeful outlook for the future. The general health will be good and the native's nervous system will be in excellent condition. Real confidence develops during this period. This influence, whether parallel or conjunction, is one of the few directions in the horoscope which will elevate the whole natal chart. This is a fine period for learning the true nature of philosophy and for expanding the mental horizons, indicating prosperity in every avenue of life's expression.

Favorable Mercury Progression to Jupiter

These are excellent vibrations for mental expansion; the native's whole outlook being cheerful, bright and intelligent, his judgment excellent, and his intuition profound. Note the other progressions (solar, lunar, or mutual) in operation during this period; everything undertaken now will prove a success, such success being limited only by the native's own desire to push ahead and by the indications of the natal chart. This is another fine period for travel and some sort of journey will doubtless be undertaken. Relationships with relatives and inferiors are at their best and the native will benefit from the efforts of new-found friends. These directions can bring long-lasting and successful attachments; in some female charts they may even bring marriage, although the student may have difficulty perceiving this relationship at first. The simplest example is perhaps that of a chart with Gemini rising, making Sagittarius the ruler of house VII cusp and the normal ruler of IX indicating an idealistic, sometimes Platonic, marriage.

Unfavorable Mercury Progression to Jupiter

In this period the native should be passive, relying on the counsel of others rather than following his own judgment, for his own perspective will be warped even though he will feel that he is right. His mental life will be marked by errors of judgment giving rise to grave anxiety. At this time he should also be on guard against the hypocrisy and deceit of others. This is a poor time to travel or to make new contacts, and care should be exercised in all legal matters for (depending on the natal chart) trouble and litigation are again indicated. There is a strong tendency to make promises which cannot be fulfilled and the native should guard against that. His reputation may be assailed, often without any justification but due largely to his own poor judgment. The opposition influence can cause difficulties with in-laws, leading to separation and litigation. Care must be exercised in all financial matters and loans should not be made. The native must be very discreet, as the emotions may be improperly aroused leading to many foolish acts. Opposition between Jupiter and Mercury often causes a conflict, within the native, of the higher and lower occult minds. Note the other directions in effect during these periods for Mercury is the most susceptible planet in the heavens.

Conjunct of Parallel Mercury Progression to Saturn

This is not considered a favorable influence, since it retards the mental faculties, makes the native apprehensive, and inhibits the full expression of his intellectual life. In nervous types this may prove a beneficent influence, provided the vibrations of other directions in effect are favorable. The outcome is to give the native a more solid intellectual nature. This vibration tends to selfishness and the native becomes suspicious of others, going as far as depression and even paranoia if accentuated by other influences (parallel or conjunction). While the native may become intellectually more ambitious; difficulties, delays, and worries may ensue. He may be burdened with domestic responsibilities and disappointments come through older people. While the native may become very critical and fault-finding, the general tendency of the vibration is restricting and limiting.

Favorable Mercury Progression to Saturn

These vibrations are nothing but valuable unless contradictory influences are in effect at the same time. The stabilizing influence of Saturn gives the native a more honest and sincere attitude toward life; he will be thoughtful, steadfast, prudent, and discreet in everything. While these influences always bring responsibilities, this is largely due to the native's capacity to take them on. The mind becomes more serious than previously and the inanities of life hold little interest. Benefit and gain come through the native's exercise of forethought. These vibrations may also make the native philosophical in his attitude toward life's problems, as well as practical (which contributes to success). Interest in philosophy and more serious matters is indicated. This is an excellent period for developing sincere mental qualities, since they will be permanent.

Unfavorable Mercury Progression to Saturn

This combination indicates hindrance, delay, difficulties, and attendant worry about personal problems. These vibrations are highly malefic because they warp the mind and give the native a suspicious nature which may stay with him for the rest of his life; he will be deceitful, treacherous, and inclined to fraud, for this depressed mentality will bring on the worst sort of despondency. Difficulties with relatives, brothers, sisters, and older people will cause him grave concern. He may be separated from loved ones. This type of vibration (despondency) is usually due more to the acts of others than to those of the native; he may be the victim of deceit or fraud and may lose financially through the signing of documents. Any matters of dispute should be avoided, and he should make a strong effort to develop a cheerful outlook. Of course, the force of these vibrations is measured largely in terms of the natal chart, sign and house positions, and other aspects. But, all in all, it is a depressing period when the native must guard carefully against mental breakdown through worry.

The delineation must be corrected to note not only the distribution of planets in quadruplicities and triplicities but also the association of the Ascendant and houses III, VI, IX, and XII with unfavorable directions involving Saturn and Mercury.

Conjunct or Parallel Mercury Progression to Uranus

Whether these vibrations will prove beneficial or harmful depends very much upon the natal horoscope and other influences from progressions operating at the same time. Both Mercury and Uranus are mental planets and their tendency, when combined, is to broaden the intellect to give deeper insight into all intellectual matters, especially in relation to philosophical subjects. Sudden and original mental changes develop in the native a previously unapparent originality and unorthodoxy. He becomes interested in occult phenomena and cosmic laws, including astrology. Withal, there is a strong tendency to irritability and lack of concentration; the native wants to know all there is to be known, often without taking the time or trouble to study. He will meet unusual people and be a party to unusual mental experiences. This period is marked by impulsiveness but, if he can control it, the native will greatly benefit. He seems to develop magnetic qualities and attracts to himself unusual persons.

Favorable Mercury Progression to Uranus

This is a fine period, but still a period of change. The native will develop an original mind which may be expressed in the form of inventions, investigation of the occult, etc. His magnetic qualities will draw others to him and he may become a metaphysical healer. His studies and relations with others bring unexpected gains. This is a period of progress in all realms of thought and the native who takes full advantage of it derives permanent gain, either materially or in the form of emotional satisfactions. Many unique attachments will be made and speculation or investment may yield unexpected gains. This influence may turn the native into a reformer with strong humanitarian impulses.

Unfavorable Mercury Progression to Uranus

This is one of the most malefic possible influences, especially if it accords the indications of the natal chart. The native must learn great self-control, as most extraordinary and sudden changes are indicated. Not only will this bring strange and unusual experiences, but the native may become involved in very destructive friendships. He may adopt an extremist attitude toward life and may become an iconoclast. Caution must be observed in all relations with others, since opposition to his plans will come from all sides and the upsetting conditions encountered may give rise to hasty action which he will regret for the rest of this life. Any inclination to conventionalism disappears and the native must fight against his strong desire to cast off the bonds of civilization. The desire is strong to act on his own which may lead to strange and even romantic developments. These periods should be studied with a view to conquering the implicit tendency of self-destruction in them. The native will have difficulty avoiding developing an eccentric streak.

Note carefully the natal positions of Mercury and Venus as well as their rulerships. These are always very important in defining the influence of progressions.

Conjunct or Parallel Mercury Progression to Neptune

Every astrological researcher has difficulty determining the influence of Mercury and Neptune aspecting each other. Neptune's elusive character makes an analytical interpretation (such as the present) very difficult to express in mere words. Its vibrations are usually regarded as malefic since so few people, apparently, can attune themselves to Neptune. Thus, consideration of vibrations will depend largely upon the native's susceptibility as shown in the radical horoscope. In charts of low vibration the parallel or conjunction of these two planets may bring weird experiences as well as much day and night dreaming. In charts of high vibration, however, where the native himself is spiritually developed, this is an inspirational influence which may confer creative and artistic abilities. One of the greatest of modern astrologers has said, "This essential mental fecundity is almost certain to produce effects of some kind in all who come under this influence, but in the less evolved it is only likely to result in a disposition to scheme for the attainment of some desired object, either personal gain or the gratification of passion." It is certain, in any case, that if afflictions are in effect at the time of these configurations of Mercury and Neptune, the native must act with great caution to avoid drug addiction or alcohol.

Favorable Mercury Progression to Neptune

Much depends on the radical horoscope, but this usually indicates a period of fanciful, mystic, and poetic consciousness from which the native's literary or artistic skill may bring him permanent benefits. He has a pleasant disposition and a keen sense of humor. In the absence of afflictions in the natal chart, this may bring pronounced good fortune. Neptune's influence is always great and has to do with large enterprises. These vibrations may lead to an association with large institutions devoted to intellectual matters.

Unfavorable Mercury Progression to Neptune

Highly malefic, for the mysterious and unfavorable influence of Neptune on the mind brings vague and indeterminate fears, longings, and aspirations. A moral dimension to the mind may be indicated, bringing sorrow and difficulty, possibly developing a mania such as hypochondria. The native's mind is overbalanced by his emotions, and if the chart is not harmonious, Neptune's added romanticism causes distorted views which harm the moral character. The native may be deserted by those whom he has trusted. It is particularly necessary to consider the natal chart in all cases in which Neptune is involved.

Conjunct or Parallel Mercury Progression to Pluto

Because Pluto intensifies all with which it comes in contact this Mercury link will bring to the native a period of mental research and analysis. This is a time of investigating the prime causes and effects of whatever deeply affects the individual. For some it may be collecting data for an anthology on Elizabethan poetry, for others a search for historical proof behind their religious belief, and for yet more a detailed study of anthropogenesis. During this brief period the mind is allowed to penetrate the veils which obscure knowledge from the outer world. On the lower planes, this can also be an aspect of utter confusion and emotional instability.

Favorable Mercury Progression to Pluto

For one who has scientific abilities and interests this is a time of fulfillment. Research papers can be easily written and will be accepted for their great value. Information arrives from the most unusual sources and the native learns to use these ideas constructively. An interest in revising the usual approach to problem solving may lead to enrollment in journaling or mind control classes.

Unfavorable Mercury Progression to Pluto

The nervous tension generated by this combination of energies or vibrations brings problems for the native and his co-workers. There is a lack of patience for even minor details. The person becomes argumentative and dictatorial in dealing with others. Everything must be scrutinized and criticized from a skeptical viewpoint. During this period the native strives to conceal his inner conflicts and fears behind an unrelenting facade. On the lower level, this time could bring serious problems in power struggles, disposition of dead bodies, tax fraud, or secret contracts signed under coercion. The restlessness of the opposition may be used, when shown natally, as impulse to accomplish long over-due projects.

Progressed Venus Aspects Conjunct Venus Progression to Natal Venus

This return of easy-going Venus to its natal location is characterized by harmony and much socializing, a time for cooperation and understanding. When in favorable direction to the natal place this brings social advantages, and these periods favor domestic matters as well as new friendships. Gain and good fortune will come along the lines indicated by house and sign positions. If directions are unfavorable, Venus will bring on emotional difficulties, grief, and disappointment.

Conjunct or Parallel Venus Progression to Mars

While the progression of Venus to the position of Mars is not as dangerous as that of Mars to the position of Venus, this is still an unpleasant direction in many ways. It intermingles the higher and esthetic nature with the lower passions or animal nature, and much depends on sign and house positions as well as on other directions in operation at the time. If properly balanced, this blending can yield a very beneficial mixture of the feelings and emotions, but Martian influence dominating that of Venus leads to danger. The native has a strong urge for sensational experiences, which will be beneficial only if he can exercise control and avoid rash conduct. It often gives rise to a joyful outlook which makes the native cheerful and happy. Frequently someone of the opposite sex crosses the native's path at this time leading to love at first sight, which may culminate in marriage if other conditions are favorable. But if the native is imprudent and rash under this direction his excesses may get him into difficulties almost impossible to escape without suffering or loss of prestige, honor, and substance. Alan Leo says that, "The inner meaning of this aspect is the conjunction of the Soul and the Senses, bringing a fuller and more sensuous expression of either than would otherwise be the case; so that much will depend upon which is the stronger force in the activity, soul, or senses. If both are evenly balanced, then a full and liberal time is before the native; if the soul is the stronger, then the senses will be raised to a higher level, and love will absorb them, but if the senses have the greater hold, then there is a liability of the soul being made captive to sensuous or sensual feelings."

Favorable Venus Progression to Mars

In all directions between Venus and Mars it is important to know which is the dominant influence for they are in eternal conflict, Venus influencing man's higher nature (which to some extent distinguishes him from the animal kingdom) and Mars having dominion over the lower nature (which strives to return to the animal nature). If these two bodies are in harmony, this can be one of the finest periods in life; their conflicting natures are in balance and the native is stimulated to a fuller and freer experience of sensation while at the same time expressing a deeper and fuller love for all that is worthy and good. His contacts with others (particularly the opposite sex) will be richer and all relationships lead to success. This often indicates marriage; or at least a union of the affections in a way that is wholesome, stimulating, and permanently beneficial.

Unfavorable Venus Progression to Mars

Here not only do the natures of the planets clash, but also the action of their vibrations. This is an evil aspect in many ways, bringing conflict between the higher nature and the passions. The keynote is impulsive action without proper forethought or consideration of the consequences. The lower nature is uppermost and passions are stimulated to a degree that will damage the native's character, if previous life experience has not taught him the self-control which steadies and stabilizes his nature. Domestic affairs and finances will be unsettled and disturbed. In the charts of married persons, this is a very dangerous direction which may bring illicit attachments ending in disgrace and scandal. Indiscretions will be multiple, with their inevitable consequences. These unfavorable directions between Venus and Mars cause emotional instability. The opposition aspect causes many disappointments affecting the emotional expression and there is a strong conflict between the native's will to do and his desire to have. These unfavorable directions almost always bring attachments and unions with others but they are usually founded upon physical desire, with its impermanence and consequent heartaches. These are dangerous periods and the wise person will meet them with a resolution not to be led into temptation. Remember also that Venus is the minor money planet; unfavorable directions with Mars will cause undue expenses and financial difficulties, often because of the native's indiscretion.

Conjunct or Parallel Venus Progression to Jupiter

While these directions, involving the two most benefic planets in the heavens, are extremely helpful, their vibrations are at such a high level that few can respond favorably in a permanent way. While this aspect brings social and financial gain or benefit, it is more through others than through the native's own efforts. This is a period more of psychological, than of material, ease and comfort. Life looks good. While this influence is long-lasting (much longer when Jupiter is passing over the natal place of Venus than vice-versa) its operation is generally to be expected only during those short periods when the Moon or other bodies are making favorable contacts with them.

Favorable Venus Progression to Jupiter

These are strongly favorable influences, particularly as they affect the native's mental outlook. They confer a philosophical attitude and deepen the intuition. All relations with others bring benefit, domestic conditions are of the best, plus social and financial gains may be expected. These are very good directions for journeys as well as for lasting attachments and friendships. The native will become more kindly; his affections will be expanded and become more sincere; and he will take a generous attitude toward religious institutions. Financial gain will come through others or through the native's own efforts. As always, house and sign positions must be noted carefully.

Unfavorable Venus Progression to Jupiter

While these vibrations are harmful or malefic in nature, little real damage can be done when two benefic planets are involved. Losses are to be expected through foolish investments, misplaced trust (especially in religious persons), and travel. Extravagance seems to be the keynote, leading to temporary losses. The native should guard against becoming frustrated due to consequent disappointment in domestic affairs and personal relationships. He does not enjoy this period of life, as sorrow often comes with the pleasures. Legal difficulties and separation from someone dear to the native may occur under the force of the opposition. During this period the native's judgment is worse than usual because of the emotional upsets brought on by his own actions.

Conjunct or Parallel Venus Progression to Saturn

These major afflictions must be guarded against, for they may permanently disturb the native's emotional expression and harm his mental or spiritual health. Much depends on the native chart; if the native is highly emotional, the restrictions imposed by this position of Venus relative to Saturn may give rise to harmful psychopathic conditions both to the native and his associates. Great loss of honor and credit may ensue. These directions also include a beneficial influence or a strong urge to thrift and economy which prove of value in certain horoscopes. Thrift should be encouraged, but it is mingled with a tendency to avarice and selfishness which can bring disappointment and trouble. The natal chart, as always, must be considered.

Favorable Venus Progression to Saturn

These are very favorable periods as the better side of Saturn comes to the fore as a stabilizing and lasting influence. The affections are steady; the native's feelings and emotions run smoothly; his fidelity to others is increased; plus the faithful and sincere regard of others is directed to him. Financial gain may come through his own efforts or through the aid of those in superior positions. This is a period in which moral character is improved and lasting friendships are formed. This is also an excellent period for the health. The native's judgment is good throughout this period and financial gain may come through careful investment especially in real estate or amusements.

Unfavorable Venus Progressing to Saturn

A hard time comes for the native's affections as all types of difficulties may be expected, depending upon the sign and house positions involved: disappointments, delays, the breaking of relations with loved ones, and even the death of the latter. He may suffer financial losses and impositions of all kinds. Great care must be exercised, for there may be strong tendencies to loss of honor, moral irresponsibility, and general ill–repute. The native may be inclined to despondency and remorse but should never succumb to these feelings (this is much stronger in angular houses and will undoubtedly bring much anxiety). Enemies may try to discredit the native and dishonor him, whether or not he deserves it, and he must take every possible precaution to ward off such unjust attacks. Note the parallel and conjunction as well.

Conjunct or Parallel Venus Progression to Uranus

These are romantic periods which can bring the native great good or great harm. Any Bohemian instincts in him will be stimulated to action and difficulties arise unless great precautions are taken. The native may encounter remarkable and extraordinary emotional experiences; he may enter into attachments of a romantic type with unusual people, under peculiar circumstances, and with unexpected results. Sudden friendships are made during such periods for, after all, Venus is a planet of impressions while Uranus is the planet of the unusual. The imagination is stimulated and idealism plays an important role in life. Many experiences will come to the native at this time and his own moral qualities determine whether they will be for good or ill.

Favorable Venus Progression to Uranus

These directions are exhilarating for the native's emotional life and beneficent in their expression, but they may end disastrously. Sudden attachments will be made, often to unusual people, but with a certain idealism which is difficult to attain. In his entertainment and social life the native displays a carefree attitude which cannot be found under any other vibrations. He will be carried away by personal feelings and must guard against being led into more serious situations. This period may be good financially, emotionally, and socially, especially if other indications corroborate. If the natal chart indicates luck in gambling, unexpected good fortune may come.

Unfavorable Venus Progression to Uranus

Except, possibly, for unfavorable Neptunian vibrations, these are the most dangerous periods in the native's emotional life, with sudden estrangement, separation, divorce, loss of friends, and unfavorable domestic conditions (whether married of single). Sudden rebound attachments may also be made, which have no permanency. While these directions often bring marriage by elopement, they usually end in repentance at leisure. There is danger from scandal and scandalmongers because the native's actions are erratic, especially where they involve emotional relations with others. Financial losses may also come, but (unless Venus rules house II, VIII, X, or VI) the problems and difficulties are primarily those arising from emotional disturbances, whether brought on by the native's sudden impulsive actions or by his peculiar attitude to all Venusian matters. Note the house rulership.

Conjunct or Parallel Venus Progression to Neptune

This combination excites very unique vibrations which usually bring some peculiar attachments of the heart which may be purely platonic. The natal chart is of paramount importance in reaching any decision here. Under the parallel or conjunction Neptunian influence may have a strongly refining impact, lifting the affections to the heights. These configurations may also give an interest in jewelry, music, painting, and all aesthetic matters.

Favorable Venus Progression to Neptune

Most astrologers agree that these are periods of great joy and deeply rooted emotional experiences, centering on love. But they have another side as well, spiritual development and a morally or spiritually elevating influence; the native undergoes an uplifting spiritual self analysis similar to the old-time conversion or the insight gained by Paul on the road to Damascus. An interest in music and the finer things of life is also common in these periods; if the native has an undeveloped musical or artistic talent, it may be developed at this time.

Unfavorable Venus Progression to Neptune

These together with the unfavorable directions of Venus to Uranus, are in the author's view the most emotionally damaging periods of life. While unusual experiences may be encountered, perversion, impurity, and dishonesty are often coupled with them. Some astrologers conclude that these directions are either so baneful as to ruin the whole of life or else they pass without any appreciable impact at all. In any case, discretion and care in all dealings with others are essential under these vibrations. All afflictions involving Neptune establish nebulous conditions.

Conjunct or Parallel Venus Progression to Pluto

During this period the native will be more romantic than usual, even surprising himself with his passionate and sensual feelings. However, it is wise to remember that love affairs begun under a progressed aspect have little chance of lasting unless the natal horoscope denotes some permanent attachments. It is important to let the object of affection be free to express his or her own personal desires; that is, the native should not give rein to his tendency to manipulate situations (which is strong at this time). Neither should he express the inward jealousy felt when friends and loved ones prefer other interests or companionship occasionally. The love nature is heightened to the point where it may transcend social and economic barriers. Romance can actually rejuvenate the native during this progression. This is a favorable period for investing in antiques or mineral rights, if the natal chart concurs.

Favorable Venus Progression to Pluto

Besides becoming more adaptable concerning the emotions, the native expresses a need for increased group activities. Friendships created now are transforming on both parties, who may later look deeply into occult phenomena. New insights lead to increased creative output. This is an excellent time to refinish antique furniture or restore old paintings. Charisma is strong so all types of people are draw to the native. He may become a champion of some cause for those more underprivileged than self. Although of short duration this can be a memorable period in life.

Unfavorable Venus Progression to Pluto

The native's own chaotic feelings lead to misunderstandings and breakups with friends and relatives alike. Because he feels the disruption in his personal affairs he expresses doubt and futility in all endeavors. During this period it is difficult to curb the strong, and erratic, sex urges. The native may be tempted to use other people for his own gratification on all levels. This can be a period of abusing or receiving abuse. Warning is given about the dangers of attempting to dominate other people.

Progressed Mars Aspects Conjunct Mars Progression to Natal Mars

Favorable directions of Mars to his radical position stimulate the native and confer on him greater mental and physical energy. He is inclined to undertake new interests and accept new responsibilities. His principal difficulty under these directions is a tendency to be overly aggressive, manifesting Martian restlessness. This is a time to exercise caution, prudence, and consideration for others.

Conjunct or Parallel Mars Progression to Jupiter

The opposed natures of these two bodies means that the combination of Martian: and Jupiterian vibrations can never be genuinely benefic. In the case of the parallel of declination and, to a lesser extent, the conjunction there is a strong tendency to waste energy, wealth, health, or whatever else is indicated by the house or sign positions involved in the direction and radical positions of the planets. Jupiter's natural tendency is to liberality and the addition of the Martian characteristics may give rise to extravagance and waste. The native should emphasize the passive side of his character; otherwise this exciting influence will involve him in insurmountable difficulties. His enthusiasm runs rampant, and probably along lines which can never be beneficial. This is a very poor period for contact with religion or religious organizations. But the native will benefit from passivity, as this will teach caution and thoughtfulness. Gain or loss may come suddenly and may give him a powerful spirit of enterprise which will send him forth later with increased energy. While this may lead to success, the native must be on guard against rashness.

Favorable Mars Progression to Jupiter

The geometrical angles formed make these vibrations favorable, but too much good cannot be expected from them, since malefic mixed with benefic does not give rise to greater benefits. The native will be generous and liberal, with a strong urge to extremism in everything. For example, in financial affairs he will be extravagant or penurious, and in health he will either follow a very rigorous or a very lax regimen. These directions often indicate social advantages as well, bringing contacts and friendships which can greatly benefit the native if he will be passive and take care not to be too aggressive. Persons of a highly religious nature become very zealous during this period, which frequently brings either a conversion or at least a strong sense of spiritual uplift. The emotional nature is stimulated to a higher plane. But in charts of lower vibration there may be a tendency to lust that will destroy everything good in the native's character. One of the foremost astrologers of modern times has pointed out that the trine of Mars to Jupiter is (theoretically, at any rate) "the only aspect that promises a fortune through speculation." He adds that "the lunar aspects must coincide and the directions tend that way to make this an accomplished fact."

Unfavorable Mars Progression to Jupiter

These directions are difficult to control and bring to the fore problems of all kinds such as loss of wealth, extravagance, legal difficulties, and even loss of liberty or false confinement. As always, much depends upon the sign and house position of the planets but, generally, everything seems to go against the native. Excesses must be avoided; the person who can control his emotions is the one who will get through this period successfully, as extreme caution must be continually exercised. The native is inclined to foolhardy bravery and will be extremely zealous in everything; however, these displays of energy will only bring trouble. This is also a period in which to guard against accidents.

Conjunct or Parallel Mars Progression to Saturn

Although these are both regarded as malefic, they tend to neutralize each other with Mars being hot and dry, while Saturn is cold and moist. The degree of their strength in these positions is indicated largely by the directions of the Moon in effect at the time. The animal side of the nature may be aroused, with resulting intemperate action leading to disaster. Again, this is a period for stressing passive qualities as the natural impulse is to act rashly, lose one's temper, and do things which are later regretted. If the houses are angular, this tendency is accentuated. The native is being tested to see if he can withstand the temptations besetting him. In horoscopes of high vibration this period is very important; the decisions taken here will make or mar the native. He should exercise every technique of self-restraint and, if he wins the battle, he will go forward to greater accomplishments along whatever lines the chart may otherwise show. Definitely this is a tense period.

Favorable Mars Progression to Saturn

This again is a blending of extremes. Although the vibrations are favorable, the malefic nature of the two planets makes it a difficult period of life. The native is torn between two extremes, causing him to be at the mercy of two opposing forces, corresponding to heat and cold, or force and inertia. The native will be courageous and any inferiority complex manifested previously will be erased from his personality. This period is marked by enterprise and enthusiasm, but withal by hard work. The intuition will be developed and the native will make many plans where success will be limited only by the steadiness of his own character. The amount of good to be anticipated from these directions is measured largely by the vibrations inherent in the natal chart which are, after all, the measure of the native's character.

Unfavorable Mars Progression to Saturn

These mark the most critical periods of life and can give rise to the greatest disasters. While their degree is indicated largely by the natal chart, at worst they lead to disgrace and ruin (if the horoscope otherwise corroborates) while at best the native either is hasty, ill-tempered, and rash, following evil impulses, or is just the reverse of slow, serious, secretive, and lacking in ambition.

These positions are highly malefic in every way and detrimental whether square, opposition, or some minor malefic aspect. They may make the native foolhardy, which will be interpreted by others as bravery. Any jealous instincts shown in the natal chart will be exaggerated during the period of these directions, stirring the native to rash actions from which he will later suffer.

Conjunct or Parallel Mars Progression to Uranus

This is another highly critical period of life during which the native should be cautious in his relations with others. Strange and unusual experiences will befall him, coming on suddenly and passing away just as quickly. New friendships should be avoided; because of the strong inclination to rash acts, in this period such friendships can lead to no good. In charts of advanced souls the mystical and occult side of life comes to the fore and this may prove to be a period of clairvoyant development. Other occult powers of less permanent value may also be developed. In charts of low vibration, and when other afflictions culminate at the same time, mental overstimulation may lead to hallucinations and other highly detrimental mental difficulties. Uranus is malefic largely because of our inability to adjust to its vibrations and, since Mars itself is malefic, the combination of Martian vibrations with those of Uranus is even more damaging to those who cannot attune themselves to the higher qualities. In these periods, care must be exercised in everything to a void nervous strain. It is also a time to guard against accidents and refrain from traveling by air.

Favorable Mars Progression to Uranus

These are stimulating directions which increase the native's vigor and determination as well as his perceptivity and intuition, resourcefulness and inventiveness. Sudden gains will occur along lines indicated by the natal chart but everything indicated by these directions is temporary and disappears as fast as it comes about. Mental activity is also stimulated and the native develops an interest in occult phenomena, astrology, and psychic matters.

He is likely to attract interesting and unusual people and will gain by friendships made during this period, particularly if they are with Martian types. These periods of opportunity, and the extent of the native's ability to take advantage of them, will be marked in the natal chart.

Unfavorable Mars Progression to Uranus

Not only are these vibrations highly malefic but their action is so sudden and unanticipated that the malefic impact is magnified. The native is strongly inclined to act with an almost insane rashness. The emotional strain on him is great and sudden disruptions in his affairs may lead to disaster. There is also grave danger of accidents involving electricity, lightning, fire, firearms, and explosives. Hence this is another period in which the passive side of the nature should be stressed. Application to some interesting area of study will be useful in helping to relieve the strain on the emotions. The conditions of the native's life will alter radically, bringing change in his mental, moral, and physical capacities. The passions must be brought under control. Depending, of course, upon radical factors as well as the house and sign positions, the avenues through which these malefic vibrations may be manifested can be determined within reasonable limits. There is danger (particularly in a female chart) of the sudden and disastrous termination of a marriage or love affair.

Any Mars Progression to Neptune

The extent of this influence, of course, will be measured largely by the strength of the direction itself, the house, sign, and other aspects in force at the time, as well as by the radical positions and relationships. They usually take effect when other directions enter into force, but for the average individual any aspect between Mars and Neptune seems to be dangerous and great caution is necessary. The effect of these vibrations is largely psychological but they may be destructive of health, intellect, and spiritual development. The native should guard carefully against developing harmful habits during these periods, particularly when the directions are unfavorable. When they are favorable, he will be cheerful, joyful, good-humored, and generally well-liked. Withal, he is strongly inclined to mix the lower or passional nature with the highest possible spiritual vibrations and this is difficult to control, requiring careful study of the natal chart.

Any Mars Progression to Pluto

A combination of these two willpower energies gives a powerful urge to assert the personal desires and ambitions. In a more animal nature, the native will be ruthless and cruel during this period of upheaval. For those attuned to the higHer or spiritual vibrations, there may be courage, self-confidence, and dynamic action. Regeneration of certain energies is possible during this physically fertile period. Desire for adventure is strong, as is sensual lust. There could be violence if the native tries to coerce others to do his bidding. This is a time to counsel patience and stress calmness if at all possible.

Jupiter, Saturn, Uranus, Neptune, and Pluto Progressions

Because of the small daily movement of the outer planets their progressed positions do not move out of orb of influence of their respective natal positions. An exact aspect, by progression, will highlight a natal contact.

Review Questions for Chapter 5

1. Synthesize progressed Mars in your horoscope through the ten steps suggested in this chapter.

2. Which factors are most relevant in discussing progressed planets?

3. When there are seeming conflicts between aspects, dignities, and the lunation how do you reconcile the differences?

4. Progress the horoscope of a male, born on March 7, 1932, in Covington, Kentucky, at 10:30 PM, CST, to 1974. Can you pinpoint a marriage breakup?

|Chapter 6|

Transits

TRANSITS ARE IMPORTANT TIMING FACTORS IN all horoscopes. As the word Transit implies, these positions are contemporary placements of the various celestial bodies at any given time. This is sometimes ref erred to as an Ephemeral position. The ephemeris gives their actual daily position at either noon or midnight for Greenwich Mean Time or Universal Time. So mathematical calculations are only required for specific timing of events.

The Moon, of course, is considered as a principal timing device for its movement is much faster than any other body. However, it is wise to consider transits following the Ptolemaic rule that the Sun, Moon, Midheaven, Ascendant, and Part of Fortune are the significators or prorogators while Mars, Jupiter, Saturn, Uranus, Neptune, and Pluto are the promittors. Of course, these last three planets were discovered since Ptolemy's day.

The duration of transitory influences is also a matter of import. Sepharial advanced the theory that transits operate from the time of a contact to the radical, or natal, position of a given planet until such transiting planet passes over the progressed, or directed, position of said body. There seems to be a reasonable basis for this observations, but the author has found that the acuteness of the influence is felt during the actual transit of the natal or progressed position, although, particularly in the cases of health factors and occasionally in purely psychological matters, there seems to be a coincidence of the continuing influence for the period suggested. Sepharial thus explained the longer endurance of influences as an individual ages. So, conditions which seem to have great effect after maturity have little effect upon growing children. It is wise to observe and note these matters, but a sure rule to follow is that transiting actions are greater at the time of the actual aspect to either a natal or a progressed planet. Sometimes the native is not even aware of the occasion of an Actual Transit which literally means within the orb of influence determined by the orbital speed of the transiting planet. Slower-moving bodies are in orb within 1 degree of aspect while this may be modified by the position of progressed bodies in relation to natal positions.

Naturally, the slower the apparent motion of a planet, the longer its transiting influence will be in operation while the opposite is true for faster-moving bodies. In the case of Stationary planets the length of time of operation is still much greater. When a planet reaches the point, or degree of the zodiac, where it seems to stand still and begin to move backward it is said to station or be stationary. Particularly is this true in the case of a transiting planet stationing when conjunct a radical planet. The same is accurate when a transiting planet stations in opposition to a natal body.[8]

It also seems well to note transiting parallels of declination. These are to be treated as a conjunction of the planets involved, although some astrologers think that when one planet is in north declination and the other in south declination they should be treated as an opposition. This point requires much more research from multiple sources. However, two planets in opposition, and having the same latitude, will be in opposite parallel of declination, which is called contraparallel. To treat such an aspect as an opposition is probably more logical than to consider it being conjunct, although research does not bear out this theory.[9]

In the meantime, treat the parallel as the inception of a new condition. Declination is simply the distance a body lies north or south of the celestial equator (see Figure 10). Since parallels are of prime importance in some charts, greater attention will be given to this matter in a later chapter.

Lunations

As timing factors, lunations and full moons are of utmost importance. Generally speaking the mundane position of a lunation indicates the avenue of expression of influences over the ensuing month. Thus, when a lunation falls in house I, it tends

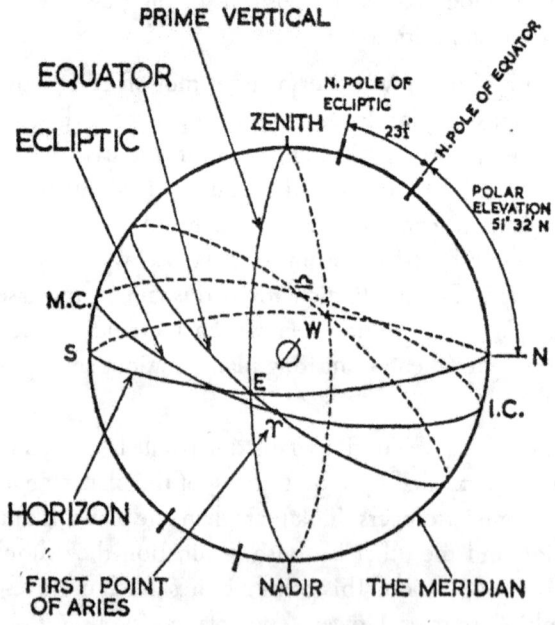

Figure 10. The celestial sphere, showing relationships between the celestial equator and other celestial reference circles.

to bring to the fore personal matters of self; in house II matters of finance; and so forth through house XII.

It has been stated in preceding chapters that a secondary progression or a radix direction (as well as primary) may be in operation over a period of two or three years. The timing of influence will largely depend upon the transiting positions of the planets and, frequently the position of a lunation or full Moon tends to hasten activity. However, do not fall into the mistaken idea that because a lunation (or full Moon) falls on a sensitive point in the horoscope it will bring great gain or cause dire distress. The lunation is simply a conjunction of the ephemeral Sun and Moon and, as such, begins a new soli–lunar cycle lasting until the next conjunction of those two bodies. As the Sun and Moon are probably the two most important timing factors in any horoscope, their arrival at the same longitude in the ecliptic is of far greater import than for either to reach this point alone. When this occurs on a sensitive point of the chart, naturally a third factor of importance is added to it and, if at the same time some other body or sensitive point is aspecting this point (either by progression, regression, direction, or transit), the influence is accentuated to the point that the vibration becomes operative in the life.

Influence of a lunation lasts until the succeeding lunation, a period of about 29 ½ days, while that of a full Moon (which is simply the opposition of the Sun and Moon ephemerally) lasts always until the next lunation (two soli–lunar weeks) but some astrologers have advanced the thought that their influence may continue until the succeeding full Moon. Here again, careful observation in experience will lead to answers having a sure foundation.

When the Sun, Moon, and Earth are in direct line, an Eclipse occurs. An eclipse of the Sun or Moon is said to be of far greater importance than a simple lunation or full Moon for it is positioned so that the influence of one or the other body is temporarily cut–off.[10] The influence of an eclipse of the Sun is considered to be in operation for as many years as minutes the eclipse is in duration; while an eclipse of the Moon will continue to be in effect for as many years as it was in hours of duration. The author's experience leads to belief that eclipses have far greater significance in mundane and other branches of astrology than they do in natal astrology. He does not consider an eclipse in itself as malefic in natal astrology, as many old authors have indicated.

The surest test of any astrological rule or aphorism is the student's own developing experience. Just as there are different methods of studying any subject so, with astrology, each teacher uses those methods with which he has found success. But, after all, experience is the best teacher and the experience one may gain by minutely studying a single horoscope in fine detail will measure well in acquainting anyone with correct horoscope interpretation. Astrology is both a science and an art. In the latter field individual techniques developed by the artist mark the success of his work to a large extent.

Lunation on Natal or Progressed Sun

This marks the inception of things to come and brings uncompleted tasks or ideas to fruition. Best results will be obtained when the native uses a clear head and some good advice when making decisions. There is an increased desire to be active, the extent of which is determined by sign and house location.

Lunation on Natal or Progressed Moon

During the month following this occurrence the native will react more according to his emotions and intuition than by logic and reason. It will not be a time for solitary activities because the need for companionship is strong. Moves or home activities are increased during this period.

Lunation on Natal or Progressed Mercury

The mind will be filled with ideas, the mouth with words,

and the pen with sentences after this new Moon. There is also an excellent chance of making one or more short trips. However, during this month it is difficult for the native to be patient or calm when faced with delays or obstacles.

Lunation on Natal or Progressed Venus

If possible, the native should plan a party or large-scale entertainment this month. A general air of joy exudes, as joy is found in simple pursuits. However, excess spending must be curbed to avoid sorrow later. There is caution about becoming romantically involved, however this is a good time for a wedding or honeymoon as the culmination of a friendship or engagement.

Lunation on Natal or Progressed Mars

An excess of energy will be available which can be used constructively or destructively according to basic inclinations. This is an excellent month to initiate tasks which demand long hours or hard work. However, involvement in wild ventures, quarrels, or debates should be avoided. Impulsiveness is fine unless carried to extremes. Physical fertility is increased.

Lunation on Natal or Progressed Jupiter

During this lucky month, the native may win a long-desired trip, find the answer to a weighty problem, or greet a new child into the family circle. This is a favorable time to register for a course of study or to mail a completed manuscript.

Lunation on Natal or Progressed Saturn

That long-deserved promotion could be received during such a period. It is also a time to care for chronic health problems and to take a needed vacation. There will be dealings with parents or older persons. Superiors observe the manner in which the native accepts responsibility. Delays are likely.

Lunation on Natal or Progressed Uranus

Inner discontent may or may not be shared, but is present.

During this time, when the unexpected becomes commonplace, the native must strive to keep his balance. Whether he can make these rapid adjustments depends on the house and sign location. News may be disruptive or welcome.

Lunation on Natal or Progressed Neptune

A sense of unreality envelops the native for a few weeks. His dream life will be enhanced but any attempt to increase alcohol or drug consumption (even vitamins) should be halted. Simple tasks require more concentration than usual because there is a tendency to be more reflective rather than logical. This is an excellent time to go on retreat, or turn to music and poetry.

Lunation on Natal or Progressed Pluto

To become involved in a power struggle is not wise just now because of the drive to be dictatorial. Answers will be found to puzzling questions and lost articles may mysteriously reappear.

Transits of the Sun

Transiting Sun to Natal or Progressed Sun

Even though the world celebrates New Year's Day on January 1 this will be the real new year for the native. What occurs here depends entirely on the character of the natal or progressed Sun, its house and sign position, and dominant aspects.

Transiting Sun to Natal or Progressed Moon

Emphasis will be on daily tasks and home concerns rather than more worldly matters during this day. When this contact is by an unfavorable aspect there will be tension in the family.

Transiting Sun to Natal or Progressed Mercury

This becomes a good day to write, travel, or talk by telephone. If the native enjoys bargain hunting this can be favorable unless the contact is by bad aspect when the native will be reckless. Signing contracts is possible as well purchasing licenses for a new business venture.

Transiting Sun to Natal or Progressed Venus

New male friends may be introduced today and the rapport will depend on the aspect being formed. There will be a definite interest in color and clothing. This is not a day for solitude.

Transiting Sun to Natal or Progressed Mars

With this contact the native acts on impulse, tries to use force, and drives things through regardless of the feelings of others. Conditions of unpleasantness may be brought about. Good aspects bring increased vigor and courage, as well as an interest in sports or physical activity. This is a good day for either surgery or hard work.

Transiting Sun to Natal or Progressed Jupiter

If there is a need for legal advice this is a good day to receive it. Good aspects between these two bodies are magnetic, drawing luck and success to the native. Wealthy friends will be inclined to make loans or donate to the native's favorite charity. Professional men are available for assistance. With unfavorable aspects there can be over-extension and personal loss.

Transiting Sun to Natal or Progressed Saturn

This is an excellent day to substitute for a superior in order to show latent talents and abilities which, unless this contact is through unfavorable aspects, could be an award winning day. All decisions should be according to previously established procedures.

Transiting Sun to Natal or Progressed Uranus

Government dealings loom on the horizon for this day. The native may add new opportunities to his agenda if this contact is through good aspects. This transit brightens the intuition, tones up the circulatory system, and adds vigor to all activities. All this energy will tend to create nervous tension which will be heightened if the contact is through bad aspects.

Transiting Sun to Natal or Progressed Neptune

This is an unreliable influence which warns the native to be skeptical about people and ideas. Suggestions will be impractical, probably appealing to the sympathies more than the mind. The native may experience a general sense of nervousness, being ill at ease or needlessly depressed. When this contact is by favorable aspect the native will be altruistic, devotional, unselfish, and charitable. Inner spiritual experiences can come under this yearly transit.

Transiting Sun to Natal or Progressed Pluto

Teamwork and group activities are highlighted during this contact, if the aspects are favorable. The native assumes the mantle of leadership easily and comfortably. There will be an increased sense of independence. Under bad aspects, this contact can be frustrating and destructive.

Transits of Mercury
Transiting Mercury to Natal or Progressed Sun

The mind is alert and open to suggestions under such a transit; however, interest is primarily personal. When the contact is unfavorable nervous tension will result, accompanied by unexplained anxiety. Other people pay heed to the native's ideas according to the type of aspect being formed; when favorable people will be more supportive.

Transiting Mercury to Natal or Progressed Moon

Conversations which pry into personal affairs need not be answered during this period, however letters and telephone conversations will be very informative. Other people tend to be openly critical under unfavorable contact, but the brevity of the transit has little lasting effect.

Transiting Mercury to Natal or Progressed Mercury

Clerical details will demand time and attention although they are of little monetary value. This is a day when much time can be wasted on endless chatter or driving about on errands. Under good aspects the mind is stimulated to be productive, if kept clear of extraneous explanations.

Transiting Mercury to Natal or Progressed Venus

A pleasant voice, calm nerves, and a jolly smile are all part of this nice blending. It is quite possible to receive good news, friendship cards, love letters, or fresh flowers on the day of this contact. This would be a good time to pay house calls, have lunch with a female friend, or wished-for invitations may arrive.

Transiting Mercury to Natal or Progressed Mars

Impulsive words will be offensive to some people under this mental stimulus. The mind will work faster than the hands, which leads to mistakes in working or typing. Unfavorable contacts cause irritability, impulsiveness, and hasty judgment. The native must make every effort to exercise diplomacy and patience during this brief jolt of energy, when his nerves are already on edge. The favorable aspects are conducive to travel if proper precautions are observed.

Transiting Mercury to Natal or Progressed Jupiter

These aspects produce hopefulness, confidence, and inner faith as well as giving positive mental action, constructive planning, and the ability to express oneself tactfully. Jupiter, depending on sign and house position, portends appreciable material and social rewards. Good aspects will bring tolerance, patience, and harmony while unfavorable contacts make people overly optimistic.

Transiting Mercury to Natal or Progressed Saturn

Being inclined to depression is a factor of this brief contact as well as aggravating chronic rheumatism, neuralgia, and toothache. This will bring a healthy skepticism which suggest spending the day in routine business affairs without being overly critical. Favorable aspects bring a steadying of mental activity, productive working with older people, and favorable results in legal matters.

Transiting Mercury to Natal or Progressed Uranus

These conditions will be excitable, irritating, nervous, and tense; with an inclination to be sarcastic, impatient, irritable, and indefinite. This period will make routine work and delays difficult for the native to endure. All aspects will bring unexpected meetings with strange people, unwanted for news, and tangled matters. Favorable aspects bring a day in which to exercise the mind to its utmost capacity.

Transiting Mercury to Natal or Progressed Neptune

This is a day to be on the lookout for deceit, quacks, frauds, and misjudgments. When the aspect is unfavorable there can be treachery, underhanded enmity, scandals, and trickery. A favorable contact can provide inspirational, spiritual, and psychic views if Neptune is well posited.

Transiting Mercury to Natal or Progressed Pluto

Whether or not the native makes permanent enemies with this transit depends on the natal position of Pluto in the horoscope. There will be the tendency to take over a situation, and unfavorable aspects bring conflict and disagreement at this point. During these periods there will be interest in reading or studying about occult phenomena.

Transits of Venus

Transiting Venus to Natal or Progressed Sun

There is an arousal of the emotional or sensual nature making the native more susceptible to beauty, music, art, the opposite sex, amusement, pleasure, love of dress and finery, and social influences. Under unfavorable aspects the love of pleasure remains but conditions are not likely to flow smoothly; there is strain or foolish action to make a point. A good time to plan social and artistic activities.

Transiting Venus to Natal or Progressed Moon

Domestic affairs find fortune as well as dealings with women in general; this being an excellent time to interview potential female employees, to request favors of friends, and to appeal to the public. Under bad aspects the native tends to indulge himself, both sensually and physically. Emotions can get completely out of control if the native is crossed by an aggressive woman.

Transiting Venus to Natal or Progressed Mercury

Favorable contacts between these two interior planets are good for expression of artistic faculties, social amenities, pleasant correspondence, associations with others, and personal contentment. When the aspects are unfavorable there will be multiple problems which are best handled by making light of them. It will be a time when easily made promises are hard to keep; a day to receive and give compliments.

Transiting Venus to Natal or Progressed Venus

Social affairs are highlighted on this day when close friends and relatives get together to enjoy companionship. There will be an abundance of genuine warmth and affection. Unfavorable aspects tend to bring separations from loved ones.

Transiting Venus to Natal or Progressed Mars

This contact, even when through good aspects, will bring impulsive actions, spasmodic bursts of affections, and lovers quarrels. The native will seek sympathy and love, being in the mood for enjoyment regardless of the consequences. During an unfavorable aspect there can be a tendency to force issues, to be impatient, passionate, and foolhardy.

Transiting Venus to Natal or Progressed Jupiter

First of all, this contact is favorable for artistic and social matters, a good influence under which to meet people, a period to make friends, and a day to be entertained. Next, it usually brings favors, kindnesses, gifts, and material gains. Old friends will appear unexpectedly; and this is a good time to patch up quarrels. When there is an unfavorable aspect it will bring boredom and social unrest. Associates can be overly conservative or too elegantly dressed. The native will be dissatisfied with his position in life.

Transiting Venus to Natal or Progressed Saturn

The less favorable contacts will bring unhappiness in the form of hurt feelings or criticism of a favorite song or idea. During this transit the native can exhibit jealousy, extreme sensitivity, stupidity, dullness, and awkward appearance. Under favorable influences this contact will bring good behavior, discretion, self-control, and association with older people.

Transiting Venus to Natal or Progressed Uranus

Very magnetic vibrations are associated with this contact. New acquaintances come into the native's life only to disappear just as rapidly, even though the relationship seems to hold promise of more to come. When there are bad aspects this will be an unconventional influence bringing erratic behavior. The native can become emotionally excited and unwilling to listen to firm advice.

Transiting Venus to Natal or Progressed Neptune

This misleading blend of energies can result in peculiar emotional states, psychic experiences, and being influenced by deceitful people. It is an unreliable and treacherous situation, thankfully of short duration. There can be self-deception as well as mysterious actions by others. Regardless of the aspect this is a day to question rather than to be trusting.

Transiting Venus to Natal or Progressed Pluto

Although this will be a productive period it can also bring embarrassing encounters with lovers or mates. It is a day to be wary and gracious all the while keeping one's own counsel. The native could be manipulated by a woman during this period.

Transit of Mars

When considering the exterior planets the effect of a transit may last from a few days to several months because of the slower orbital speed along the ecliptic.

Transiting Mars to Natal or Progressed Sun

In addition to bringing additional zest and physical energy this conjunction gives a positive attitude and increased drive. Even though there will be the impetus for participating in sports and games it is also an accident potential. During unfavorable contacts of Mars to the Sun the native will be argumentative, competitive, rash, and aggressive. If illness coincides there will be high fevers. Favorable aspects bring new people, particularly men, into the life.

Transiting Mars to Natal or Progressed Moon

This contact stirs up the emotions and the senses; uncontrolled urges can lead to dangerous excesses, petty violence, displays of temper, and domestic quarrels. There may be trouble with women or the public in general. Domestic affairs can be unsettled and troublesome; and digestive upsets are common.

Transiting Mars to Natal or Progressed Mercury

The whole nature of this contact will irritate the nerves, intensify mental action, and be annoying. Correspondence or travel plans bring troubles, worries, and confusion. Petty affairs are apt to become involved; and written words give offense. This is not a period for the native to handle legal affairs, write important documents, make relevant decisions, or expound new ideas.

Transiting Mars to Natal or Progressed Venus

During this time of increased popularity the native will be quite impressionable. He must be able to differentiate between excitement and reality in making declarations of permanent commitments. There will be increased sexual interest and a need to be around other people, especially of the opposite sex. Under negative aspects there can be severe emotional strain. Impulsiveness leads to excessive spending on frivolities.

Transiting Mars to Natal or Progressed Mars

This contact stirs up energies which need to be controlled by diplomacy and caution. Accidents are possible through carelessness and recklessness. Cuts and abrasions are common during these few days. Much depends on the natal position and aspects of Mars.

Transiting Mars to Natal or Progressed Jupiter

When the feelings are expanded there can be either generosity or extravagance determined by the type of aspect. Unfavorable contacts lead to heavy expenses, unsatisfactory purchases, theft, financial risk, and impulse spending. This is not time for speculation. Favorable aspects bring courage and true heroism, nobility of action, magnanimity, hospitality, kindness, and tolerance of others. There may be heavy expenses, but not losses.

Transiting Mars to Natal or Progressed Saturn

This brings a period of in harmony when the native expresses bitterness or feels abused. Work may not seem to flow smoothly, there is treachery or jealousy, and serious accidents are possible. During these days the temper can get out of hand if care is not exercised; brooding is a problem.

Transiting Mars to Natal or Progressed Uranus

The contact between these two aggressive energies brings impulsive actions. When the aspects are unfavorable the native may be disagreeable, vicious, and antagonistic. Utmost caution is needed to prevent taking wild chances.

Transiting Mars to Natal or Progressed Neptune

The emotional nature is aroused in peculiar ways by this contact so there will be a tendency toward self-gratification. For the duration of this aspect avoidance of any type of drugs or narcotics would be wise. The imagination and the dream life will be overly activated so the native needs to take care not to become hysterical about suggestions. Under extremely unfavorable contacts the temper is easily aroused and quickly dispersed.

Transiting Mars to Natal or Progressed Pluto

With such a strong sense of competition aroused there will be drastic attempts both by the native and against him to determine directions and power. Under unfavorable aspects permanent changes should not be made even though the circumstances seem to demand them. This can indicate surgery to clear up chronic conditions. There will be a decided sense of restlessness as well as a desire to rebel. Favorable aspects direct these energies toward more productive paths.

Transits of Jupiter

Because Jupiter completes a complete revolution around the Sun or, geocentrically, along the ecliptic, in 11.86 years it remains in each zodiacal sign for approximately a year. Retrograde positions cause variances in this figure but it may be generally assumed. Thus, transits of Jupiter will be considered as they extend through the houses as well as when they are in aspect to a natal or progressed planet.

Transiting Jupiter to Natal or Progressed Sun

When under favorable aspects these are markedly good periods of the life, when health is satisfactory, spirits are above par, finances are prosperous, and new opportunities are arising. The native will be in favor with his superiors; and this is an advantageous time to enter new partnerships with successful men. When this contact is adverse there can be trouble with the blood, such as severe anemia; an opposition or square predisposes to congestion. In general, during unfavorable aspects between these two life-giving planets there will be a trend where high hopes are not realized, there is more expense than profit, there are certain forms of limitations, and the native feels harassed.

Transiting Jupiter to Natal or Progressed Moon

This contact is fortunate for dealings with the public, for travel, domestic affairs, personal happiness, relations with women, health, and affairs of female relatives. The senses are under control, the instincts are normal, habits are well regulated, living mode is improved, and personal affairs are generally peaceful. However, if these aspects are unfavorable, domestic affairs may be tampered with by interfering women; conservative concepts prevail over more liberal leanings; and the mother's health can be affected.

Transiting Jupiter to Natal or Progressed Mercury

By removing mental problems this contact brings benefit through writing, literary endeavors, study, increased efficiency, consultations, advice or counsel, and legal matters. During this period the native will be able to sort out his ideas and information in order to use them in a profitable way. Afflicting aspects between these planets bring bad periods for making financial decisions, wrong conclusions, red tape in legal dealings, wasted effort, and confusing correspondence.

Transiting Jupiter to Natal or Progressed Venus

Pleasure, social amusements, holidays, friendship, success in artistic endeavors, and gifts all can come during such contact. This is an extremely pleasant time under favorable aspects when the native is surrounded by comforts, kindness, and consideration. During these periods friends and acquaintances bring benefits, reconciliations, marriages, trips, gifts, and sometimes renewed health. However, when these planets are in an adverse relationship there can be period of association with boring people, unwanted invitations, expense-generating travel, and lack of spontaneity.

Transiting Jupiter to Natal or Progressed Mars

When adverse these contacts can bring heavy expenses and losses; a theft or robbery is possible; and carelessness leaves the native open to endangering exposure. Under favorable conditions there can be acts of courage, generosity, religious enthusiasm, activity in business, strength, and initiative.

Transiting Jupiter to Natal or Progressed Jupiter

When the conjunction occurs this period is considered as the Jupiter return and will emphasize whatever is promised by the sign and house position of natal Jupiter. It is usually considered lucky unless there are extremely bad afflictions natally. In any case, one or more major ambitions come to fruition and travel conditions are favored. Adverse contacts bring disappointments, increased expenses, and excessive enthusiasm. It is these Jupiter returns upon which the Chinese 12–year cycle of the animal zodiac is founded.

Transiting Jupiter to Natal or Progressed Saturn

Good aspects tend to emphasize economy, prudence, and care in financial matters. This contact is generally restrictive, favors dealing with older people, gives gain or loss in real estate transactions, and is an advantageous time to begin savings programs. Under evil aspects these planets together are delaying, hampering, annoying, and frustrating.

Transiting Jupiter to Natal or Progressed Uranus

This contact, by favorable conditions, brings financial gain through inventions, discoveries, new enterprises, and corporations. The native can be placed in a position of power or authority; inheritances or legacies are possible; study of astrology or engineering is favored; and unexpected monies may arrive. Unfavorable aspects bring sudden loss of funds, spasmodic financial states, and do not favor speculation.

Transiting Jupiter to Natal or Progressed Neptune

When favorable, this contact awakens the altruistic nature, making the native charitable and unselfish. This can be a spiritualizing influence when the higher nature is allowed to dominate; otherwise psychic talents simply are enhanced. A danger from adverse aspects is being misused or deceived by others.

Transiting Jupiter to Natal or Progressed Pluto

Changes are likely to take place under this long–lasting transit, but their effect will be determined by the strength of Pluto in the nativity. The native will learn the true meaning of compromise, under good aspects, or of coercion, under adverse contacts. Disturbing elements erupt under unfavorable relations between these planets, although this same energy can be creative through trines or sextiles. Under bad conditions scandals are remotely possible.

Transiting Jupiter Through the Houses

Jupiter through house I brings increased vitality, overweight problems due to retention of fluids, cheerfulness, and social opportunities.

Jupiter through house II brings opportunities to make additional money, along with the desire for impulse spending for lovely possessions.

Jupiter through house III brings frequent short journeys, abundant correspondence, and increases the interest in writing.

Jupiter through house IV brings religious discussions into the home, additions to the family or house, and domestic contentment.

Jupiter through house V brings a winning streak, honors through children, and increased pleasure or profit through self-expression.

Jupiter through house VI brings good health, improved working conditions, helpful co-workers or employees, and revival of meaningful customs.

Jupiter through house VII brings romance and weddings for the single, unity and amity through partners for couples, and luck in legal disputes.

Jupiter through house VIII brings inheritances, financial increase for the partner, psychic investigations, banking favors, and psychological understanding.

Jupiter through house IX brings inspiration, opportunities for long voyages, friendship with foreigners, and philosophic acceptance.

Jupiter through house X brings honors, social acceptance, career advancement, fame or infamy, and public exposure.

Jupiter through house XI brings new friends and associations, realization of fondest hopes and ambitions, and support for interests.

Jupiter through house XII brings spiritual support, secret romance, exposure of enemies, and compassion for the unfortunate.

Transits of Saturn

One of the most difficult periods of life comes when Saturn returns to the natal position in its orbital cycle of 29.46 years. The second and third returns are not as troublesome and disturbing as the first one. Of course, retrograde periods cause the exact timing to vary from chart to chart.

Transiting Saturn to Natal or Progressed Sun

Having a debilitating effect on the physical vitality is the least of the limitations brought about when Saturn is conjunct or in adverse aspect to the Sun. This contact is depressing, devitalizing, lowering of the entire vibratory rate, retarding, and restrictive. Nothing will go just right and all conditions are delayed by obstacles and hindrances. The native will receive blame for mistakes which were not his responsibility. For women especially, there can be problems or illness for the men in her life. Reputation and business affairs can suffer; new ventures should not be initiated; and misunderstanding can break up relationships. Good aspects are fairly restrictive, bringing caution, prudence, and stability.

Transiting Saturn to Natal or Progressed Moon

Personal depression and discouragement come with this lengthy contact between Saturn and the Moon. This unfavorable aspect can also be unfavorable for domestic affairs, indicate trouble with women, loss through real estate, and bring abuse from others. The native will experience dissatisfaction with his home life and be anxious to travel or move. Marriage under this transit will prove to be a burden as well as be restricting for both partners. Favorable aspects show periods for dealing with elderly women, exhibiting self-control, and being cautious.

Transiting Saturn to Natal or Progressed Mercury

Memory and concentration can be strongly affected by this contact as well as making obstacles difficult to overcome. Adverse contacts bring pessimism, incredulity, scepticism, unbelief, doubt, mental distress, and moodiness. The native should make every effort to avoid legal matters during this transit. Good aspects tend to bring mental continuity, patience, perseverance, earnest study, and careful research.

Transiting Saturn to Natal or Progressed Venus

When there is a conjunction or an adverse aspect there will be problems with the affections, over social matters, and through female friends. The native can become more sensitive, easily slighted, and feel unloved. Because he expects too much of friends and relatives he is hurt by indifference, lack of response to his demands, and neglect. Sorrows may be through death of a loved one or merely separation by distance. Favorable aspects bring the ability to control one's affections, regulate emotions, associate with older and wiser people, prevent impulsive attachments, and help withstand temptations.

Transiting Saturn to Natal or Progressed Mars

While favorable aspects are restraining and regulating, the unfavorable ones will bring abuse, ill treatment, treachery, jealousy, enmity, revenge, bitter feelings, cruelty, and trying experiences. During this period the native should be careful of potential accident situations and express himself less harshly than he feels.

Transiting Saturn to Natal or Progressed Jupiter

Even though Saturn slows down financial affairs it also brings a tendency toward economy, prudence, caution, and circumspection. Financial straits are caused primarily by the square aspect which brings great expense. Property can need repairs, interest payments will be delayed, and honors will not be forthcoming - truly a test of the native's faith. Favorable aspects are good for all matters pertaining to land and property, even when the returns are slow but steady.

Transiting Saturn to Natal or Progressed Saturn

When conjunct there will be a long period of reexamination of decisions made over the past thirty years, with the native being unusually strict about himself. Restrictions in the career can cause loss or change of job because of dissatisfaction, lack of freedom, and increased responsibility without additional pay. Under favorable aspects efforts can bring rewards in paid debts, promotions, completed obligations, and a sense of inner dignity.

Transiting Saturn to Natal or Progressed Uranus

Basically this contact is a strong impetus toward independence and change in life style. During the period of its effect the native can either learn to balance his need for security and stability versus his desire for freedom and personal control or else search out a situation better suited for his present requirements. During adverse contacts there can be danger of loss, troubles with coworkers and superiors, accidents and quarrels which lead to violence, delays which build up tension, loss of a parental figure, physical handicaps or nervous disorders, as well as added burdens which are resented. When the aspects are favorable Saturn brings exciting changes, the ability to organize and use innovative ideas, chances to develop the insight, increased concentration, and control which brings out the logic of shrewd calculations.

Transiting Saturn to Natal or Progressed Neptune

Someone seems to be trying to force the native's innovative spirit into a mold during such a contact: to question his faith, to structure his free time and space, to channel his psychic abilities, to smooth over their own fraudulent practices toward him, and, through hidden schemes, to show up his incompetent behavior at work. Adverse aspects lead to apprehension about personal ability, feelings of anxiety and frustrations, schemes and scandals from unexpected sources, an inability to create order out of chaos, incompetent coworkers and superiors, and lack of free time. When the contacts are favorable there can be a harmony of life style which brings increased self-confidence and deeper understanding. The native will be encouraged to be more realistic about his dreams and ideals. This blending of energies can enhance the basic faith and strengthen religious convictions.

Transiting Saturn to Natal or Progressed Pluto

When these energies meet adversely there can be great demands for overwhelming changes, struggles against authority, frustration of ambitious desires, elimination of useless people and activities, attempts at manipulation, and violence or traffic accidents. The native should be warned against robberies, loans, or attempts to borrow funds. Under favorable contacts there can be conservation of the energies, a certain emotional detachment, fulfillment of long-standing goals, and success at self-understanding.

Transiting Saturn through the Houses

Saturn through house I brings depression, decreased physical vitality, added responsibilities, and a cautious frame of mind.

Saturn through house II brings concern with income, emphasis on savings, decreased impulse spending, and a diminishing source of funds.

Saturn through house III brings obstacles and delays through travel, disappointments about brothers and sisters, difficulty in expressing self, and research into serious study.

Saturn through house IV brings older people into the home, domestic troubles, unusual expenses through houses or real estate, and bereavements.

Saturn through house V brings loss of children through marriage or boarding school, lack of opportunities to express personal creativity, financial suppression, and unsatisfied needs for affection.

Saturn through house VI brings chronic illness to the fore, trouble with co–workers and employees, care with diet and exercise, and loss of job.

Saturn through house VII brings separations, misunderstandings with the spouse, grief in domestic situations, partnerships with older persons, and lack of public confidence.

Saturn through house VIII brings troubles with taxes or legacies, some serious connection with occult phenomena, and financial losses for the mate.

Saturn through house IX brings legal disputes, delays in long-distance travel, problems with foreigners, and questioning of religious affiliations.

Saturn through house X brings delay of promotions, lack of recognition for completed projects, trouble with superiors, and loss of dignity.

Saturn through house XI brings deception through friends, failure of hopes and wishes, older persons into the social sphere, and lack of invitations.

Saturn through house XII brings work with institutions and hospitals, illnesses or operations, frightening mystical experiences, and the desire for solitude.

Transits of Uranus

Transits of Uranus are both important and interesting because this planet brings latent talents to the surface and augments power of the other bodies. The 84.01 year orbital cycle of Uranus promises that it will reside about 7 years in each house.

Transiting Uranus to Natal or Progressed Sun

This very important contact will bring people into the native's sphere of activity who can afford to finance and develop his abilities. Mentors may be involved in government matters, large corporations, engineering companies, or research facilities. Things which occur are not in accord with preconceived plans. Favorable contacts bring unique persons, fulfillment of cherished dreams, and unusual opportunities. Blending by adverse aspects can bring disturbing influences, obscure complaints, restlessness, dissatisfaction with present conditions, desire to be impractical, lack of caution, antagonism for coworkers, and fraudulent advice. Older men may exit from the native's life; whereas with women this contact can be disruptive to the marriage. New acquaintances are not to be trusted.

Transiting Uranus to Natal or Progressed Moon

Conjunctions or unfavorable aspects are not good for the general health pattern, bringing illness not only to the native but also to his wife or mother. There can be disturbances for home, domestic affairs, and personal feelings. When the contact combines through good aspects there can be travel, interesting experiences, exciting new women friends, broader mental views, uplifting of the soul, and interest in humanitarian groups.

Transiting Uranus to Natal or Progressed Mercury

Through favorable contacts there will be mental advancement, new research projects initiated, an added interest in scientific pursuits, patenting of inventions, invitations to lecture, and introduction to clever people. However, adverse aspects are disturbing to the mind and the nerves, bringing worry, confusion, excitability, disorder, distractions, tension, unwelcome experiences, sarcasm, and misunderstandings.

Transiting Uranus to Natal or Progressed Venus

Personal magnetism can be one of the strongest attributes from this contact; during this period the native can meet those of the opposite sex who have great personal appeal. It may be difficult to differentiate between fascination and love although there is always mental rapport and mutual understanding. Artistic and literary matters are favored. Under unfavorable contacts unconventional emotional experiences are possible, which often cause the native to break free of normal conventions and bonds to his later sorrow.

Transiting Uranus to Natal or Progressed Mars

While good aspects bring out bold actions, courage, fame, bravery, and adventure the unfavorable contacts between these two energetic bodies can be devastating. Bad or difficult aspects portend to recklessness, lack of prudence, danger, impulsiveness, lack of common sense, foolhardy action, aggressiveness, love of excitement, and quick tempers.

Transiting Uranus to Natal or Progressed Jupiter

Unwarranted speculation, financial losses, introductions to schemers, loss of legal suits, unfortunate property deals, and general lack of good judgment come along with unfavorable contacts between these planets. A good Uranus transit to Jupiter can, however, turn this picture around by bringing the desire to work on behalf of others, developing the latent spiritual powers, broadening the compassion, and causing the native to be less self concerned.

Transiting Uranus to Natal or Progressed Saturn

This contact can bring troubles through older people, property, business affairs, and financial investments. Many things which were thought to be secure can be lost during this period. If the contract is through trine or sextile aspects older friends often come to the aid of the native during troubled times, and help him be more realistic about what is possible. A solid foundation is required of all ideas and plans before they can be implemented.

Transiting Uranus to Natal or Progressed Uranus

Only those individuals who reach the ripe age of 84 have a conjunction of transiting Uranus to its natal position. However, the squares and semi–squares will occur more often during the lifetime, bringing changes, moves, rebellion against authority, urges for freedom, competition from more progressive individuals, and unexpected events. The good aspects can be quite creative, making the native aware of his unique potential and bringing assistance in the form of exciting, supportive people.

Transiting Uranus to Natal or Progressed Neptune

When this contact occurs there can be psychic experiences and occult pursuits, along with confusion according to the house and sign affected. Changes will occur in private and secret agreements will come to light. Deception can occur among bad aspects.

Transiting Uranus to Natal or Progressed Pluto

Adverse contacts can be extremely dangerous for the native can throw caution to the wind. Under some conditions there can be instances of violence. Good contacts may be the drive behind creative activity; there will be a need for reevaluation of direction; and opportunities for change are presented.

Transiting Uranus through the Houses

Uranus through house I brings unexpected moves or changes in the personality, participation in weird experiments, and a desire to be independent.

Uranus through house II brings financial chaos, a change in the value system, and loss of favorite possessions, either willingly or forced.

Uranus through house III brings interesting studies for the native, mental stimulation, and spontaneous travel.

Uranus through house IV brings changes in the overall family structure, realigning of parent-child relationships, and problems with real estate.

Uranus through house V brings loss through speculation, changes through children, excitement in the love life, and frequent change of partners.

Uranus through house VI brings changes of occupation, conflict with co–workers, desire for freedom from routine jobs, and possible accidents.

Uranus through house VII brings separation from partners, tensions with superiors, arguments with friends, and exciting new encounters.

Uranus through house VIII brings troubles with legacies, psychic experiences in groups, and problems with the partner's money.

Uranus through house IX brings unusual modes of transportation, unexpected gifts of travel, and investigation of other religions.

Uranus through house X brings loss or gain of great prestige, changes of profession, encounters with the government or with superiors, and restrictions from a parental figure.

Uranus through house XI brings unusual new friends, increased teamwork, separation from old friends, and participation in a revolt.

Uranus through house XII brings secret enemies into the public eye, surprise visits to hospitals, danger of arrest, and karmic encounters.

Transits of Neptune

All aspects from Neptune to a natal or progressed planet bring a certain amount of confusion to the matter determined by planet, sign, and house. The 164 year orbit of Neptune around the Sun assures that this outer planet will remain in each zodiacal sign approximately 14 years thus prohibiting much variety in the aspects made by its transit. Mundane affairs over centuries of time show delineations more clearly than do natal horoscopes.

Transiting Neptune to Natal or Progressed Sun

This peculiar and disintegrating influence tends to destroy the willpower, as it acts upon the psychic and emotional nature. Often people are exposed to strange actions because of the confused motives of others. The native should avoid drugs, beware of supposedly alluring romances, deny any attempts to be self-sacrificing, and avoid the exotic. Favorable aspects bring spiritual enlightenment, altruistic aims, poetic phrases, musical inspiration, and psychic experiences on a high plane.

Transiting Neptune to Natal or Progressed Moon

The women who are introduced into the native's life can be either impractical or inspirational. Often strange experiences come through female relatives. Good aspects favor meditation, universal understanding, increased faith, and uplifting experiences; while unfavorable contacts may bring frightening clairvoyant contacts, nightmares, and indulgence.

Transiting Neptune to Natal or Progressed Mercury

Besides clouding the mental processes, unfavorable contacts from Neptune can bring false conclusions, irregular data, deceit, impractical fields of study, waste of time, day-dreaming, deception, and fraud. Favorable aspects tend to bring periods of contemplation which are later productive, spiritual investigation and study, informative insight, and idealistic teachers.

Transiting Neptune to Natal or Progressed Venus

The native can become entrapped in deceptive love affairs with this transit, when he deserts home and family for an elusive romance. These mysterious escapades can be exciting and unique but are not long lasting. Good aspects bring spiritual friends whose bond is on the higher planes.

Transiting Neptune to Natal or Progressed Mars

Regardless of the contacts formed there can be serious quarrels because of complete misunderstanding of purpose, high fevers from infectious diseases, accidents around bodies of water, sexual disappointments, and fanatic attachments formed to impractical ideals or persons.

Transiting Neptune to Natal or Progressed Jupiter

Other people will impose on the native under adverse contacts or help him during good transits. There can be opportunities for dishonesty, fraud, generosity, charitable contributions of both time and money, compassion or emotionalism, and serious spiritual sentiments.

Transiting Neptune to Natal or Progressed Saturn

When these two serious influences blend there can be discredit, loss of prestige, denial of promotions, trouble with superiors, and imagined lack of attention. Favorable contacts can bring inspirational solutions to problems, a serious consideration of religious experiences, and cooperation with beautiful women on a Platonic level.

Transiting Neptune to Natal or Progressed Uranus

There will be few aspects formed between these two outer planets during a lifetime but the primary effects can be increased investigation of occult phenomena, inspired research in technical fields, increased nervous tension, freedom through solitude, and acceptance of dream messages.

Transiting Neptune to Natal or Progressed Neptune

Neptune reaches an opposition with its natal position in 82 years, so few aspects are made on this level which is mainly an entire generation rather than an individual. Effects of the natal Neptune would be highlighted, according to sign and house location.

Transiting Neptune through the Houses

Neptune through house I brings scandals and deceit through personal action, a desire for solitude, and an illusion of glamour to the appearance.

Neptune through house II brings confusion in financial affairs, robbery or loss of valuables, and demands for charity.

Neptune through house III brings confusion over affairs of brother and sisters, confidences from other people, and unsigned letters.

Neptune through house IV brings water damage in the home, drugs and alcohol problems for a parent or relative, and confusion of basic beliefs.

Neptune through house V brings misinformation or rumors about children, desire to gamble, and idealism or deceit in romance.

Neptune through house VI brings a weakening of the body's immune system, surfacing of allergies, and disappointment through a co-worker.

Neptune through house VII brings complete misunderstanding of a partner, with deception possible on both sides of any encounter, and spouse can be hospitalized.

Neptune through house VIII brings medical expenses which affect the mate, fraud from banking institutions, and possible psychological counseling.

Neptune through house IX brings a questioning of childhood beliefs, long and tedious study, and confusion about travel.

Neptune through house X brings ill-use by superiors, discouragement on the job, the dissolution of a corporation, and alcohol problems at work.

Neptune through house XI brings danger of deceit through new friends, false enticements, losses through business loans, and need for society.

Neptune through house XII brings visits to the hospital for drug abuse or overdose, emotional confusion, rumors and scandals from secret sources, and questioning of basic concepts.

Transits of Pluto

With the outermost known planet making a complete revolution of the Sun in approximately 248 years it will not move far from the natal position during the average lifetime. Because of its unusual declination and varying distances from the Sun, Pluto remains in a particular sign of the zodiac from 12 to 30 years. Natal aspects and house positions will hold true for transiting effects as well.

Example for Transit Action

Information has been gathered on the life of former President Franklin D. Roosevelt to illustrate the combination of natal, progressed, and transiting horoscopes in action. No attempt at delineation of these charts is made here because method of calculation is being dealt with rather than interpretation.

When Mr. Roosevelt consulted an astrologer, through friends, he furnished birth time as 7:45 PM. His mother said the birth was at "about 8:00 PM." The generally accepted rectified birth time is 7:41 PM, EST on January 30, 1882, in Hyde Park, New York (73°W56', 41°N47').

The natal, progressed, and transiting charts of the late president are given in Figure 11. However, the progressed time is not calculated for his birth anniversary, but rather for the date of his transition on April 12, 1945, according to the following method.

January 30, 1945, marked his sixty–third birthday. Calculate the Sidereal Time for his progressed horoscope as of that date and for the same moment, longitude, and latitude, as birth. Sidereal Time moves forward 3 minutes and 56 seconds each day, which represents one progressed year. For all practical purposes this can be considered as 4 minutes, or 240 seconds. One degree can be dropped for each 3 months after the birthday for which the progression is calculated.

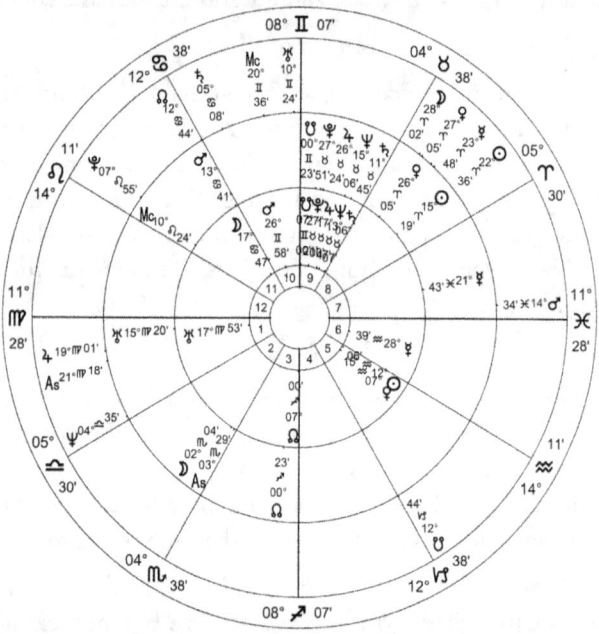

Figure 11. A chart combining natal, progressed, and transit positions for former president Franklin D. Roosevelt. The inner wheel contains radical planets; the middle wheel is progressed planets, Ascendant, and Midheaven for April 12, 1945, at 4:35 PM, EWT, in Warm Springs, Georgia (84°W41', 32°N53'). Progressed points are placed within natal house cusps. The outer wheel contains planets and house cusps for transits at the time and place of death. April 12, 1945, at 4:35 PM, EWT in Warm Springs, Georgia (84W41', 32°N53').

If the horoscope progresses 240 seconds in 12 months, then it moves 20 seconds in 1 month or 2/3 seconds a day. President Roosevelt died on April 12, 1945, just 2 months and 12 days after his birth anniversary. Then the progressed Sidereal Time moved forward 48 seconds in that interval (for closer correction use 47 seconds). This figure will be added to the progressed sidereal time for his sixty-third birthday.

Time of birth was 7:41 PM, EST, which equals 0:41 Greenwich Mean Time on January 31, 1882, for natal positions. As the progressed chart moves 1 day for a year, it moves 2 hours for a month, or 4 minutes in a day. Summarizing then, to calculate the progressed cusps for any date after the birth anniversary, add to the progressed Sidereal Time for the birthday at a rate of 20 seconds per month, then calculate for present location.

Transits are calculated for the time of death at 4:35 PM, EWT, in Warm Springs, Georgia (84°W41', 32°N53'). Place these data, including house cusps, in the outer ring of Figure 11. The natal horoscope is given in the inside ring surrounded by progressed planets, progressed Ascendant, and progressed Midheaven in the center circle, within the natal house cusps. Events may be considered from all three positions.

Other information on former President Roosevelt is provided for additional research on progressed positions as they affected his life.

In 1900 he finished preparatory course at Groton School, presumably during June.

In 1904 he graduated from Harvard University with A.B. degree, also presumably was during June.

In March 17, 1905, Mr. Roosevelt married Anna Eleanor Roosevelt, a distant cousin.

In 1907 he was admitted to New York Bar following study at Columbia University School of Law.

In 1910 he was elected to the New York State Senate, presumably on the first Tuesday in November.

In March 17, 1913, he was appointed Assistant Secretary of the Navy by President Woodrow Wilson.

In 1918 he was placed in charge of inspection of U.S. naval forces in European waters, July-September (foreign travel).

In July 7, 1920, he was nominated for Vice President by the Democratic National Convention, at San Francisco as the running mate of James M. Cox.

In November 2, 1920, he was defeated in a Republican Landslide.

In August 21, 1921, Roosevelt was stricken with infantile paralysis and paralyzed from the waist down, keeping him in retirement until 1924.

In June 27, 1924, he nominated Alfred E. Smith for President at the Democratic National Convention in New York City.

In June 28, 1928, he nominated Alfred E. Smith for President at the Democratic National Convention in Boston, Massachusetts.

In October 3, 1928, he was nominated for Governor of New York at Democratic State Convention and was elected Governor on November 6, 1928.

In July 1, 1932, he was nominated for Governor of New York at Democratic National Convention in Chicago, and flew by airplane to Chicago the following day from his home at Hyde Park.

In November 8, 1932, Mr. Roosevelt was elected President of United States.

In November 3, 1936, Mr. Roosevelt was re-elected President.

In November 5, 1940, Mr. Roosevelt was re-elected President.

In November 7, 1944, Mr Roosevelt was re-elected President.

On April 12, 1945, Mr. Roosevelt died in Warm Springs, Georgia (84°W41', 32°N53') at 4:35 PM, EWT (3:35 PM, EST).

Review Questions for Chapter 6.

1. Look at the transit positions for President Roosevelt's illness beginning on August 21, 1921. Compare these effects with the patterns on July 1, 1932, when he was nominated for United States President. If an older ephemeris is available, use progressions also.

2. Compare the natal, progressed, and transit charts for another President who died in office: John Fitzgerald Kennedy, born on May 29, 1917, in Brookline, Massachusetts, at 3:15 PM, EST. He was assassinated on November 22, 1963, at 12:45 PM, CST, in Dallas, Texas. Are there any similar factors in the deaths of the two presidents?

|Chapter 7|

Birth Diurnal Charts

METHODS OF BRINGING THE NATAL HOROSCOPE up to a given date are all based upon specific cycles which are in turn related to the rotation of Earth on its axis as it goes whirling along in space. Yet at the same time they are related to the annual cycle of the Sun. When it is recalled that the Sun is the source of all life in our solar system, the logic of these procedures will be readily recognized and accepted. Remember that truly astrology is the science of cycles· and all existence moves along in this fashion. Night follows day, season follows season; as each cycle is completed another begins.

But go further than these symbolic relationships for the Sun, Moon and planets which continue in their apparent courses day after day, week after week, month after month, and year after year; each has a different cycle related directly to the time it requires for a complete revolution in its orbit. In the case of the Moon, the orbit is as it revolves around the earth; and in the case of all planets, their orbits as they revolve around the Sun (Table 3). Thus, the Moon makes one complete cycle or revolution around the earth in about 27 ⅓ days; while it takes Neptune about 164 years to make one complete revolution or return around the Sun in its orbit, thus passing through all 12 signs of the zodiac. So this leads to the consideration of the birth diurnal cycle.

Calculating Birth Diurnal Charts

The first cycle completed after birth is based upon the rotation of the earth, which causes all celestial bodies of the solar system to appear to rise in the east, ascend to the Midheaven, descend to the west, pass under the earth, and rise in the east again. Using the Sun as an example, for it is the yardstick by which this cycle is measured, watch as the Sun returns to the same mundane position every day. The birth diurnal chart is simply the calculation of a chart for the 24 hour cycle based on the rotation of the earth. Thus, it ignores the ephemeral apparent motion of celestial bodies through the zodiac, so the natal positions of the planets continuously appear to rotate around the earth retaining their identical relationship to each other, but moving forward clockwise at identically the same rate as the increase in sidereal time in direct motion, and moving backward, opposite or counterclockwise when calculated in regressed or converse motion. As clock or solar time is used in the initial calculation of sidereal time for the moment of birth, however, it is necessary to use that same time converted to the place of residence, in the erection of birth diurnal charts.

Every point in the natal horoscope moves forward approximately one degree in mundane motion each day, so that in the course of a year each celestial body and sensitive point conjuncts every other point in the chart, forms every aspect to every other position, and returns to its natal mundane place.

It has been discovered that when sensitive points in the chart reach the angles, house cusps, or other sensitive points in such motion and, if there are contacts made at the same time by transit, then influences indicated in the natal and progressed charts are brought into play and events occur.

While both Sepharial and Alan Leo have referred to birth diurnals in their writings, it remained for Keye Lloyd, an American astrologer, to carefully investigate them and present his findings for their advancement in this country.

The process of calculation is very simple. Simply convert the time of birth into Local Mean Time at the place of residence by subtracting four minutes for each degree of longitude the residence is west of the birthplace, or adding four minutes for each degree of longitude the residence is east of the birth place. Both of these local mean times are for the same Greenwich Mean Time, so a natal relationship to the point of birth is actually maintained, while it is at the same time coordinated to the place of residence, or that place where any influence will be manifested. By converting birth time to Greenwich Mean Time any location or system may easily be used.

When the new Local Sidereal Time is ascertained, calculate the cusps of the houses for that LST at the new latitude and longitude correction. With Mr. Lloyd's express permission, the following is quoted from him:

"When the native moves away from his birthplace, the chart is automatically set forward or backward, according to a move east or west. Therefore, allowance must be made for geographical location. The most accurate way of erecting the diurnal chart for a given day is to calculate it for the birth time, converted into the corresponding time at the place he is then located.

After the cuspal degrees are all calculated, place in the chart any natal planets that receive aspects (1 degree orb) from any of the diurnal cusps, then add any of the transiting planets which aspect diurnal cusps.

Events happen in a native's life when the degree on a diurnal cusp aspects or conjoins a natal planet – particularly the degree on the Midheaven and Ascendant, which are the most powerful and important cusps of all.

When a transiting planet conjoins or aspects a diurnal cusp it is of very little effect unless it is a major planet and in close aspect to a natal planet; in which case, of course, the natal planet would also be aspected by the cusp.

When a natal planet is aspected by a diurnal cusp, and is not at the same time receiving an aspect from a transiting or progressed planet, there may be a very minor event partaking of the nature of the planet and the cusp.

When there is an existing aspect from a transiting planet to a natal planet, lasting over a period of days, that aspect will operate strongest on the day that the transiting and natal planet are brought into one degree aspect to a diurnal cusp.

When an aspect from a transiting planet to a natal planet apparently fails to operate, or is very light on its feet, it is because the aspect does not tie up with any diurnal cusp during the period of its existence. On the other hand an aspect from a minor planet transiting that ordinarily would be of no consequence, might become quite strong if closely combined with the diurnal Midheaven or Ascendant.

While the direct, or clockwise annual return of the natal chart seems quite logical and reasonable, there is also a counter-clockwise, or converse annual return, which does not seem logical, but which has been found by observation to take place. This converse motion is just as important as the direct and, to have the complete picture of the most powerful cosmic influences in the life of an individual on a given day, both the converse and direct diurnal charts should be erected.

Calculating Converse Diurnal Charts

On each birthday of the native the direct and converse diurnal charts will exactly coincide, forming one chart. On the day after the birthday the direct chart will have rotated approximately four sidereal minutes forward, and the converse chart exactly the same distance backward, and so on through the year until they again coincide on the next birthday.

To find the correct Sidereal Time to use to create the converse diurnal chart for a given day, proceed as follows:

(1) Calculate the Sidereal Time of the direct chart for that day.

(2) From that time deduct the Sidereal Time of the diurnal chart for the last previous birthday.

The remainder will be the amount of Sidereal Time which measures the forward motion of the direct chart and also measures the backward motion of the converse chart. Therefore, deduct the remainder from the Sidereal Time of the previous birthday diurnal chart. The result will be the Sidereal Time to use for the erection of the converse chart.

Example: Birth on July 30 of any year. Required is the Sidereal Time for the converse diurnal chart on February 14 of any year. Assume that the Sidereal Time for the direct diurnal chart, for February 14 has been found to be 17 hours 30 minutes, 47 seconds. Then:

17:30:47 ST of direct chart on February 14

-4:26:13 ST of diurnal, last birthday, July 30

13:04:34 forward motion

04:26:13 ST of diurnal, last birthday, July 30

+24:00:00 (in order to subtract one day)

28:26:13

-13:04:34 converse motion

15:21:39 ST for converse chart for February 14

After one fully understands the working of the above process the same result may be obtained by multiplying the Sidereal Time of previous birthday diurnal chart by 2, and from that amount subtracting the Sidereal Time of the direct diurnal chart for the given day in the following manner:

    04:26:13 ST of diurnal chart, last birthday, July 30
    <u>X   2   </u>
    08:52:26
    <u>+24:00:00</u>
    32:52:26
    <u>-17:30:47</u> ST of direct chart, February 14
    15:21:39 ST of converse chart, February 14

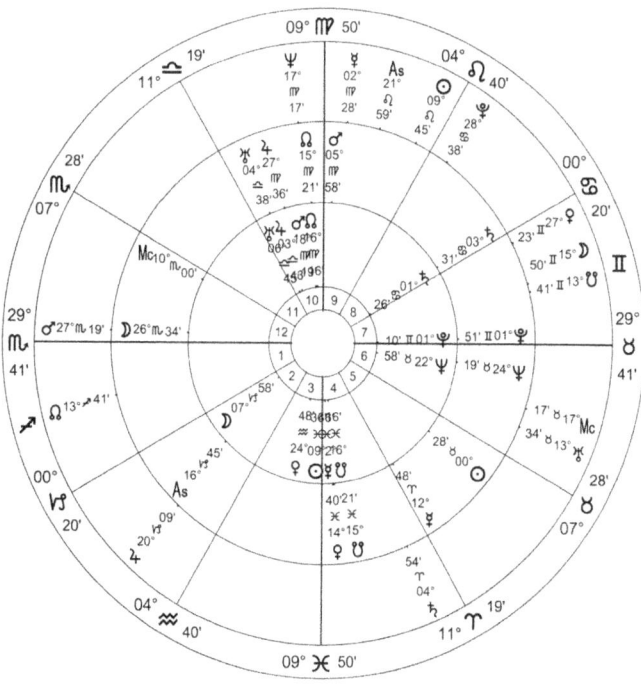

Figure 12. Natal, secondary progressions and transits for August 2, 1937 for Supreme Court Justice Hugo Black.

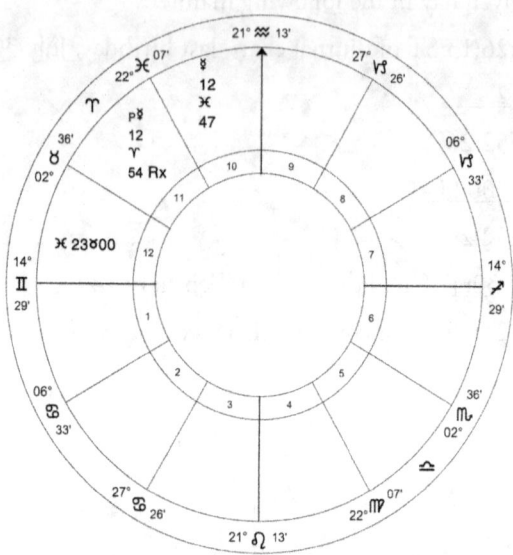

Figure 13. Birth diurnal for Hugo Black on August 2, 1987, in Washington, DC 77°W01', 38°N53'.

(3) Proceed to calculate house cusps in the regular manner for Hugo Black, associate justice of the US Supreme Court from 1937 until 1971. He was born on February 27, 1886, at 11:57 PM, CST in Ashland, Alabama (85°W50', 33°N 17;) and died in 1971. Justice Black became a Supreme Court member on August 2, 1937, in Washington, DC (77°W01', 38°N53'). It is for the latter date that the birth diurnal chart is erected. Natal, secondary progression to birth anniversary in 1937, and transits for August 2, 1937, are given in Figure 12. The birth diurnal chart is in Figure 13.

Justice Black had an exceedingly difficult natal chart and is used here as a fine illustration of how obstacles may be overcome. It is the typical horoscope of a politician; note Uranus in house X conjunct Jupiter, ruler of the Ascendant. The latter planet doubtless led Mr. Black into the field of law, while the

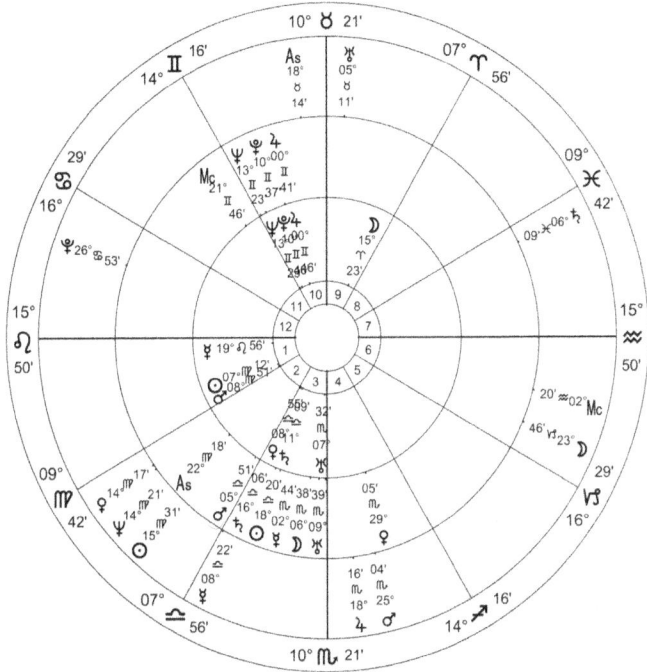

Figure 14. Natal, secondary and transits for former Senator Huey Long. Progressed to 9:20 PM, CST, September 8, 1935, in Baton Rouge, LA.

trine of the Moon to the Midheaven brought him before the public.

Jupiter, ruler of the Ascendant, being angular in Libra with Mars culminating on the Midheaven in Virgo, trine to Neptune in house VI was undoubtedly the key to success in this man's life. Very little contact is made in the secondary progressions at the time of Black's transfer from the Senate to the Supreme Court bench, except that the progressed Sun was within one degree of a sextile to natal Sun.

The birth diurnal chart seems to indicate that birth oc-

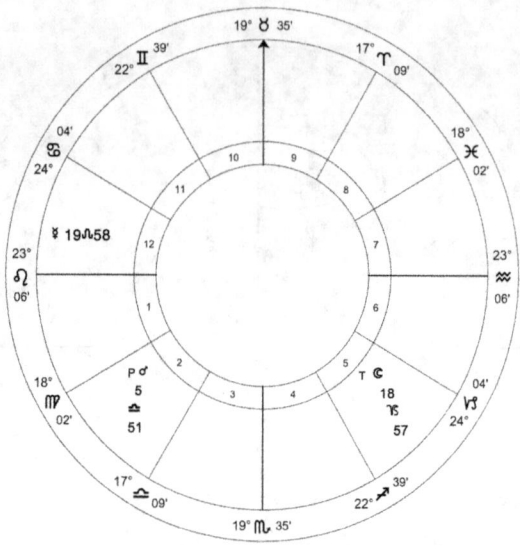

Figure 15. Birth diurnal for shooting of Senator Huey Long on September 8, 1935, in Baton Rouge, LA. 91°W11', 30°N27'.

curred about four minutes earlier; if so, natal Mercury (ruler of the Midheaven) would be square the diurnal Ascendant on the day of his nomination, with progressed Mercury sextile the same point. This, and the square of natal Neptune with the birth diurnal Midheaven explains the attacks made on Justice Black after his nomination to this high position (he was accused of having been a member of the Klux Klan). On this very day (birth being four minutes earlier) transiting Moon was conjunct the birth diurnal Ascendant in Gemini.

At the time of his nomination the progressed Moon had moved into Scorpio and at the time when his appointment was confirmed by the Senate, it was close to a conjunction with his natal Ascendant (which frequently brings about changes in life).

A calculation of the solar return for the previous birth anniversary will show that at this time Jupiter was conjunct the Midheaven presignifying matters of this nature during the ensuing year culminating suddenly and secretly (transiting Uranus was in the solar return house I sextile the Sun in Pisces in house XI of friends, hopes, and wishes). In the rotational diurnal chart for the day of his nomination the Moon and Venus were in rapt parallel, i.e., the Midheaven was precisely on the midpoint between these two bodies, while Venus was on the solar return Ascendant.

Also, on the day of the nomination, transiting Neptune was conjunct natal Mars, while Jupiter transited in trine to this position and was at the same time trine to natal Neptune.

In the birth diurnal chart, which is based upon essentially the same factor as primary directions (the rotation of the earth), four minutes of time is the equivalent of one day; thus, exceedingly fine precision can be obtained without application of greater mathematical knowledge than is required to calculate the ordinary chart. By this method the most trivial events of life are indicated more clearly; strong or powerful configurations need not be in operation to time an influence or an event to the very day, even to the time of day.

The student may regard diurnal charts as difficult and confusing at the outset but practice (especially on his own horoscope) will enable him quickly to calculate birth diurnals, to observe the significant natal or progressed, or regressed positions and transits, and to obtain excellent results.

Always bear in mind that in birth diurnal charts an aspect to a house cusp, especially an angle must be within one degree of exact on the date of operation of the influence. In calculating such a chart for the time of birth converted to the place of residence, if a given planet is two degrees from conjunction with the Ascendant for the date which this planet might signify, the time of birth must be in error about eight minutes of time (longer for signs of long ascension and shorter for signs of short ascension).

If the planet is two degrees above the Ascendant, the time of birth should be earlier; if two degrees below the Ascendant, the time should be later.

Huey Long, U.S. Senator from Louisiana, was born at 4:07 AM, CST on August 30, 1893, at longitude 92°W38', latitude 31°N55'. He was shot by an assassin in Baton Rouge, Louisiana (91° W11', 30°N27'), at 9:20 PM, CST, on September 8, 1935, and died at 4:06 AM, CST, on the morning of September 10, 1935.

His natal chart, progressions, transits, and birth diurnal chart for the date he was shot are given in Figures 14 and 15. The probability of a gunshot wound is clearly shown in the nativity by the angular square of Mars and Jupiter from houses I to X; this is further intensified by the conjunction of Mars and the Sun in house I, Mars being ruler of house IV cusp.

Long's is a most interesting chart and, when compared with his life's course, brings out the astrological principles involved. He was egotistical, (Leo Ascendant, with Sun in house I conjunct Mars), rash, (Sun and Mars square to Jupiter), bombastic, selfish, and self-centered, with an excellent mind, (Moon in house IX trine Mercury ascending; Libra on house III cusp with Venus in house III; Uranus in house III original–sextile Sun and Mars). While Jupiter in Gemini is afflicted and in its detriment, it is highly elevated and rules his house V – the son took Long's place in the U.S. Senate. Note also Neptune in house X; while not in orb of conjunction with Jupiter, it is in square aspect to the Sun and Mars in house I, making the native a tricky kind of individual.

At the time of the assassination his progressed Moon was applying to a conjunction with Uranus which is conjunct the Nadir; progressed Mars had been semi-square natal Mercury in the Ascendant (Mars co–rules his house IV natal cusp).

The full Moon before the event occurred on August 14, 1935, at 20°♒00' in opposition to natal Mercury. The lunation on August 28, 1935, at 4°♍00' conjuncted his natal Sun and was at the midpoint of the square aspect to Jupiter. At the time of the lunation Mars and Jupiter were transiting in conjunction with one another.

The birth diurnal chart indicates (from this one event alone) that birth may have been a few minutes earlier (to bring natal Mercury into conjunction with the Ascendant) or a few minutes later (either to make the aspect of natal Mercury with the birth diurnal Nadir more precise or, still later, to bring transiting Mars into conjunction with the birth of Nadir). However, using the stated time, Mercury did square the Nadir, and progressed Mars was inconjunct the Midheaven, while transiting Mars was just outside the orb of the square of the birth diurnal Ascendant. Two minutes later it would have been within the orb.

The student can find many other factors in effect at this time, but knowledge of other events would be needed to be certain of rectification.

Review Questions for Chapter 7

I. Erect a birth diurnal chart for the death of Senator Huey Long on September 10, 1935, in Baton Rouge, LA. Calculate also the converse birth diurnal chart for death.

2. Erect a birth diurnal for marriage or birth of a child for yourself or a friend. Also a converse birth diurnal.

|Chapter 8|

Symbolic Directions

SINCE THEIR GENERAL ACCEPTANCE THERE HAVE been some improvements in secondary progressions by the adoption of certain primary methods, but the author is frank to confess, secondary progressions or regressions sometimes are not sure indicators. Consequently, the same controversy that inspired Placidius to write his Primum Mobile in 1652, is still apparent in astrological circles. With the advances made during the past generation in research, however, certain methods of progressing horoscopes, generally categorized as Symbolic Directions have been developed. Perhaps the most important of these are Radix Directions and Solar Arc Directions in addition to previously mentioned primary directions.

Serious research minded students of this important problem have given much time to a solution. Among the foremost was English astrologer Sepharial, who introduced the fundamental principles of a new system in 1918, now known as the radix system. This method is by far the most logical and practical of the various methods of symbolic directions advanced during recent years. Sepharial argued that to maintain consistency in any method of direction, the relationship of the planets in the radical horoscope must be maintained. He contended, and the author agrees that no direction (regardless of strength) can produce an event denied by the natal chart and that the influence of a planet under direction must be in definite accord with its radical strength and signification.

"The main features of any consistent measure of time must, in my belief, show all calculations to be directly related to the radical horoscope, i.e., the horoscope for the moment of birth, and the indications derived from calculation must be in terms of that radix. No system which does not maintain the radical relations of the planets can lay claim to integrity or consistency. For it is above all things certain that the radical imprint of the heavens is that from which the argument is derived as to tendency, aptitude, opportunity, and circumstance, in the character and life of an individual, we may therefore direct Jupiter to the Midheaven, or the Ascendant, or to the good aspect of the Sun or Moon; but the detached significance of the planet cannot be rightly judged apart from a consideration of its radical relations and affections, and this is the chief cause of expectancy being disappointed in many cases. Nor can a planet that is radically well aspected indicate by malefic direction any serious hurt, for with its direction to the conjunction or opposition it will simultaneously bring up the sextiles and trines by which it was attended at birth."[11]

Solar arc directions are employed primarily by exponents of cosmobiology and the Uranian system of astrology. In this instance the actual arc, or movement, between the natal Sun and the progressed Sun is determined. Then the actual arc is added to all other points in the horoscope.

Radix Directions

In progressing a horoscope by primary directions the Ptolemaic measure of one degree of right ascension (the longitude of the ecliptic measured along the equator) is taken as the basis of one year. By secondary progressions, as has already been pointed out, the 24–hour motion of each celestial body after birth is taken as the principal basis for progression of the chart for one year. The radix method combines some of the better features of both these systems, while it simplifies mathematical problems involved in each. It further carries out the principle so strongly advocated by Sepharial that in directing the planets the relationship between them which existed at birth must be retained throughout life. Two measures of directions are therefore used. The first, or Major Arc, is based upon the apparent mean motion of the Sun through the zodiac and the second, or Minor Arc, is based upon the apparent mean motion of the Moon.

Through Vivian Robson's research, improvements have been made upon the original findings of Sepharial, and while secondary progression is the preeminent method of directing horoscopes in the western world today, it is fitting that students should learn of other methods which have a sound basis in logic and reasoning.

"During the Middle Ages and through the classical period of the seventeenth century the Regiomontanus system of house division held the field, and the chief predictive method was that of primary direction under the poles of the planets, with which the solar return and projections were employed as subsidiary aids. At a rather later date the Placidean house cusps began to be extensively used, and with them the primary semi–arc system came to the fore. The solar return still held its place, but projections fell into disuse. The substitution of semi–arc directions for polar ones was an improvement in method, but it did not touch the basic principles of primary direction, namely the employment of the earth's rotation as the sole factor in the formation of directions, and the use of one degree as the equivalent of a year of time. It is true that small variations were introduced from time to time in this measure, but the principle has remained unchanged from the earliest times to the present day.

"Somewhat about a century ago, however, a new system began to spread. This was the secondary system, of Arabian origin, in which the planetary positions on each day after birth are taken to measure a year of life, and directions are formed by the movement of the planets in their orbits after birth instead of by the earth's rotation. From the point of view of results the adoption of the secondary system was not a progressive step. The directions formed by this method have not the power of primaries, and are not usually so definite in their effects. This was well known in the early days of their use, but is not so generally recognized today, because comparatively few astrologers use or understand the primary system. The reason for the rapid spread of the secondary method was not due to any idea of its superior merit, but chiefly because it overcame two distinct drawbacks to all primary systems. Primary directions depend entirely upon the absolute accuracy of the time of birth, for an error of about four minutes will in many cases throw out the date of direction by as much as a year. This is rather a serious drawback, because birth times are not usually recorded with such a degree of accuracy and, in the case of a young person, rectification by events is frequently impossible owing to lack of data. The secondary system however, afforded an easy means of obtaining directions in cases where the birth time was only very approximate, because the minor directions are formed by the Moon, and an error of two hours in the birth time alters the Moon's place by only about one degree, and throws the events out by no more than a month. The second disadvantage of the primary systems is that they all require considerable calculation, necessitating the outlay of a great deal of time, and the possession of, if not mathematical ability, at least a good head for figures. Here again the secondary system scored because of its ease of working, and the facility with which the directions for any given year could be obtained without laborious calculation.[12]

During the course of one year, a little over 365 days, the Sun appears to move through 360 degrees of longitude, with a mean motion of 59 minutes and 08 seconds daily.[13] This distance is taken as the measure of one year of life for the major arc of direction. The Moon appears to move through the 350 degrees of longitude in slightly over 27 days, or with a mean motion of 13 degrees 10 minutes and 35 seconds daily, which is taken as the minor arc of direction for one year of life. Thus, when the radical horoscope is calculated, the student has little further need to refer to the ephemeris for the motion of each planet. The Midheaven and the cusp of each house progressed identically for each year of life.

Major Arc of Direction

In Chapter 1 (Figure 1) the horoscope for a birth in New York City on November 7, 1930, was progressed to 22 years of age by secondary progressions. Now progress the same horoscope to 22 years of age by the radix directional method. If the major arc for one year of life is 59 minutes and 08 seconds, the arc for 22 years will be 21 degrees 40 minutes and 52 seconds (59'08" x 22). This measure is added to each house cusp and each planet. As the cusp of the radical Midheaven was 4° Scorpio 23, the cusp of the directed Midheaven will be 26° Scorpio 04; of house XI; 20° Sagittarius 02; of house XII 10° Capricorn 30; of the Ascendant, 1° Aquarius 25; of II, 12° Pisces 53; of III, 24° Aries 19. Likewise, the same arc of direction is added to the position of each radical planet. Whereas the Sun was 14° Scorpio 32 at birth, its directed position will be 6° Sagittarius 11'52"; which the observing student will notice is only 30 minutes less than the Sun's progression by the secondary session. Mercury, which was 14 Scorpio 52 at birth, would be directed to 6 Sagittarius 32, and the same increment of 21 degrees 40 minutes and 52 seconds is added to the natal position of the Moon and remaining planets.

A second Ascendant is added to the horoscope which is called the **Oblique Ascendant.** No calculation is necessary. Simply ascertain the radix directed Midheaven and turn to the table of houses for the latitude of birth; copy into the horoscope the Ascendant given for that Midheaven. In this case the directed

Midheaven is 26° Scorpio 00 and the oblique Ascendent thus obtained will be found to be 4° Aquarius 48. Following is a completed list of the natives' progressed chart using the radix directional method including house cusps:

Mc: 26°♏04'   Asc: 1°♒25'   2nd: 12°♓53'   3rd: 24°♈19'

4th: 26°♉04'   5th 20°♊02'   6th 10°♋30'   7th 1°♌25'

8th 12°♍53'   9th 24°♎19'   11th 20°♐02'   12th 10°♑30'

☉ 6°♐12'   ☾ 21°♊08'   ☿ 6°♐32'   ♀ 28°♐27'   ♂ 29°♌33'

♃ 12°♌11'   ♄ 29°♑36'   ♅ 3°♉53'   ♆ 27°♍11'   ♇ 12°♌31'

Oblique Asc 4°♒28'

To apply the principle of timing future direction, find the age of the native when Mars will direct to a conjunction with natal Neptune. For ease of calculation use the conversions in **Table 4**.

Neptune   5°♍31' = 155°31'

Mars   7°♌52' = 127°52'

           Result: 27° 39' Arc of Direction

By reference to the arc of direction (Tables 5–7) it is seen that 27 degrees and 36 minutes covers 28 years; the remaining 3 minutes covers 19 or 20 days.

A further example is Sun directing to Saturn in 54 years, 2 months and 6 days, on January 12, 1985:

Saturn   7°♑56' = 277°56'

Sun   14°♏32' = 224° 32'

           Result: 53° 24' Arc of Direction

53° 13' = 54 years

10'   = 2 months

01'   = 6 days

53°24' = 54 years 2 months 6 days.

Table 4. Arc conversion table.

° OPP. SIGNS	♈ °	♉ °	♊ °	♋ °	♌ °	♍ °	♎ °	♏ °	♐ °	♑ °	♒ °	♓ °
	0 : 1	0 : 30	0 : 60	0 : 90	0 : 120	0 : 150	0 : 180	0 : 210	0 : 240	0 : 270	0 : 300	0 : 330
1	1 : 2	1 : 31	1 : 61	1 : 91	1 : 121	1 : 151	1 : 181	1 : 211	1 : 241	1 : 271	1 : 301	1 : 331
2	2 : 3	2 : 32	2 : 62	2 : 92	2 : 122	2 : 152	2 : 182	2 : 212	2 : 242	2 : 272	2 : 302	2 : 332
3	3 : 4	3 : 33	3 : 63	3 : 93	3 : 123	3 : 153	3 : 183	3 : 213	3 : 243	3 : 273	3 : 303	3 : 333
4	4 : 5	4 : 34	4 : 64	4 : 94	4 : 124	4 : 154	4 : 184	4 : 214	4 : 244	4 : 274	4 : 304	4 : 334
5	5 : 6	5 : 35	5 : 65	5 : 95	5 : 125	5 : 155	5 : 185	5 : 215	5 : 245	5 : 275	5 : 305	5 : 335
6	6 : 7	6 : 36	6 : 66	6 : 96	6 : 126	6 : 156	6 : 186	6 : 216	6 : 246	6 : 276	6 : 306	6 : 336
7	7 : 8	7 : 37	7 : 67	7 : 97	7 : 127	7 : 157	7 : 187	7 : 217	7 : 247	7 : 277	7 : 307	7 : 337
8	8 : 9	8 : 38	8 : 68	8 : 98	8 : 128	8 : 158	8 : 188	8 : 218	8 : 248	8 : 278	8 : 308	8 : 338
9	9 : 10	9 : 39	9 : 69	9 : 99	9 : 129	9 : 159	9 : 189	9 : 219	9 : 249	9 : 279	9 : 309	9 : 339
10	10 : 11	10 : 40	10 : 70	10 : 100	10 : 130	10 : 160	10 : 190	10 : 220	10 : 250	10 : 280	10 : 310	10 : 340
11	11 : 12	11 : 41	11 : 71	11 : 101	11 : 131	11 : 161	11 : 191	11 : 221	11 : 251	11 : 281	11 : 311	11 : 341
12	12 : 13	12 : 42	12 : 72	12 : 102	12 : 132	12 : 162	12 : 192	12 : 222	12 : 252	12 : 282	12 : 312	12 : 342
13	13 : 14	13 : 43	13 : 73	13 : 103	13 : 133	13 : 163	13 : 193	13 : 223	13 : 253	13 : 283	13 : 313	13 : 343
14	14 : 15	14 : 44	14 : 74	14 : 104	14 : 134	14 : 164	14 : 194	14 : 224	14 : 254	14 : 284	14 : 314	14 : 344
15	15 : 16	15 : 45	15 : 75	15 : 105	15 : 135	15 : 165	15 : 195	15 : 225	15 : 255	15 : 285	15 : 315	15 : 345
16	16 : 17	16 : 46	16 : 76	16 : 106	16 : 136	16 : 166	16 : 196	16 : 226	16 : 256	16 : 286	16 : 316	16 : 346
17	17 : 18	17 : 47	17 : 77	17 : 107	17 : 137	17 : 167	17 : 197	17 : 227	17 : 257	17 : 287	17 : 317	17 : 347
18	18 : 19	18 : 48	18 : 78	18 : 108	18 : 138	18 : 168	18 : 198	18 : 228	18 : 258	18 : 288	18 : 318	18 : 348
19	19 : 20	19 : 49	19 : 79	19 : 109	19 : 139	19 : 169	19 : 199	19 : 229	19 : 259	19 : 289	19 : 319	19 : 349
20	20 : 21	20 : 50	20 : 80	20 : 110	20 : 140	20 : 170	20 : 200	20 : 230	20 : 260	20 : 290	20 : 320	20 : 350
21	21 : 22	21 : 51	21 : 81	21 : 111	21 : 141	21 : 171	21 : 201	21 : 231	21 : 261	21 : 291	21 : 321	21 : 351
22	22 : 23	22 : 52	22 : 82	22 : 112	22 : 142	22 : 172	22 : 202	22 : 232	22 : 262	22 : 292	22 : 322	22 : 352
23	23 : 24	23 : 53	23 : 83	23 : 113	23 : 143	23 : 173	23 : 203	23 : 233	23 : 263	23 : 293	23 : 323	23 : 353
24	24 : 25	24 : 54	24 : 84	24 : 114	24 : 144	24 : 174	24 : 204	24 : 234	24 : 264	24 : 294	24 : 324	24 : 354
25	25 : 26	25 : 55	25 : 85	25 : 115	25 : 145	25 : 175	25 : 205	25 : 235	25 : 265	25 : 295	25 : 325	25 : 355
26	26 : 27	26 : 56	26 : 86	26 : 116	26 : 146	26 : 176	26 : 206	26 : 236	26 : 266	26 : 296	26 : 326	26 : 356
27	27 : 28	27 : 57	27 : 87	27 : 117	27 : 147	27 : 177	27 : 207	27 : 237	27 : 267	27 : 297	27 : 327	27 : 357
28	28 : 29	28 : 58	28 : 88	28 : 118	28 : 148	28 : 178	28 : 208	28 : 238	28 : 268	28 : 298	28 : 328	28 : 358
29	29 : —	29 : 59	29 : 89	29 : 119	29 : 149	29 : 179	29 : 209	29 : 239	29 : 269	29 : 299	29 : 329	29 : 359

This procedure may be followed for any given date with all of the celestial bodies.

The student who masters radix directions will have additional method to substantiate secondary progressions. It would not be advisable, however, to eliminate secondary progressions, but rather to use radix directions as supplementary. Many com-

YEARS	MAJOR ARCS ° ' "	MINOR ARCS ° ' "	YEARS	MAJOR ARCS ° ' "	MINOR ARCS ° ' "
1	0 59 08	13 10 35	46	45 20 08	246 07 10
2	1 58 16	26 21 20	47	46 19 16	259 17 45
3	2 57 24	39 31 55	48	47 18 24	272 28 20
4	3 56 32	52 42 30	49	48 17 32	285 38 55
5	4 55 40	65 53 05	50	49 16 40	298 49 30
6	5 54 48	79 03 40	51	50 15 48	312 00 05
7	6 53 56	92 14 15	52	51 14 56	325 10 40
8	7 53 04	105 24 50	53	52 14 04	338 21 15
9	8 52 12	118 35 25	54	53 13 12	351 31 50
10	9 51 20	131 46 10	55	54 12 20	4 42 25
11	10 50 28	144 56 45	56	55 11 28	17 53 00
12	11 49 36	158 07 20	57	56 10 36	31 03 35
13	12 48 44	171 17 55	58	57 09 44	44 14 10
14	13 47 52	184 28 30	59	58 08 52	57 24 45
15	14 47 00	197 39 05	60	59 08 00	70 35 20
16	15 46 08	210 49 40	61	60 07 08	83 45 55
17	16 45 16	224 00 15	62	61 06 16	96 56 36
18	17 44 24	237 10 50	63	62 05 24	110 07 05
19	18 43 32	250 21 25	64	63 04 32	123 17 40
20	19 42 40	263 32 00	65	64 03 40	136 28 15
21	20 41 48	276 42 35	66	65 02 48	149 38 50
22	21 40 56	289 53 10	67	66 01 56	162 49 25
23	22 40 04	303 03 45	68	67 01 04	176 00 00
24	23 39 12	316 14 20	69	68 00 12	189 10 35
25	24 38 20	329 24 55	70	68 59 20	202 21 10
26	25 37 28	342 35 30	71	69 58 28	215 31 45
27	26 36 36	355 46 05	72	70 57 36	228 42 50
28	27 35 44	8 56 40	73	71 56 44	241 52 55
29	28 34 52	22 07 15	74	72 55 52	255 03 30
30	29 34 00	35 17 50	75	73 55 00	268 14 05
31	30 33 08	48 28 25	76	74 54 08	281 24 40
32	31 32 16	61 39 00	77	75 53 16	294 35 15
33	32 31 24	74 49 35	78	76 52 24	307 45 50
34	33 30 32	88 00 10	79	77 51 32	320 56 25
35	34 29 40	101 10 45	80	78 50 40	334 07 00
36	35 28 48	114 21 20	81	79 49 48	347 17 35
37	36 27 56	127 31 55	82	80 48 56	0 28 10
38	37 27 04	140 42 30	83	81 48 04	13 38 45
39	38 26 12	153 53 05	84	82 47 12	26 49 20
40	39 25 20	167 03 40	85	83 46 20	39 59 55
41	40 24 28	180 14 15	86	84 45 28	53 10 30
42	41 23 36	193 24 50	87	85 44 36	66 21 05
43	42 22 44	206 35 25	88	86 43 44	79 31 40
44	43 21 52	219 46 00	89	87 42 52	92 41 15
45	44 21 00	232 56 35	90	88 42 00	105 52 50

Table 5. Major and Minor arcs by years.

MONTHS	MAJOR ARCS ' "	MINOR ARCS ° ' "	MONTHS	MAJOR ARCS ' "	MINOR ARCS ° ' "
1	4 56	1 05 53	7	34 30	7 41 11
2	9 51	2 11 46	8	39 25	8 47 03
3	14 47	3 17 39	9	44 21	9 52 56
4	19 43	4 23 32	10	49 17	10 58 56
5	24 38	5 29 25	11	54 12	12 04 42
6	29 34	6 35 18	12	59 08	13 10 35

Table 6. Major and Minor arcs by months.

DAYS	MAJOR ARCS ' "	MINOR ARCS ° ' "	DAYS	MAJOR ARCS ' "	MINOR ARCS ° ' "
1	10	2 12	16	2 38	35 08
2	20	4 24	17	2 48	37 20
3	30	6 35	18	2 58	39 32
4	39	8 47	19	3 07	41 44
5	49	10 59	20	3 17	43 55
6	59	13 11	21	3 27	46 07
7	1 09	15 23	22	3 37	48 19
8	1 19	17 34	23	3 47	50 31
9	1 29	19 46	24	3 57	52 42
10	1 39	21 58	25	4 06	54 54
11	1 48	24 10	26	4 16	57 06
12	1 58	26 21	27	4 26	59 18
13	2 08	28 33	28	4 36	1 01 29
14	2 18	30 45	29	4 46	1 03 41
15	2 28	32 57	30	4 56	1 05 53

Table 7. Major and Minor arcs by days.

manner as the **Major Directional Chart,** using the mean motion of the Moon in 24 hours, or 13 degrees 10 minutes and 35 seconds, as the arc of direction for all planets, cusps, and sensitive points compared to the major arc of 59 minutes and 8 seconds to a year.

In a desire to carry out the principles of primary directions, such directions as **Zodiacal Parallels, Mundane Parallels,** and **Rapt Parallels** have been investigated. It is not believed these have sufficient value to warrant their inclusion in a volume such as this, although it might be well to define each so that the research-minded student can investigate these at his leisure.

When celestial bodies have the same declination, either north or south of the equator, they are said to be parallel. By progressed position a planet may come to the same declination as a radical or progressed planet. These really belong to secondary progressions and not to the radix method.

Mundane parallels, as their name implies, relates to the distance planets are found on either side of the angles of the horoscope. It is an indication that their mundane positions are equidistant from an angle. While usually calculated in relation to the Midheaven and Nadir, they may also be calculated in a relationship to the Ascendant or Descendant. These are not measured in longitude, but in right ascension, needing tables of right ascension for calculation.

Rapt parallels are calculated as in primary directions and are formed when a directed angle reaches a point midway between two planets so that they are equidistant from directed position.

The major directions in the radix method of directing are the same as in primary directions. In fact, it is primarily an adaptation of the principles of primary directions. These major factors are the Sun, Moon, Midheaven, and Ascendant, plus the Part of Fortune. Of course, precise data are needed for the last three more so than for the Sun and Moon, although the chart should be rectified if correct time is unknown. As pointed out by Ptolemy, and continued in the usual terminology of the radix method, they are the significators for they relate to very definite phases of life. All other celestial bodies are termed promittors because they are the indicators of the nature of influences that will affect the significators, thus causing events. In a broader sense, however, in recent years the faster–moving planet has generally come to be known as a significator, while the slower moving planet has been considered as a promittor.

Solar Arc Directions

In the use of the actual solar arc for directing the horoscope

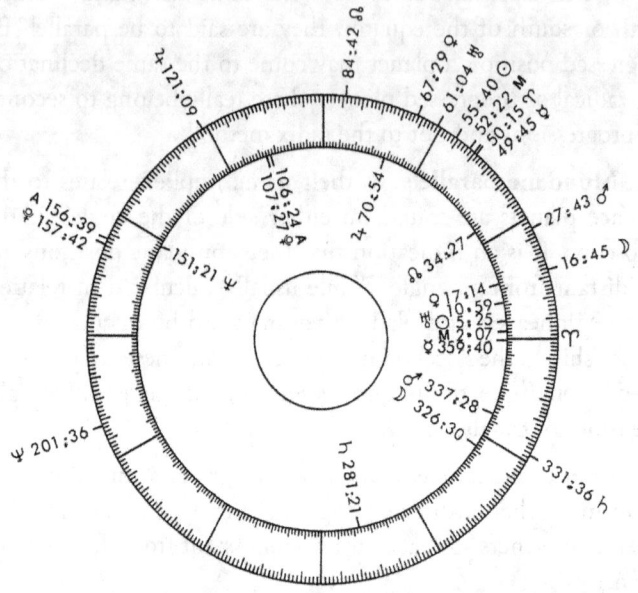

Figure 16. The 360 degree dial (horoscope) for Sandra Day O'Connor, born March 26, 1930, at 12:22 MST, in Phoenix, AZ. Directed to her inauguration as a Justice of the U.S. Supreme Court at 7:15 PM, EDT in Washington, D.C., on September 25, 1981 (directed points on outer ring).

the basic premise of the radix method is employed with one major difference. The actual movement of the Sun from its natal position to its progressed position is used as the arc of direction to be added to all planets, luminaries, and angles. Because this method belongs to the schools of astrology termed cosmobiology and Uranian, the only house cusps to be considered are the Midheaven and Ascendant.[14]

The horoscope of the U.S. Supreme Court Justice Sandra Day O'Connor is shown on the Uranian 360-degree dial with her natal planets positioned in the inner wheel and the solar arc directions in the outer wheel in Figure 16. Transits for her inauguration as a Supreme Court Justice, September 25, 1981, in Washington, D.C., at 2:15 pm EDT, were:

Sun	2°♎33	Saturn	11°♎33
Moon	3°♍40	Uranus	24°♏12
Mercury	28°♎34	Neptune	22°♐13
Venus	14°♏50	Pluto	23°♎25
Mars	14°♑47	Nodes	28°♋20
Jupiter	16°♎46		

So it is obvious that multiple contacts were made that day between the directed, natal, and transiting planets. Some of the most obvious are transiting Jupiter to directed Moon, transiting Sun to natal Midheaven (in these systems squares, semi-squares, sesquiquadrates, and oppositions are considered as major aspects of equal strength), directed Saturn to midpoint of natal Moon and Mars, directed Sun to midpoint of natal Sun and Ascendant, and directed Mercury to midpoint of natal Jupiter and Mars. This is a valuable system which may be used within the framework of traditional astrology as well.

Primary Directions

There is a vast difference between secondary progressions and primary directions but, as their titles imply, they are based upon the second and first apparent motion of the heavens in relationship to the place on Earth for which the chart is calculated. It is therefore essential at the outset to clearly understand the difference.

In the system of secondary progressions the only factors taken into account are longitude and declination of the Sun, Moon, each of the planets, Midheaven and other house cusps, Part of Fortune, Moon's Nodes, and, in very advanced work, the fixed stars. It is based upon the apparent motion of celestial phenomena in the ecliptic, that is, in the distance such phenomena would be from Zero Degrees of Aries if the planet or point were actually at the nearest point in the ecliptic from its actual apparent position or, in the case of declination, its distance from

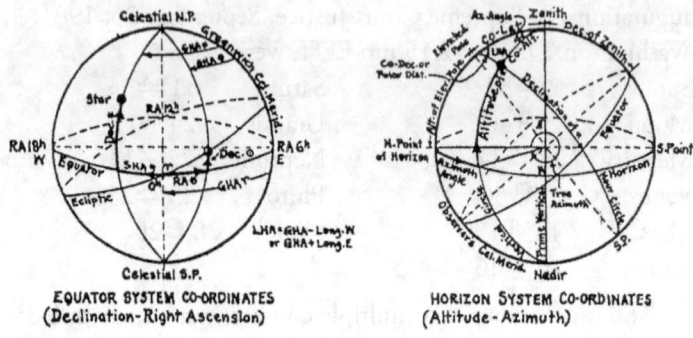

Figure 17. Astronomical coordinate systems: A) the equatorial or right ascension–declination system; B) the horizon system.

the equator. The daily motion thus measured is the equivalent of one year of life.

Thus, no account is taken of the latitude of celestial phenomena in calculation of moving positions by secondary progressions. Stated otherwise, it is the calculation of the degrees and minutes existing between progressed positions (on the basis of one day's apparent motion as, the equivalent of one year) and natal or radical positions of celestial bodies.

In secondary progressions only the ephemeris and a diurnal motion table, or a good table of logarithm are necessary to determine any planetary position. But in primary directions the calculations are not so simple for the latter case deals with the doctrine of the sphere, and this has been the source of endless controversy among astrologers as well as astronomers for many centuries of time. Yet, it now appears, that primary directions were perhaps the only method used by the ancients. It is now established that secondary progressions are a matter of comparatively recent development, but it is not the author's opinion that this impairs their validity. They are of great value in the determination of present influences operating in a horoscope.

Primary directions are based upon the initial, or primal,

apparent motion of all celestial phenomena in relationship to the location for which the chart is calculated. That is to say, it is a method based upon the rotation of the earth, and as the earth rotates on its axis at near right angles to the poles, all measurements are calculated in right ascension, or the distance from Zero Degrees of Aries as measured on the celestial equator. The student must always bear in mind that the celestial equator is simply the projection of the earth's equator into space. In view of the fact that practically all births occur at some distance from the equator, calculations must be in semi–arc as there is a difference in time from sunrise to sunset and sunset to sunrise, except on the Vernal or Autumnal Equinoxes (see Figure 18).

There is a vast difference in method of calculation, for in the average period of six hours after birth, some 90 degrees of the ecliptic will cross the Midheaven of the horoscope and, as each degree represents one year of life, the changed position of the heavens within six hours after birth is the equivalent of about 90 years of life.

In both systems of calculation the planets conserve their radical character, but they acquire various additional properties in proportion as they advance in the theme of the nativity and, thus, they may set into action new forces. This is true evolution with the development of new karmic conditions to be faced later. The groupings of these newly combined energies are the cause of the multiple phases of existence. Indeed, they are the application of universal rhythm to individuals. These latter are the real causes for new events coming into personal lives by combining the primal causes of exterior origin with the secondary causes from individual free will. And, in this connection, it seems wise to state that all methods of progressing or directing the horoscope are really just symbolical.

There are meritorious objections to both of these systems of advancing the horoscope. In the case of secondary progressions, the objection hinges on the fact that the motion of the

Sun does not correspond every day to exactly one degree and therefore, as all progression must hinge upon the apparent motion of the Sun, the progression of one day per year is not strictly exact. Also, though the ephemeris gives the rate of progression of planets by longitude, it will be easily understood that planets do not move by longitude, it will be easily understood that planets do not move by longitude on the ecliptic, but rather on their semi–arc parallel to the equator.

The difficulty with primary directions hinges on the fact that rarely is the precise moment of birth known. Consequently, while primary directions are founded upon a truly scientific basis, the rotation of the earth on its axis causing all points in the heavens to advance parallel to the equator – the slightest variation from true time of birth causes timing of influences to vary widely from time of operation. Four minutes variation from the correct moment of birth changes the mundane position of all celestial bodies, as well as the Midheaven to vary approximately one degree – the equivalent of a full year of life – which is a handicap, astrologically. A second difficulty to the use of primary directions is the tremendous amount of detail involved in calculating the various arithmetical computations necessary. Few astrologers can afford to devote so much time to a single prediction.

To give a home illustration that may make more clear the difference between these two methods, consider the following:

A stranger asks the distance he will have to cover in the course of a day in order to reach a certain city. He is told first, that he will find the crossroad leading to the city somewhere between ten and fifteen miles from this point, and that the town is just a little way down that crossroad. This is not very accurate information but it is somewhat helpful. Another person speaks up and tells the stranger that if he drives his automobile at the rate of 15 miles an hour and meets no traffic lights to delay him, he will arrive at this city in just 53 minutes and 42 seconds, which is exact.

In the first case, the stranger could drive back and forth between the ten and fifteen mile extremes until he found the correct crossroad to use. But, in the second case, should he increase or decrease the speed of his automobile, he would either pass or not arrive at the city in the time given. Thus, he would not arrive at the crossroad at the time given and so might completely miss the correct turnoff.

Thus, exactitude carried too far may be productive of inexactitude and in this fact lies the danger of employing primary directions when the birth time is not accurately known. However, in those horoscopes where the birth time is accurately known either through correct timing at birth or through proper rectification, directions are far more apt to give the dates of events with much greater precision than secondary progressions.

The student should obtain trigonometrical tables which exist in all languages. Because of the wealth of other astrological material contained in it, the author recommends Simmonite's Arcana of Astrology, although there are many other good books containing the same mathematical data.[15]

Trigonometry was originally a branch of astrology, probably of early Babylonian origin. The first scientific exposition of trigonometry is given by Ptolemy in his Almagest, wherein he divided the circle of the heavens into 360 degrees, each degree into 60 minutes, and each minute into 60 seconds. Trigonometry was used for the measurement of a chord of the circle corresponding to a given angle, and it is just this purpose to which it is put in calculating primary directions. Ptolemy prepared a table of these chords.

The sine is of ancient origin and antedates some of the other mathematical facts which have been developed through time. The sine of the complementary angle is the cosine. The tangent was developed mathematically by the Arabs. It was Copernicus, another great astrologer and mathematician who introduced the secant. While still another astrologer, Regiomontanus, first made trigonometry a separate science, by detaching it from astrology. Presently, however, trigonometry is a hybrid form of mathematics which borrows from algebra plus synthetical and analytical geometry.

Because this is not a course of instruction in trigonometry, every effort has been made to simplify so that the principles and rules laid down may be carried out by any student having the patience to follow through. Therefore this chapter contains calculations which will be given only for the nearest minute of arc to simplify matters, which is sufficient for most charts. For the student who desires greater exactitude to express his results in seconds of arc, the author recommends the detailed explanations given in the introductory pages to Chamber's Seven–figure Mathematical Tables, and the English publication of mathematical tables.

In primary directions first calculate a table called a Speculum, which is simply a visual presentation giving details of the many conditions necessary for accurate calculation of mundane and zodiacal positions of all celestial bodies in the horoscope. These must be used in calculating primary directions. There are several modes of setting forth the speculum which includes latitudes, declinations, right ascensions, meridian distances, the diurnal and nocturnal semi–arc, and ascensional differences. It is also convenient to add ternary proportional logarithms of the right ascensions, meridian distances, and the semi–arcs as in Table 8.

The 11 formulae followed in calculating primary directions are:

FORMULA 1: *To convert longitude into right ascension without latitude:* When longitude is between 0 Aries 00 and 0 Cancer 00 or 0 Libra 00 and 0 Capricorn 00; Log cosine of obliquity of the ecliptic (23 degrees 27 minutes) plus log tangent longitude equals log tangent of right ascension from Aries

	Latitude	Declination	R.A.	M.D.	S.A.	Cuspal Distance
☉						
☽						
☿						
♀						
♂						
♃						
♄						
♅						
♆						
♇						
ASC						
M.C.						
I.C.						

Table 8. A sample speculum.

or Libra. When longitude is between 0 Cancer 00 and 0 Libra 00 or 0 Capricorn 00 and 0 Aries 00; Log cosine of obliquity of ecliptic plus log cotangent equals log contangent from Cancer or Capricorn.

If in Aries, Taurus, or Gemini, the answer will be the right ascension required. If in Cancer, Leo, or Virgo add 90 degrees. If in Libra, Scorpio, or Sagittarius add 180 degrees. If in Capricorn, Aquarius, or Pisces add 270 degrees.

FORMULA 2: *To convert right ascension into longitude without latitude:* When right ascension is between 0 Aries 00 and 0 Cancer 00 or 0 Libra 00 and 0 Capricorn 00; Log cosine

Degrees to be Added to Right Ascension of Midheaven	Which Equals House Cusp
30	XI
60	XII
90	I or Asc.
120	II
150	III

Table 9. Right ascension corrections for intermediate house cusps.

of obliquity of ecliptic plus log cotangent right ascension from Aries or Libra equals log cotangent of longitude from Aries or Libra. When right ascension is between 0 Cancer 00 and 0 Libra 00 or 0 Capricorn 00 and 0 Aries 00; Log cosine of obliquity of ecliptic plus log tangent of right ascension from Cancer or Capricorn equals log tangent of longitude from Cancer of Capricorn.

Right ascension of 0 Aries 00 is 0 degrees, of 0 Cancer 00 is 90 degrees, of 0 Libra 0 is 180 degrees, and of 0 Capricorn 00 is 270 degrees.

FORMULA 3: *Longitude being given, to find declination without latitude:* When longitude is between 0 Aries 00 and 0 Cancer 00 or 0 Libra 00 and 0 Capricorn 00; Log sine of obliquity of ecliptic plus log sine longitude from Aries or Libra equals log, sine of declination.

When longitude is between 0 Cancer 00 and 0 Libra 00 or 0 Capricorn 00 and 0 Aries 00; Log sine obliquity of ecliptic plus log cosine longitude from Cancer or Capricorn equals log sine of declination.[16]

FORMULA 4: *Declination being given, to find longitude,* *without latitude:* When longitude is between 0 Aries 00 and 0 Cancer 00 or 0 Libra 00 and 0 Capricorn 00; Log sine of declination minus log sine of obliquity of Ascendant equals log sine of longitude from Aries or Libra.

When longitude is between 0 Cancer 00 and 0 Libra 00 or 0 Capricorn 00 and 0 Aries 00; Log sine of declination minus log sine of obliquity of ecliptic equals log cosine from Cancer or Capricorn.[17]

FORMULA 5: *To find ascensional difference:* Log tangent of declination plus log tangent of latitude of birthplace equal log sine of ascensional difference.

FORMULA 6: *To find oblique ascension:* With north declination, right ascension minus ascensional difference equals oblique ascension. With south declination, right ascension mnius ascensional difference equals oblique ascension.[8]

Table 9 contains the right ascension corrections for intermediate house cusps.

FORMULA 7: *To find the semi-arc:* For diurnal semi-arc, with north declination, 90 degrees plus ascensional difference.

For diurnal semi-arc, with south declination, 90 degrees minus ascensional difference.

For nocturnal semi-arc, with north declination, 90 degrees minus ascensional difference.

For nocturnal semi-arc, with south declination, 90 degrees pl us ascensional difference.[19]

FORMULA 8: *Oblique ascension being given, to find the degree of longitude on the cusp of any house:*

A) When oblique ascension is from 0 Aries 00 to 0 Cancer 00 or 0 Libra 00 to 0 Capricorn 00; Log cosine oblique ascension from Aries or Libra plus log contangent of pole of the house equals log contangent of first angle. Call this A.

When oblique ascension is from 0 Cancer 00 to 0 Libra 00

or 0 Capricorn 00 to 0 Aries 00; Log sine oblique ascension from Cancer or Capricorn plus log contangent of pole of the house equals log contangent of first angle. Call this A.

The pole of the Ascendant is always the latitude of the birthplace. The Midheaven has no pole. The poles of the other houses are given in Table 10.

B) If the oblique ascension is less than 90 degrees or more than 270 degrees, then A, plus the obliquity of the ecliptic (23 degrees 27 minutes), equals B. If the oblique ascension is more than 20 degrees and less than 270 degrees, then the difference between 23 degrees 27 minutes and A equals B.[20]

C) When oblique ascension is from 0 Aries 00 to 0 Cancer 00 or 0 Libra 00 to 0 Capricorn 00; Log cosine of B, (arithmetical complement –a.c.), plus log cosine A plus log tangent oblique ascensions from Aries or Libra equals log tangent of longitude from Aries or Libra.

Poles of Houses

When oblique ascension is from 0 Cancer 00 to 0 Libra 00 or 0 Capricorn 00 to 0 Aries 00; Log cosine of B (a.c.) plus log cosine A plus log Cotangent of oblique ascension from Cancer or Capricorn equals log cotangent of longitude from Cancer or Capricorn.[21]

When the right ascension of the Midheaven (RAMC) is exactly 0 degrees (or 360 degrees) or 180 degrees then the log sine obliquity of ecliptic plus log tangent latitude of birthplace equals log cotangent of ascending degree from nearest equinox point – 0 Aries 00 or 0 Libra 00.

FORMULA 9: *Right ascension and declination being given, to find the longitude and latitude:*

A) When right ascension is from 0 Aries 00 to 0 Cancer 00 or 0 Libra 00 to 0 Capricorn 00; Log sine right ascension

Poles of Houses

Asc. or Lat.	Pole of XIth & IIId Houses		Pole of XIIth & IId Houses		Asc. or Lat.	Pole of XIth & IIId Houses		Pole of XIIth & IId Houses		Asc. or Lat.	Pole of XIth & IIId Houses		Pole of XIIth & IId Houses	
1	0	21	0	42	21	7	20	14	24	41	16	29	30	25
2	0	41	1	22	22	7	43	15	7	42	17	5	31	20
3	1	00	2	00	23	8	5	15	50	43	17	42	32	18
4	1	21	2	41	24	8	30	16	36	44	18	20	33	15
5	1	41	3	23	25	8	54	17	22	45	18	58	34	13
6	2	00	4	00	26	9	17	18	5	46	19	37	35	10
7	2	21	4	40	27	9	43	18	52	47	20	19	36	10
8	2	41	5	21	28	10	8	19	37	48	21	3	37	12
9	3	2	6	2	29	10	32	20	21	49	21	46	38	12
10	3	23	6	43	30	10	59	21	9	50	22	33	39	14
11	3	43	7	24	31	11	26	21	56	51	23	21	40	18
12	4	4	8	5	32	11	54	22	46	52	24	12	41	24
13	4	24	8	45	33	12	23	23	36	53	25	6	42	32
14	4	45	9	26	34	12	51	24	25	54	26	1	43	39
15	5	7	10	10	35	13	26	25	15	55	26	59	44	48
16	5	29	10	50	36	13	51	26	5	56	28	1	45	59
17	5	49	11	30	37	14	18	26	55	57	29	6	47	13
18	6	12	12	14	38	14	52	27	48	58	30	15	48	27
19	6	34	12	57	39	15	24	28	40	59	31	29	49	44
20	6	57	13	41	40	15	56	29	32	60	32	48	51	4

Table 10. Table of poles of houses from Pearses' Textbook of Astrology. The pole of house V is the same as house XI and the pole of house IX is the same as house III, while the pole of house VI is the same as house XII and the pole of house VIII is the same as house II.

from Aries or Libra plus log cotangent of declination equals log tangent of Angle A.

When right ascension is from 0 Cancer 00 to 0 Libra 00 or 0 Capricorn 00 to 0 Aries 00; Log cosine right ascension from Cancer or Capricorn plus log contangent of declination equals log tangent of angle A

B) Right ascension and declination either both north or both south (if R.A. is less than 180 degrees call it north; if more than 180 degrees call it south); then A plus obliquity of ecliptic equals B. If right ascension and declination are one north and one south, the difference between A and obliquity of ecliptic (23 degrees 27 minutes) equals B.

C) When right ascension is from 0 Aries 00 to 0 Cancer 00 or 0 Libra 00 to 0 Capricorn 00; Log Sine of A (arithmetical complement) plus log sine B, plus log tangent right ascendant from Aries or Libra equals log tangent longitude from Aries or Libra.

When right ascendant is from 0 Cancer 00 to 0 Libra 00 or 0 Capricorn to 0 Aries 00; Log sine of A (a.c.) plus log sine B, plus log cotangent right ascendant from Cancer or Capricorn equals log cotangent longitude from Cancer or Capricorn.

D) For latitude: Log cosine A (arithmetical complement) plus log cosine B plus log sine declination equals log sine latitude.[22]

FORMULA 10: *Longitude and latitude being given, to find right ascension and declination:*

A) When longitude is from 0 Aries 00 to 0 Cancer 00 or 0 Libra 00 to 0 Capricorn 00; Log sine longitude from Aries or Libra plus log tangent obliquity of ecliptic (25 degrees 27 minutes) equals log tangent of angle A. When longitude is from 0 Cancer 00 to 0 Libra 00 or 0 Capricorn 00 to 0 Aries 00; Log cosine of longitude from Cancer or Capricorn plus log tangent obliquity of ecliptic equals log tangent of angle A.

B) Longitude and latitude are both the same name (if longitude is less than 180 and latitude is north or more than 180 degrees and latitude is south) then 90 degrees minus latitude equals B. If longitude and latitude are of different names (if longitude is less than 180 and latitude is south or if the longitude is more than 180 degrees and latitude is north) then 90 degrees plus latitude equals B. Then, B minus A equals C.

C) For declination: log; cosine A (arithmetical complement) plus log cosine C plus log cosine obliquity of ecliptic (23 degrees 27 minutes) equals log sine declination.

D) For right ascension: When longitude is from 0 Aries 00 to 0 Cancer 00 or 0 Libra 00 to 0 Capricorn 00; Log cosine declination (arithmetical complement) plus log cosine longitude from Aries or Libra plus log cosine latitude equals log cosine right ascension from Aries or Libra. When longitude is from 0 Cancer 00 to 0 Libra 00 or 0 Capricorn 00 to 0 Aries 00; Log cosine declination (a.c.) plus log sine longitude from Cancer or Capricorn plus cosine latitude equals log sine right ascension from Cancer or Capricorn.

FORMULA 11: *Longitude, latitude and declination given, to find right ascension*: When longitude is from 0 Aries 00 to 0 Cancer 00 or 0 Libra 00 to 0 Capricorn 00; Log cosine (arithmetical complement) of declination plus log cosine latitude, plus log cosine longitude from Aries or Libra equals log cosine right ascension from Aries or Libra.

When longitude is from 0 Cancer 00 to 0 Libra 00 or 0 Capricorn 00 to 0 Aries 00; Log cosine (a.c.) declination plus log cosine latitude, plus log sine longitude from Cancer or Capricorn equals log sine right ascension from Cancer or Capricorn.

A sample speculum is shown on the following page for the late King George V, of England, born on June 3, 1865, at 1:18 AM, GMT, at Marlborough House. Cuspal distance defines the distance a planet lies above or below a given house cusp, particularly the angles.

The great astrological thinkers, such as Leo and Sepharial, proposed the system of primary directions as the principal technique for rectifying a time of birth. As already pointed out, this method is based upon the rotation (or first apparent motion) of the earth. The calculation of a speculum, various geometrical and trigonometrical factors which are constant for each horoscope, is a long and tedious system whose study can be recommended only to the student with mathematical inclinations. In this system an error of only four minutes in the time of birth is equivalent to approximately a year of life, thus 20 seconds is equivalent to about one month.

It is rare indeed for a secondary progressed aspect to be

	Latitude	Declination	R.A.	M.D.	S.A.	Cuspal Distance
☉		22°N 18'	70°58'	19°54'	58°57'	0°15' above III
☽	2°S 27'	2°S 40'	179°59'	89°08'	93°22'	4°14' below VII
☿	3°S 18'	14°N 10°	46°57'	43°54'	71°29'	3°45' below II
♀	1°S 30'	13°N 17'	37°43'	53°08'	72°44'	4°39' above II
♂	1°N 27'	20°N 17'	128°20'	37°28'	62°19'	4°05' below VI
♃	0°N 27'	22°S 57'	265°18'	5°34'	57°51'	5°34' from X
♄	2°N 40'	6°S 51'	203°16'	67°56'	81°18'	13°42' above VII
♅	0°N 12'	23°N 39'	88°30'	2°21'	56°35'	2°21' from IV
♆	1°S 29'	2°N 39'	9°55'	80°57'	86°40'	5°43' from I
ASC		0°N 50'				
M.C.		23°N 27'	270°52'			
I.C.			90°52'			

precise within a minute of arc in identifying the operation of an influence or the occurrence of an event. Lunations, full Moon, eclipses, and transiting planets often bring a secondary progressed aspect into play before the date on which it is precise; they can also delay its action until the aspect has passed.

Review Questions for Chapter 8

1. Describe the major difference between secondary progressions and symbolic directions.

2. Calculate your personal radix directions to an eventful year of life. By major arc and then by minor arc.

3. Now calculate the solar arc directions for the same year and compare the results with the radix method.

4. Repeat the exercises in questions 2 and 3 for Sandra O'Connor for these events:

Graduation from Stanford University in 1952; Arizona Assistant Attorney General from 1965 through 1968; appointed to Arizona Senate in 1969; elected Majority Leader of Arizona Senate in 1973; named to state appeals court in 1979.

|Chapter 9|

Cyclic Charts

CYCLIC CHARTS ARE BASED ON THE importance of any planet or relevant point in the horoscope returning to its natal longitude in a given period of time. This would, of course, resemble the earth beginning a new cycle of activity each season, predictable on the whole but with ever varying nuances, delightful surprises, and anxiety-causing mishaps. Without this variation there would be no growth through experiences to be encountered.

Because the Sun and the Moon are closely related to man's personality and emotional well-being they are most frequently used when considering the cycles of life. However, cyclic charts can be calculated for any of the planets, or the Midheaven and Ascendant. Each celestial body deals primarily with the energies which it beams toward the earth and its inhabitants. Also, the yearly revolution of the Sun and the monthly revolution of the Moon are more easily considered than the irregular patterns of Mercury and Venus or the longer cycles of exterior planets. Some few astrologers do compute the biennial energy cycle of Mars as it deals with the work environment.

During the early part of the 20th century a great controversy arose concerning methods of computing planetary returns. One body of astrologers contended that all factors should be

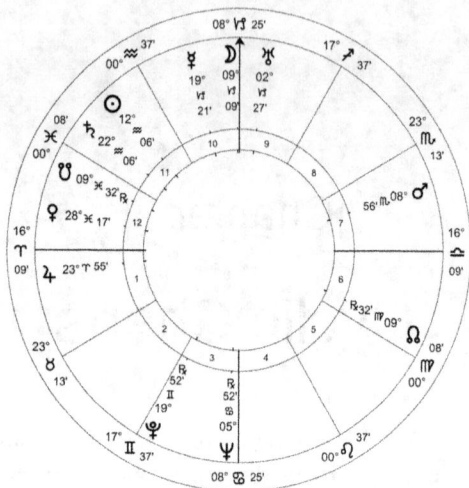

Figure 18. Solar return for the year 1905, for former President Franklin D. Roosevelt.

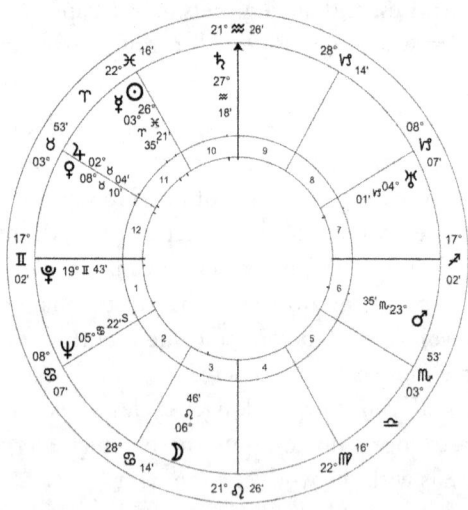

Figure 19. Rotational diurnal for former President Franklin D. Roosevelt on his wedding day of March 17, 1905.

kept within the confines of the tropical zodiac while another group stated quite firmly that the precession of the equinoxes must be considered in any return situations. Thereby the term solar and lunar returns was assigned to the tropical calculations; while solar and lunar returns is the terminology preempted by astrologers who factor in movement of this entire system against the greater band of heavenly fixed stars when considering cyclic charts.

Solar and Lunar Returns

Sometimes referred to as "solunars". It should be pointed out that at the original writing of this book, the authors noted a difference in the terms solunars and solar and lunar returns. Returns were calculated with additional factors such as precession, and revolutions were not. Today, many practicing astrologers use only returns, and do not factor in precession. As with other such topics, the student should try them both and note the results. The lesson will be given for both situations. The general trends for the year are suggested by relationship of the planets to each other as well as the house positions, in a return chart. Planets posited in the northern hemisphere will be less obvious in their activity, while those bodies above the horizon suggest the native's public exposure for the ensuing year. Basic areas of life handled by each house are the same as in a natal horoscope, with special emphasis on the Ascendant as the focal point of the year. When this compares favorably or blends with the natal characteristics the native feels much more content than when these factors are in conflict.

Synthesis of the solar and lunar return is carried out by observing first the sign of the Ascendant, then the hemisphere emphasis, and finally any groupings or planets in a house or quadrant. Aspects are less relevant than patterns of the planets in the return charts. Any planet falling in house I will be emphasized during the year according to the natal location and strength.

The position of the Sun in the solar return is important from the viewpoint of understanding in which category of life

Table 11. Solar return additives

Years of Age	Hours to be added	Minutes to be added	Years of Age	Hours to be added	Minutes to be added
1	5	49	46	3	46
2	11	38	47	9	36
3	17	28	48	15	25
4	23	17	49	21	14
5	5	06	50	3	03
6	10	55	51	8	53
7	16	45	52	14	42
8	22	34	53	20	31
9	4	23	54	2	20
10	10	12	55	8	10
11	16	02	56	13	59
12	21	51	57	19	48
13	3	40	58	1	37
14	9	29	59	7	27
15	15	19	60	13	16
16	21	08	61	19	05
17	2	57	62	0	54
18	8	46	63	6	44
19	14	36	64	12	33
20	20	25	65	18	22
21	2	14	66	0	11
22	8	03	67	6	01
23	13	53	68	11	50
24	19	43	69	17	39
25	1	32	70	23	28
26	7	21	71	5	18
27	13	11	72	11	07
28	19	00	73	16	56
29	0	49	74	22	45
30	6	38	75	4	35
31	12	28	76	10	24
32	18	17	77	16	13
33	0	06	78	22	02
34	5	55	79	3	52
35	11	45	80	9	41
36	17	34	81	15	30
37	23	23	82	21	19
38	5	12	83	3	09
39	11	02	84	8	59
40	16	51	85	14	48
41	22	40	86	20	37
42	4	29	87	2	27
43	10	19	88	8	16
44	16	08	89	14	05
45	21	57	90	19	54

will the native be working out basic character lessons or problems during the following 12 months. If the Sun is on a cusp, that may indicate activities in both spheres of influence.

More detailed activities can be seen by erecting lunar return charts for each month and examining them in a similar manner. Here, of course, the position of the Moon is the most important factor.

Calculating Solar Returns

The method for calculating solar returns is simple. Turn to the ephemeris for the year the birthday map is desired and ascertain the day on which the Sun will hold closest to exact longitude it held at birth. This will not necessarily be on the birthday but within a day or two of it. The first step is to find the time when the Sun returns to the same degree, minute, and second of its natal longitude.

When the time is determined, a horoscope is calculated for the new time adjusted to the present location of residence. While most astrologers, in the past, calculated the solar return for the birthplace, it seems more logical if calculated for the present location of the native. Certainly the transitory positions of the planets will exert their influence where the individual is at that time.

For each successive year after birth the solar return will be found to occur about 5 hours and 49 minutes later than the previous year. Thus, if the natal Sun is found in house X, the solar revolution for the first birthday will find the Sun somewhere in house VIII.

Table 11 is of practical value for all cases where the native continues to live in his birthplace. If, however, he moves to a distant location, the time element must be adjusted by adding 4 minutes for each degree of longitude east of birthplace or subtracting 4 minutes of time for each degree of longitude west of the birthplace.

Taking the chart of late President Roosevelt as an example, his natal Sun is posited at 11°Aquarius 05' 41", (Figure 11). He was married on March 17, 1905, at his birthplace, during the year following his birth anniversary of January, 1905. Looking at the ephemeris for January 31, 1905, the Sun is seen to be 10° Aquarius 27' 53" while February 1, 1905, the Sun is posited at 11° Aquarius 28' 48"; between these two positions is the birth longitude of the Sun.

Sun on February 1, 1905 = 11°♒28' 48"
Sun on January 31, 1905 = 10°♒27' 53"

Result: 1° 00'55" Sun's diurnal motion

At the rate of 1 degree and 55 seconds a day, how long it would take the Sun to move to its natal longitude is shown by:

Natal Longitude = 11°♒05' 41"
January 31, 1905 = 10°♒27' 53"

Result: 37'48" Motion to natal longitude

Convert the "motion to natal longitude", 37'48" to seconds only, by multiplying the minutes column by 60, then adding the seconds column to the sum, which in this example is 37 X 60 = 2220 + 48 = 2268. Do the same to the daily motion of the Sun, 1°00'55": 60 X 60 = 3600 + 55 = 3655. Divide the motion to natal longitude by the Sun's diurnal motion: 2268 ÷ 3655 = .6205198. Multiply this sum by 24 (hrs) to get: 14.89. Now we have 14 hours and we need the minutes: .89 X 60 = 53. So the new Greenwich Mean Time for the solar return is 14:53 o'clock. The natal coordinates were 73°W 56' and 41°N 47', subtract 5 hours from the time to adjust for EST. Additional calculations will be needed to complete the solar return, which will be explained further.

The rotational diurnal chart for the day of FDR's marriage, on March 17, 1905, would be calculated for the same time as the 1905 solar return. This chart is presented in Figure 19.

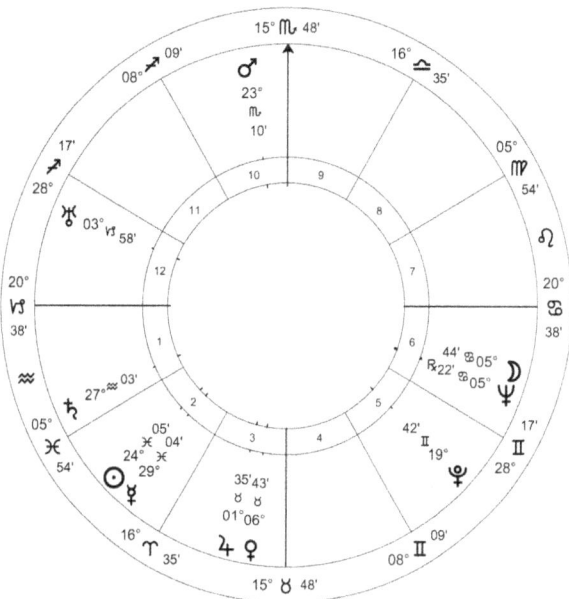

Figure 20. Lunar return of former President Franklin D. Roosevelt.

Lunar Returns

In Ptolemy's aphorism #87 he refers to lunar returns. These are calculated in the same manner as solar returns, only based upon cycles established by the return of the Moon to its natal position each month. These are usually calculated to minutes of arc as the motion of the Moon is so rapid. President Roosevelt's lunar return for March 15, 1905, is shown in Figure 20.

A solar return chart can be cast for each birthday for the time when the transiting Sun returns to its natal position in the fixed zodiac. The lunar return, likewise, is calculated for the actual transit of the Moon over its natal locations. For this reason, these charts are often called sidereal solar returns (SSR) and lunar returns (SLR).

Year	Pisces, Mean Value	Year	Pisces, Mean Value
1900	6° 39' 04"	1960	5° 49' 06"
1910	6° 31' 15"	1970	5° 40' 39"
1920	6° 22' 23"	1980	5° 32' 28"
1930	6° 14' 24"	1990	5° 23' 46"
1940	6° 05' 44"	2000	5° 15' 49"
1950	5° 57' 32"	2010	5° 06' 56"

Table 12. Synetic vernal points at 00:00 GMT January 1.

Table 13. Ayanamsa conversion table.

Year	Degrees of Difference
1700	20d33m08s
1710	20d41m41s
1720	20d49m46s
1730	20d58m32s
1740	21d06m24s
1750	21d15m20s
1760	21d23m08s
1770	21d32m03s
1780	21d39m54s
1790	21d48m45s
1800	21d56m44s
1810	22d02m24s
1820	22d13m37s
1830	22d21m58s
1840	22d30m29s
1850	22d38m37s
1860	22d47m20s
1870	22d55m15s
1880	22d03m24s
1890	23d12m00s
1900	23d20m54s
1910	23d28m43s
1920	23d37m35s
1930	23d45m34s
1940	23d54m14s
1950	24d02m26s
1960	24d10m52s
1970	24d19m19s
1980	24d27m30s
1990	24d16m12s
2000	24d44m09s
2010	24d53m02s

Table 13. Ayanamsa conversion table.

LONGITUDE NORTH NODE	CORRECTION IN SECONDS	LONGITUDE NORTH NODE
0°	− 0" +	360°
30°	− 8" +	330°
45°	− 12" +	315°
60°	− 15" +	300°
90°	− 17" +	270°
120°	− 15" +	240°
135°	− 12" +	225°
150°	− 9" +	210°
180°	− 0" +	180°

Table 14. Correction for lunar nutation. Enter Table 14 with the tropical longitude of the Moon's North Node. Add or subtract the seconds from Table 14 to the mean SVP from Table 12. Interpolation is required to result in the true SVP.

Return charts are particularly useful to timing events provided an accurate birth time is known, yet can be helpful in rectification of unknown birth times. That solar and lunar returns accurately describe events has been convincingly demonstrated over and over by those pioneers such as Donald Bradley, Ciral Fagan, Carl Stahl, and Brigadier R.C. Firebrace of the system during the middle of this century.

Although precession of the equinoxes was briefly described in Volume I of this series it is important to repeat the primary factors involved in this phenomenon. The earth, in its motion about its own axis, revolves around the Sun spinning somewhat like a top, i.e., wobbling about its own polar axis. Because of this wobble an imaginary extension of the north and south poles inscribes two large circles in the heavens over a 26,000 year period. For example, at the present time the north polar star is Polaris, while by the year AD 14,000 the star Vega will be the earth's north pole star (see Figure 24). This creates a shifting of the apparent positions of planets and luminaries against the constellations which amounts to approximately one degree every 72 years. Because of this factor the tropical zodiac is now nearly a whole degree from constellations having the same titles though the two last coincided about AD 217.

This difference between the tropical zodiac and the signs of the constellations is called precession and must be taken into account when considering a planet's return to its native position. During the early years of life this variation will make little difference but by age 72 there would be an entire degree conflict. The actual variation is called the ayanamsa (or ayanamsha).

To calculate a solar or lunar return the student must know the amount of precession between the day of birth and the year under consideration.[24] Tables have been established of the synetic vernal point, or movement of the vernal equinox against the constellations which is used to calculate the ayanamsa.

30 degrees − synetic vernal point = ayanamsa

For example, in Table 12 the synetic vernal point for January 1, 1980, is 5 degrees 32 minutes and 28 seconds of the constellation of Pisces. The corresponding ayanamsa for that date

Figure 22. House emphasis for solar and lunar returns.

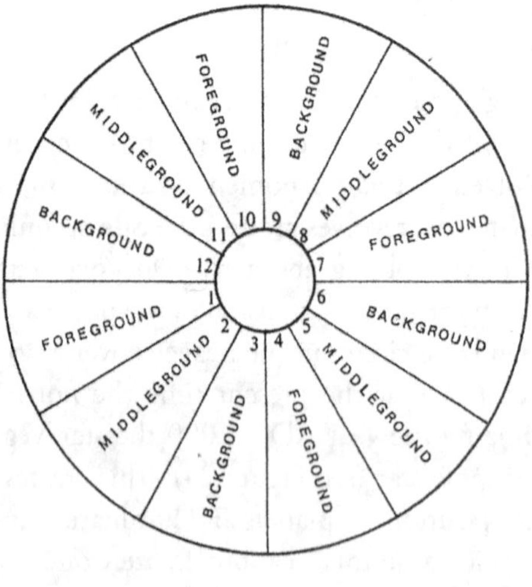

is 24 degrees 27 minutes and 32 seconds, which would be subtracted from any tropical positions to find the sidereal position. Ayanamsa conversions from 1700 to 2010 are given in Table 13.

Add or subtract the seconds from Table 14 to the mean Synetic vernal point, (SVP) from Table 12. Interpolation is required to result in the true SVP.

However, returns need not be placed in the sidereal zodiac so long as precession is taken into account. For an example, a native born on August 26, 1926, at 12 noon CDT has the following ayanamsa by August 26, 1982:

1) Computed SVP from Table 12 = 6°17'35" 1926 position

2) Correction from Table 14 = −16" For 8/26/1926

        Result: = 6° 17' 19" SVP 8/26/1926

3) Sun Tropical longitude = 2°♍41'40"

4) Add SVP from step (2) = 6° 17' 19"

           8°♍58'59"

(5) Subtract 1 whole sign = 30

        Result: 8°♌58'59" Sidereal Sun position

(6) Compute SVP from Table 12 for 1982 = 5°30'40"

(7) Correction from Table 14 = −16

        Result: 5°30'24" SVP for Aug. 26, 1982

(8) Difference between the two SVP's is:

    August 26, 1926 = 6°17'19"

    August 26, 1982 = 5°30'24"

        Result: 46'55"

(9) To locate the Sun's tropical longitude for a 1982 return consider the following factor:

    Natal Sun tropical = 2°♍41'40"

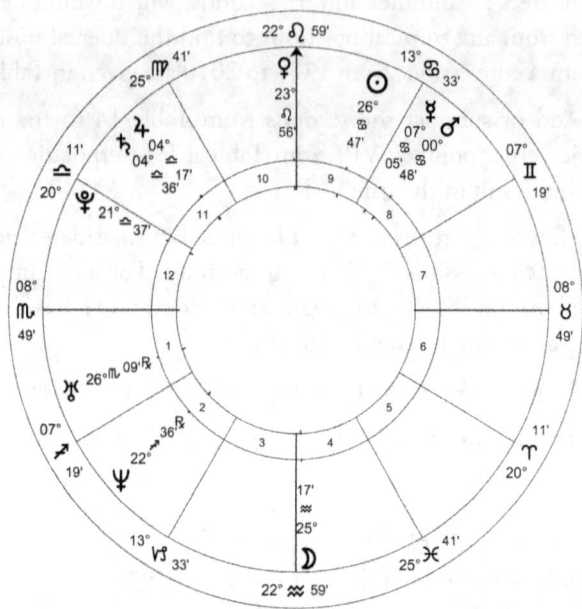

Figure 23. Lunar return for Lady Diana Spencer just prior to her wedding.

Precession Correction = + 46' 55"
Result: 3°♍28'35"

Therefore, calculate the return for August 26, 1982, as though the natal Sun position were tropical 3 Virgo 28'35" which will be 1:45 Greenwich Mean Time on August 27, 1982.

There has been developed a method of delineation with solar and lunar returns which differs from the natal horoscope reading. First, house rulerships are not considered, the energy in the chart being stored in planetary aspects with only certain aspects involved. Importance is placed in squares, conjunctions, oppositions, trines, and sextiles. The unique way in which energy is defined as producing a positive or negative potential is from the nature of the forecasted event. When two planets are

Figure 24. Birth chart of Lady Diana Spencer who became the Princess of Whales. Born July 1, 1961, 7:45 PM, BST, at Sandringham 0°W06', 52°N38.'

beneficial in nature the event is presumed to be positive, regardless of nature of the aspect; the reverse is true for malefic planets. In general, then Mars trine Saturn would be expected to bring difficulty, while Venus square Uranus can produce exhilaration, sudden love, and unforgettable events.

If the planets determine the nature of the happening and the aspects decide when it will occur, then the dynamics of this blending are shown by the unique sidereal technique of dividing the horoscope into areas called foreground, middle ground, and background. Whether a solar and lunar period is going to be eventful is determined by the position of planets in the foreground of the chart (see Figure 22). The foreground is described as being about 15 degrees on either side of the angles of the

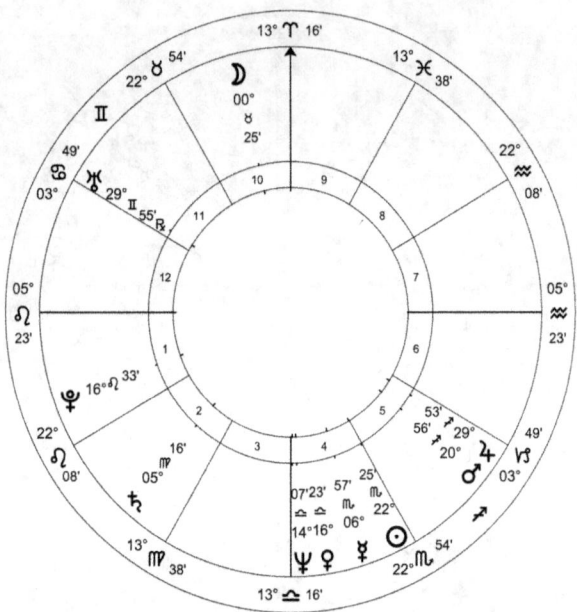

Figure 25 above: Birth chart for Charles, Prince of Whales.

horoscope followed by sections called middle ground which are each in turn followed by background segments of the horoscope. Places of maximum activity are within 5 degrees on either side of the angles where planets posited there are said to be In Mundo. The middle ground areas are not as strong and the background areas have little effect.

Finally, it is important to adhere to the good practice of not reading into a planet an event which does not match its actual quality. For example, accidents, surgery, cuts, or fever are qualities of Mars and should not be assigned to Venus, Jupiter, or Saturn.

The lunar return for Lady Diana Spencer (natal horoscope given in Figure 26) was cast for a transit of the Moon over her natal Moon previous to her celebrated marriage to Charles, Prince of Wales, which occurred on July 29, 1981, at 11:00 AM,

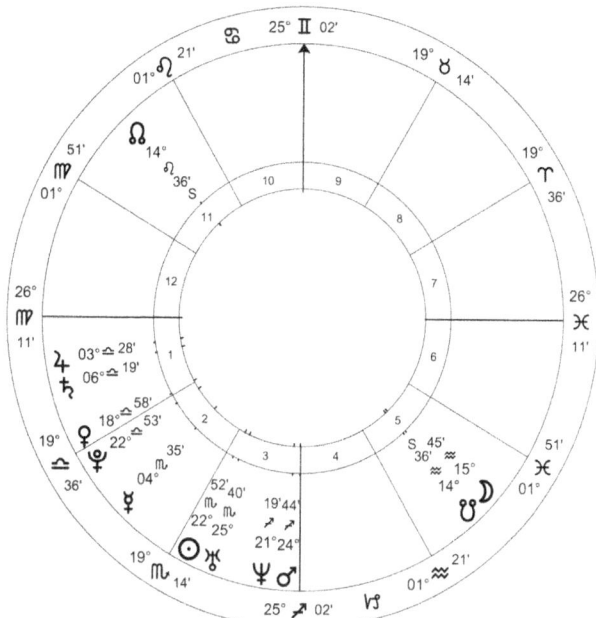

Figure 26 below: Solar return for Charles, Prince of Whales, for 1980-81.

BST in St. Paul's Cathedral, London. The lunar return (Figure 27) occurred on July 19, 1981, at 1:53 PM, Greenwich Mean Time, just 7 days before the wedding ceremony.

In Lady Diana's lunar return, Venus is within 1 degree of the Midheaven opposite the Moon which is with 2 ½ degrees of the IC. A foreground Moon brings out feelings and denotes a period when the native is intimately and vividly conscious of all experiences. The foreground of house IV brings changes in domestic surroundings and emotions associated with these changes are vivified.

Venus, the ruler of love and marriage, is clearly in a definitive position highlighting the lunar return and showing the coming wedding. The energy of the event lies in the Moon–Venus aspect which shows the upcoming change of status both at home and in the world. Foreground Venus in house X indicates Lady Diana's manner of presenting herself to the world as well as the affection and adoration she so widely received. Added certification concerning the importance of this lunar period is shown by Uranus being square to both Moon and Venus which enhances the excitement and unforgettable exhilaration surrounding the public spectacle. Other dynamic aspects are Mercury conjunct Mars in square to Jupiter and Saturn in background areas.

Finally, Lady Diana's natal Neptune conjuncts the Ascendant of the lunar return. Although Neptune is normally considered malefic and would indicate a period of setbacks or a time of self-abasement, here this is clearly not the case. Yet Neptune's fated location does bring to mind the question of what sacrifices had to be made to bring together in love two very prominent persons destined to affect future events in what was obviously a marriage dictated by political necessities.

Prince Charles' solar return poses a more difficult problem. Provided his time of birth at 9:14 PM, Greenwich Mean Time on November 14, 1948, is correctly given by palace sources, (Figure 28) then Prince Charles had far more than just his marriage to deal with in 1980 and 198 I. His solar return (given in Figure 29) does show Jupiter with Saturn in the foreground of house I which speaks for fame and happiness, but also health concerns, responsibility, and behavior draw resistance through Saturn as well as criticism. In addition to popularity and public sanction in 198 l, there is another matter which occupies Charles' attention; a matter of perhaps great importance relating to his health and psychological well-being, shown by the Mars-Neptune conjunction in minutes of the IC. Mars in the foreground rules a period in which the native is aggressive and less prone to· show caution. Physical energy can be shown through the temper, injuries, cuts involving bleeding, and falls. It was reported in the press that, during the weeks preceding the wedding, Charles sustained several falls from a horse. With Neptune in the picture, the solar return promises a year in which some situations will be threatening. There certainly will be intrusions into his personal life which cause him mental concern.

Both the Prince and Princess of Wales are shown in the tropical zodiac although solar and lunar returns are normally presented in sidereal positions. They do, however, adhere to the tradition of using Campanus house cusps with solar and lunar returns.

Rotational Timing Method

Insofar as natal astrology is concerned, the rotational timing method has a direct relationship to the solar return chart, while in mundane affairs it is related to a map of the heavens for the moment of the Vernal Equinox. The development of practice with the birth diurnal chart seems to be of greater value in natal astrology, but completeness of teaching requires that all methods be taught. While the principles of the rotational timing method are not a new discovery, astrologers like Sepharial, John Hazelrigg, and George J. McCormack, FAFA, worked for its ultimate perfection. Through years of laborious research Mr. McCormack, President of the American Academy of Astrologians and former President of the American Federation of Astrologers, brought this method of timing influences to its present high degree of efficiency. Mr. McCormack extended permission to incorporate his own instructions on this method into this volume although his explanation of it is detailed primarily on mundane affairs. Therefore, to quote directly from his findings as published in the American Academy of Astrologians, Inc. Astro–scientific series:

"The rotational timing method relates to the clockwise rotation of certain horoscopic maps whereby they are caused to complete an axial rotation of 360 degrees within a year, or other prescribed period of time. The cycle of time required for completing an axial rotation depends in each instance upon the subject involved, as later explained under the various classifications. In the course of a rotation every significator in the map perfects all possible geometrical

angles or aspects with the Midheaven, Ascendant, or other cardinal points of the horoscopic scheme. Similarly, the ephemeral Sun forms the conjunction and all other possible configurations with each radical position in the key map. This method is applied principally to Vernal Ingress charts and solar returns, but it may be extended to other maps according to the cycles of time involved.

"Fundamentally, the axial rotation method is not a modern discovery. Certain principles have been applied to solar returns since the time of Ptolemy. This statement may be verified by referring to Ptolemy's aphorisms number 24, 35, 58, 81, and 87.23 In recent years progressive applications of these principles have been extended to other cyclic charts and developed through the coordinated researches of various technical astrologers. The late Sepharial expounded certain principles involved. Those simple instructions, vague as they were, served as valuable leads to subsequent investigators under this subject. It may be of interest to mention also, that nearly forty years ago, a brilliant American astrologer named Cunningham, used this method with amazing success in forecasting the exact time and character of outstanding political and mundane events in the United States. and his remarkable predictions attracted nation-wide interest. Although Cunningham imparted certain details of axial rotation timing in articles contributed to an astrological publication entitled The Star of the Magi in 1900. he seemingly guarded the modus operandi very carefully,

"Following these leads, John Hazelrigg and the writer in 1916 conducted experimental researches under this subject by rotating the Vernal Ingress charts in the ratio of one degree daily and tabulating aspects formed by the radical positions of the planets to the angles during the period of annual rotation. The aspects thus formed were then checked as time markers of important events. We also observed transits of the ephemeral Sun over critical points - chiefly the positions held by planets at the time of the Vernal Ingress and over degrees in critical aspect to them - as additional time indicators of important mundane events. We were unable at that time to account for certain discrepancies in our observations with regards to the particular character and time of certain events and so did not deem our findings inclusive. The writer personally resumed these investigations in 1925 in connection with weather researches but was unable to continue the studies owing to other responsibilities.

"For the past three years the author has applied the principles daily in connection with astro–economics, together with mundane and astro–meteorological observations. In recording our observations we have developed some personal findings which we submit herewith for consideration. It has been demonstrated by practical application that the rotational method affords opportunities of timing events not merely to days but even to minutes of time.

Annual Revolutions

1.1 The ingress of the Sun into the first point of Aries, about March 21 each year, is the annual return as applicable to mundane events. The exact hour and minute of this Vernal Ingress marks the beginning of the astrological year at any place of observation.

l.2 In the annual cycle the Sun's ingress into Aries is regarded as holding chief rank among the solar ingresses into cardinal signs, similarly as the new Moon has dominion among the four lunar quarters in the monthly return, save when the Moon is eclipsed at the full. All through existence these interlinking cycles in the cosmic scheme affect both time and destiny, and from these cycles we seek to observe and interpret greater causes which, through the larger entity affect the component parts thereof.

A figure of the heavens is erected for the date, hour, and exact minute of the Vernal Ingress at any desired place of observation. Such maps are usually set up for the capitals of countries, as for Washington, D.C., in this country, but may conveniently be transposed to the capital of any state, for any important city or for any geographical meridian in longitude, if so desired.

1.4 The longitude of the planets will remain the same in all such maps for the same ingress, regardless of the geographical position for which they are calculated. Only the cusps of the houses will

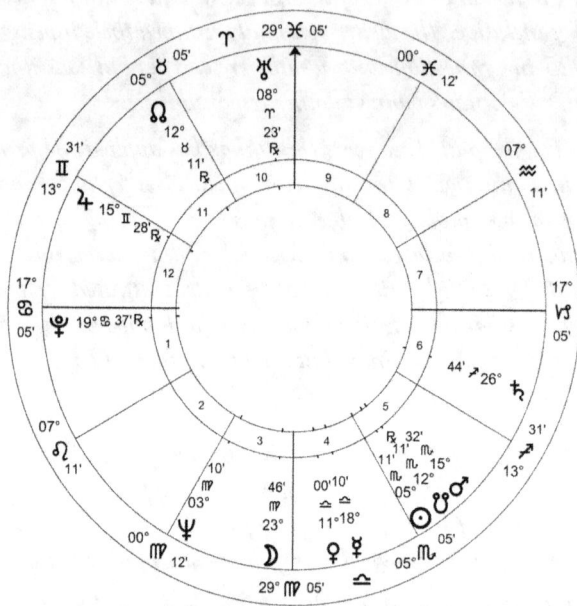

Figure 28. *Rotational diurnal chart for October 28, 1929, 9:37 PM, EST, Washington, DC.*

differ as the charts are transposed for different points of geographical longitude and latitude. It is understood, however, that these horoscopic maps shall be computed for local mean time (corrected from standard time by deducting or adding the necessary time adjustment of four minutes for each degree of longitude) in order to ensure for accuracy in computing the midheaven - an important point for timing major events during the year to follow.

1.5 The hour and minute and the place of assumed observation should be carefully recorded and the elements of this chart will then be used as radical positions when preparing subordinate maps under this series during the year following. This rule applies likewise to solar returns and all others included in the annual return series. Figure 22 shows the chart for the Vernal Ingress as calculated for Washington, DC, on March 21, 1929, 9:37 PM, EST. This chart

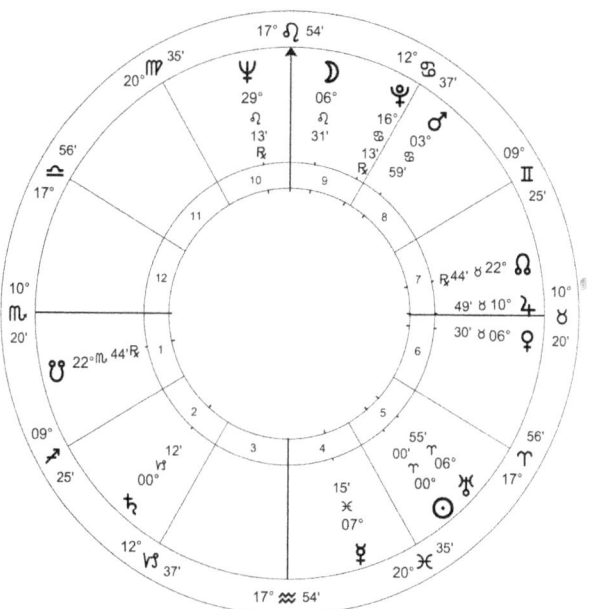

Figure 27. Vernal ingress chart for March 20, 1929, 9:37 PM, EST, in Washington ,DC, 77°W01', 38°N53'.

is deemed a most interesting and instructive illustration since it preceded the historical Wall Street panic of October, 1929. The panic was, of course, primarily influenced by the solar eclipse of April 28, 1928, which fell in 7 Taurus 46, but the Sun's position in house V (speculation) in exact square with Saturn in the second mansion, square Mars in house VI II and conjunct Uranus in the critical fifth sector, showed very strikingly how the important developments of the year were focused through house V.

l.6 Of chief consideration is the house position of the Sun, for, as we shall illustrate later, the solar orb remains in approximately the same position in the chart while advancing through the twelve signs during the entire return, unless it happens to be placed close to the horizon or a house cusp in the radical figure for the annual return. Therefore, major events of the ensuing year will be focused *through the house occupied by the ephemeral Sun at the place of observation. During the process of axial rotation the ephemeral Sun forms conjunctions and all other possible aspects with the radical significators from approximately the same house position it occupies in the Aries Ingress or any other annual return under consideration.*

Axial Rotation

Owing to the rotation of the annual return maps the radical positions of the planets will appear to move clockwise round the circle and eventually form all possible aspects with the Midheaven, Ascendant, and other angles during the year. These configurations are regarded as primary time markers and indicators of major events. Conjunctions or oppositions with the Midheaven or the Sun are especially powerful, particularly when such configurations concern the major planets Neptune, Uranus, Saturn, Jupiter, or Mars. Angles of 60, 120, 30, and 150 degrees are favorable and range in strength in the order given. Angles of 90, 45, and 135 degrees are adverse, in strength as in the order given. The radical positions of planets should be inserted in their appropriate places outside the circle on all rotational diurnal maps prepared during the annual cycle.

The sensational Wall Street panic of October, 1929, originated from multiple astrological causes which were detailed in an article under the heading "Astro–Science and the Wall Street Debacle, which was published in Mercury. December 1929. The panic definitely started during the reaction on October 3, 1929, when Neptune opposed the Midheaven in the diurnal map for that date but the spectacular selling wave on October 29, when a total of 16,388,700 shares were transacted and the industrial averages (Dow–Jones) declined 42 points during the session, affords an interesting time marker regardless of the directions of worldwide significance then operating in the Great Mutation chart or various other major causes concerned. Interest in definite time markers shows there had been a previous selling wave on October 23–24 but the Sun sextile Neptune configuration immediately following had assisted further professional manipulation, particularly when the transiting Moon over Neptune tended to excite this influence. The diurnal (Figure 28) for October 28–29 shows that the Midheaven then reached 29° Pisces 06' and squared the midway point between the ephemeral Saturn (26° Sagittarius 45') and the radical place of Saturn in 0° Capricorn 12' when the Midheaven would also form a conjunction with the radical Sun. It was applying to a square with radical Mars. A striking testimony is the fact that the Moon (ever significant of the public) was then ruling the Ascendant in the diurnal map, hence the Moon's transit over the place of Neptune was extremely critical at this time. (Compare this diurnal with the inauguration chart of President Hoover, March 4, 1929, 1:16 pm EST in Washington D.C.) From the moment of that event on March 4, the Moon, ruler of the Ascendant and conjunct Saturn in house VI, foreshadowed public depression.

It will be noted in the example charts that Figure 28 is calculated for the same moment of the day (October 28, 1929) as the chart for the Vernal Equinox (March 20, 1929).

Applying these principles to the natal chart, the time of day must be determine when the Sun will return to the precise point it held at birth. The Sun must IN ALL INSTANCES be calculated to seconds of longitude for precision work, otherwise Table 11 additives will suffice.

Whichever technique the student prefers to consider, these cyclic charts are another tool which may be used in considering the trending of a coming year or an ensuing month. When used alone, or added to another system, they substantiate dates for future events.

Review Questions for Chapter 9

1. Compute a rotational diurnal chart for December 7, 1941, at the onset of the surprise attack on Pearl Harbor. How does this compare with the chart for the Autumnal Ingress the preceding October?

2. Compare a lunar revolution or a lunar return for a wedding in your own family? Do the same for the birth of a child, enrolling in college, accepting a new position, and loss of a loved one.

3. Begin by computing the solar revolution or solar return for a given year; then calculate the lunar returns or lunar returns for the entire year and compare your predicted dates with the actual time of events during that 12 month period.

|Chapter 10|

Summary of Data

THUS FAR ALL PROBLEMS HAVE NECESSARILY had to deal with the mathematical phases of progressing or directing a horoscope. As a consequence, it may appear that there are such a bewildering number of forces at play that the task of separating them seems impossible. If a systematic method of arranging all of this information is not used one may very easily become lost in a maze of non–essential data. This chapter, brief as it may seem, is of utmost importance in that it presents a systematic arrangement to be followed in setting down data in order to better interpret the nature of all influences obtained for a given date. As experience develops, the use of tabulated forms becomes unnecessary. At the outset though, they are of great value in establishing proper habits of coordinating essential data.

A resume of various data is needed to consider timing in reference to any horoscope.

(1) The natal chart with house, sign, planetary positions, and aspects, including parallels, stelliums, or any peculiar combinations of planets is that which depicts the innate qualities, capacities, and character of the native. It is the pattern with which he starts life.

(2) The secondary progressed chart with house, sign, and planetary positions, as well as directions both between the pro-

gressed sensitive points and the radical or natal chart sensitive points, is the chart which depicts the progress of the native in the development of innate qualities, capacities, and character shown in the radical chart. Within rather broad limits, relatively speaking, it indicates the ever-changing vibrations of a gradual character which brings the influences of life into their proper sequence (and, esoterically speaking, developing karma).

(3) The radix directional chart with its house, sign, and planetary positions, as well as directions, both between the signs and cusps of the radix directional and the entire natal chart, is a complete system of progression in itself and should not be confused in interpretation with the secondary progressed chart. It is a relatively new system, being only some 200 years old. The author usually considers this less important than the secondary progressed chart. It probably has greater accuracy when planets of a particular chart have little latitude and are therefore very close to the Sun's apparent path in the ecliptic, in which case it is essentially following the method of the primary directional system.

(4) The birth diurnal chart, which is based on the rotation of the earth on its axis, marks the return of celestial phenomena to the mundane positions held at birth converted always to the place of residence. Its house, sign, and planetary positions are considered in relationship to angles and intermediate house cusps as well as natal and progressed planets. This is calculated either in direct motion or in converse (regressed) motion. It deals essentially with the transiting positions of the planets, often referred to as their ephemeral positions, and relates these to the natal and progressed charts. Birth diurnal charts can be related to both the natal and secondary progressed charts, or to the natal and radix progressed charts.

(5) Cyclic charts based upon the Sun or Moon returning to the same longitudinal position it held at birth may be calculated also for any planets returning to the same longitude they held at

birth, which are of same value in detailed work. But the cyclic charts of the two most important bodies in the heavens to us, the Sun and the Moon, have a definite value. Solar or lunar returns are interpreted in their relation to the radical or natal horoscope. It seems safe to assume, insofar as our present knowledge goes, that if there is not a striking parallelism between some phases of the solar or lunar return chart and the natal or progressed chart, that year or month in the life of the native is destined to be more matter of fact and following usual routine than otherwise.

(6) The rotational diurnal chart, which is simply a chart of the transiting positions of the heavenly bodies calculated for the same time of day as the solar return, is essentially the birth diurnal chart of the solar cycle and should be considered in its relationship to both the solar return and the secondary progressed chart as well as the radical horoscope. It has never come to our knowledge that anyone has tested these charts with the radix system of directing.

(7) The solar arc directions, solar and lunar returns, and primary directions are tools which are used independent of other systems but are also related to the natal horoscope.

These foregoing methods all deal with horoscope calculation of one kind or another. In addition there is always the transiting or ephemeral position of the planets to be considered in relationship to the natal and progressed chart, whether or not other charts are calculated. Indeed, most professional work deals almost entirely with the natal, secondary progressed, and transits. Professionals with a clientele requiring more specific timing use the birth diurnal system as timing factor for by it, if absolutely precise birth data is available, events cannot only be timed to the day, but frequently to the hour of the day when they will operate. Thus for all practical purposes there are three factors to be considered.

Use of the tabular forms in Tables 15, 16, and 17 is primarily intended to develop within personal thinking a systematic method of approach. Many students with keen analytical minds can quickly ascertain the combinations in effect from planetary positions for any given time without the help of aids. The observing and patient student will soon learn to develop this for himself. But to those who desire a brief, concise method, it cannot be too strongly emphasized that the ultimate advantages of learning a precise tabular form for setting forth data will repay the student many times over.

Three forms are presented. Table 15 deals with the progressed horoscope in relationship to the natal chart. After calculation of progressed planetary positions for either primary directions, secondary directions, or the radix directional method, the data can be set forth covering the period of a full year. In

Table 15. Progressed horoscope form

Month and Year	PROGRESSED MOON		LUNATIONS				
	Sign and Degree	Directions	New	Directions	Full	House	Transits

PROGRESSED HOROSCOPE FOR _____ YEAR _____ Secondary Radix System
Abbreviations: N---Natal; P---Progressed; T-Transit.
Monthly motion of Sun ° ': Moon ': Mercury ': Venus ': Mars

addition, it provides space for indicating degrees, aspects, and positions of all lunations and full Moons during the year as well as aspect which transits make to both the natal and progressed chart.

In calculating the progressed chart, the position of the Moon for the next succeeding birth date should always be determined. Difference in its position for two successive years indicates motion during that year. Dividing this by 12 determines

Table 16. Solar return form.

Solar Revolution Form for _____ Years of age _____ Year _____
Abbreviations: N — Natal   P — Progressed   T — Transit   Solar Arc Directed

Directions to Natal Chart

	☉	☽	☿	♀	♂	♃	♄	♅	♆	♇	M.C.	ASC
☉												
☽												
☿												
♀												
♂												
♃												
♄												
♅												
♆												
♇												
MC												
ASC												

Directions to Progressed Chart

	☉	☽	☿	♀	♂	♃	♄	♅	♆	♇	M.C.	ASC
☉												
☽												
☿												
♀												
♂												
♃												
♄												
♅												
♆												
♇												
MC												
ASC												

Table 17. Rotational diurnal chart form.

Rotational Diurnal Chart for _____ Years of age ___ Year ___
Abbreviations: N — Natal   P — Progressed   T — Transit   (It may be preferrable to use this form for three or six month periods, rather than the full year. Be sure and indicate dates.)

	☉	☽	☿	♀	♂	♃	♄	♅	♆	♀	M.C.	ASC
☉												
☽												
☿												
♀												
♂												
♃												
♄												
♅												
♆												
♀												
M.C.												
ASC												

the progressed Moon's mean monthly motion, so that it may be added to the progressed position, thus indicating in any month particular configurations to be made. This can also be done for the Sun, Mercury, Venus, and Mars. The remaining bodies have such small apparent motion in one day that it can be mentally determined.

Table 16 provides a concise method for setting forth the relationship of the solar revolution to the natal chart and/or the progressed chart. This form is simply an adaptation of the form used with many horoscope blanks indicating aspects between planets in the natal chart. Of particular emphasis are conjunctions and oppositions, although all directions should be carefully indicated.

Table 17 provides a method of showing the relationship of the rotational diurnal chart particularly to the solar return for, as such, it is a major timing factor. It can be used also to indicate similar information in comparing the birth diurnal chart to the natal or progressed, though in this case it is better practice to use the charts themselves from the outset. It is also well to show directions to the progressed and radical charts as well as to the solar return.

Some astrologers use a straight chronological method of arranging data. That is, for each day of the year when directions are formed, whether progressed or transiting, to set forth their degree as conjunction, opposition, sextile, trine, etc., plus the date, in simple chronological order.

With the completion of Volume IV of this textbook series the student can proceed further, depending on his objectives and interests; studying advanced synthesis which deals entirely with delineation; branching into horary, electional or mundane astrology; specializing in synastry, astro–meteorology, medical, psychological, or any of the other main fields of astrology. A thorough understanding of the basic concepts and methods of calculation presented in this course of study is necessary to move further into either counseling, research, or teaching. Whether astrology is studied purely for

Review Questions for Chapter 10

1. Briefly review the purpose of these different techniques:

(a) the natal horoscope;

(b) secondary progressed planets, Ascendant and Midheaven;

(c) radix directional charts; (d) solar arc directions;

(e) diurnals, both birth and rotational; (f) primary directions;

(g) transits;

(h) solar and lunar returns;

(i) ingress charts;

2. Progress your own horoscope for the next ten years.

REFERENCES

1) Vivian E. Robson. The Radix System. Darr, Toledo, OH, 1974 reprint.

2) Sepharial. The Science of Foreknowledge. Health Research, Mokelumne, CA, 1918 facsimile reprint.

3) Carolyn Dodson. Horoscopes of the U.S. Cities and States. Dodson, Nashville, TN, 1975.

4) Alan Leo. The Progressed Horoscope. L.N. Fowler & Co., LTD; London, 1969, Pl 17.

5) This principle is somewhat modified in the discussion of transits, when additional factors must be brought in the equation. It is fundamentally correct, however, for present purposes.

6) This is an analytical statement of the Moon's progressions. If the Sun and Moon are square in the natal chart, the influence of the trine, or of any other favorable progression is somewhat mitigated, although still favorable to the native. Similarly, if other progressions harmonize with the Moon's favorable aspect to the Sun, its strength is increased, and it will be along the lines indicated by the other progression.

7) These progressions occur approximately every seven years so the student must learn how to differentiate the various periods when these influences are in effect on the basis of other conditions operating in the horoscope and of indications in the natal chart.

8) For further study of transits see the following references:

Clara Darr. Transits. Darr Publications, Toledo, OH, I 971.

Robert Hand. Planets in Transit. Para-Research, Rockport, MA, 1976. Lois Rodden. Modern Transits. AFA, Tempe, AZ, 1978 .

Francis Sakoian, and Louis Acker. Transits Simplified. Sakoian, Arlington, MA, 1976.

Sepharial. Transit and Planetary Periods. Samuel Weiser, Inc., NY, I 970.

Dr. Herbert Smith. Transits. AFA, Tempe, AZ.

Noel Tyl. Integrated Transits. Llewellyn Publications, St. Paul, MN, 1974.

9) Roger Hutcheon. Planetary Pictures in Declination. ATS Press, Cambridge, MA. 1976

10) For further study of lunations and eclipses see the following refer-

ences:

Sam Bartolet. Eclipses and Lunations in Astrology. AFA, Tempe, AZ.

Robert Jansky. Interpreting the Eclipses. Astor-Computing, San Diego, CA, 1977.

Raymond A. Merriman. Evolutionary Astrology. Seek-It Publishing Co, Rochester, Ml, 1977.

Sepharial. Eclipses. Signs and Symbols, Van Nuys, CA, 1973; and Mundane Data: Lunations and Eclipses. AFA, Tempe, AZ, yearly.

11) Sepharial. The Science of Foreknowledge. Health Research, Mokelumne Hill, CA (1918 facsimile reprint), p 132, 133.

12) Vivian E. Robson. The Radix System. Darr Publications, Toledo, OH, 1974 reprint, pp 1–3.

13) This figure of 59 minutes and 08 seconds is known as the Naibod rate.

14) Reinhold Ebertin. Directions. Ebertin-Verlag, Germany, 1976.

Doris Greaves. Cosmobiology. Regulus Astrological Publications, Australia, 1979.

Roger A. Jacobson. Language of Uranian Astrology. Uranian Publications, Franksville, WI, 1975.

Kimmel, Eleanora A. Fundamentals of Cosmobiology. Cosmobiology Center, Denver, CO, 1975.

15) Other sources for tables and information about primary directions are:

Robert DeLuce. Complete Method of Predictions. ASI, New York, 1978.

Ivy Goldstein Jacobson. Turn of a Lifetime Astrologically. Jacobson, Temple City, CA, 1964.

Alan Leo. The Progressed Horoscope. L. N. Fowler & Co., LTD, London, 1969.

Lynne Palmer. ABC of Major Progressions. AFA, Tempe, AZ, 1970.

W. J. Simmonite. Arcana of Astrology. New Castle Publishing Co., Inc., Yan Nuys, CA, reprint 1974.

16) These first three formulae are used in the case of the Sun, or any heavenly body without latitude, or when considered as having no latitude, or of the degree on the cusp on the Midheaven, or of any degree in the ecliptic which may be taken without latitude.

17) This formula is used for the Sun or for any celestial body without latitude or for any degree of the zodiac considered without reference to latitude.

18) This is for places in northern latitudes; for southern latitudes, reverse the formula, adding instead of subtracting, and subtracting instead of adding.

19) This is for places in northern latitudes. For southern latitudes, reverse the rule, adding instead of subtracting and subtracting instead of adding. Either semi–arc subtracted from 180 degrees gives the other semi-arc.

20) This formula is for places in northern latitudes. For southern latitudes, the rules must be reversed.

21) If B exceeds 90 degrees, take log. sine (arithmetical complement) of its excess. The longitude will then fall the reverse way from which the oblique ascension is taken.

The arithmetical complement of a logarithm is the logarithm subtracted from 10.000000 (in the case of seven–figure logarithms – 10.0000000). It is most rapidly found by subtracting each figure of the logarithm successively from 9, beginning at the left hand, and finally subtracting the last figure at the right hand from 10. Using the arithmetical complement in place of the logarithm is the equivalent of dividing instead of multiplying by the number which the logarithm represents.

22) If B exceeds 90 degrees, use the cosine of its excess in section C and its sine in section D. The latitude will then be of the opposite declination (latitude south if declination is north and vice versa).

23) #24 An eclipse of the luminaries, if in the angles of the nativity, or of an annual revolution, is noxious; and the effects take place according to the space between the Ascendant and the place of eclipse. And as, in a solar eclipse, a year is reckoned for an hour, so likewise, in a lunar eclipse, a month is reckoned for an hour.

#35 When the Sun arrives at the place of any star, it excites the influence of that star in the atmosphere.

#58 Observe the place of an aspect, and its distance from the Ascendant of the year; for the event will happen when the profection may arrive thither.

#81 Times are reckoned in seven ways; viz. by the space between two significators; by the space between their mutual aspects; by the approach of one to the other; by the space between either of them and the place appropriated to the proposed event; by the decension of a star, with its addition or diminution; by the changing of a significator; and by the approach of a planet to its place.

#87 Monthly revolutions are made in twenty-eight days, two hours and about eighteen minutes. Judgment is also made by some persons by means of the Sun's progress; that is to say, by his partial equations to that degree and minute which he might hold at the beginning.

24) Donald A. Bradley. Solar and Lunar Returns. Llewellyn Foundation, Los Angeles, CA., 1948.

James A. Eshelman. Interpreting Solar Returns. Astro-Analytics, Van Nuys, CA, 1979.

Cyril Fagan and Brigadier R. C. Firebrace. Primer of Sidereal Astrology. Littlejohn Publishing Co., Isabella, MO, 1971.

www.ingramcontent.com/pod-product-compliance
Lightning Source LLC
Chambersburg PA
CBHW070341240426
43671CB00013BA/2387